DATE DUE

Demco, Inc. 38-293

University Press of America,® Inc.
Lanham · Boulder · New York · Toronto · Plymouth, UK

Copyright © 2007 by
University Press of America,® Inc.
4501 Forbes Boulevard
Suite 200
Lanham, Maryland 20706
UPA Acquisitions Department (301) 459-3366

Estover Road
Plymouth PL6 7PY
United Kingdom

Library of Congress Control Number: 2006933307
ISBN-13: 978-0-7618-3622-3 (paperback : alk. paper)
ISBN-10: 0-7618-3622-5 (paperback : alk. paper)

⊖™ The paper used in this publication meets the minimum
requirements of American National Standard for Information
Sciences—Permanence of Paper for Printed Library Materials,
ANSI Z39.48—1984

CONTENTS

What is remarkable about Western music is that through its scales and forms it has raised the expressive power of music to heights and depths unattainable in other cultures.

Jacques Barzun

Preface to Second Edition

The Heritage of Musical Style was first published by Holt, Rinehart & Winston in 1970; reissued in 1980 by the University Press of America. The present edition, like its predecessor, is designed for students in introductory music history courses and for general music lovers. My aim was to write a concise, integrated text. Hence, the present edition is a "slimmed-down" version to make the volume more easily portable and handy to read. Written in the humanities spirit and focusing upon musical styles and their cultural background, the book traces the development of music from the Baroque period (1600-1750) to the present.

Completely revised and updated, the opening chapters introduce the elements of music in a new and stimulating manner—through *aesthetics* as opposed to the traditional theoretical approach emphasizing musical notation, keys etc. Recent studies and research have indicated the need to do more with the introductory phases of music appreciation, specifically, to direct the listener through the "how" and "what" of musical enjoyment. Thus, the opening section discusses the "heart" (emotional) and "mind" (cognitive) approach to musical understanding with explicit examples and suggestions to follow.

Holding to the concise, integrated idea, the book bypasses a comprehensive historical survey in favor of a more concentrated emphasis on the periods of music most often encountered in the concert hall and listening. Furthermore, ever conscious of the need to do more with value in studying the humanities, I begin the book with some of the principles underlying great music, which, I believe, sets the direction and purpose of the book

The final chapters on the music of the modern period, reflect the dramatic changes in the avant-garde and audience tastes. Critics' and historians' views are examined with an attempt to cut through the complexities of the contemporary music scene. To help the reader in this endeavor, the philosophy from the opening pages is reconsidered and applied to selected works, thereby suggesting possible answers to some of the "big" questions facing interested listeners today.

Donald H. Van Ess
Weaverville, N.C.
06/06

Acknowledgments

I wish to thank the following for generous assistance: Patti Belcher, Acquisitions Editor, and other members of the publishing staff at the University Press of America; my wife, Jan, for her ever helpful criticism and support; the library staff at the University of North Carolina, Asheville; and the students in the courses at the College for Seniors at the University of North Carolina, Asheville, whose stimulating questions motivated my renewal of interest in writing and research.

CHAPTER ONE

INTRODUCTION

Our experience of fine art removes us temporarily
out of the commonplace world of cause and effect,
and immerses us in a rarer state of concentrated
vision.　　Harold Osborne, British aesthetician

WHY STUDY MUSIC HISTORY?

A Great Musical Heritage

For many followers of classical music the answer to our opening question is
aesthetic enjoyment. This is a special kind of musical enjoyment that results
from an understanding of the composer's art and a feelingful response to the
elements of music. The focus of this type of pleasure rests upon significant
works mirroring emotional life at a higher plane than what we would expect in
our daily existence.

Edward Lippmann (*A Humanistic Philosophy of Music*) comments on the
value of music history and its aesthetic pleasure. Music history, he writes, is the
source of our enjoyment; it illuminates the created work, and places it in a
cultural setting that deepens and enriches the meaning of the music.

The historical periods chosen for this study—the Baroque, Classical,
Romantic, and Twentieth Century—fulfill the expectations of our aesthetic
definition. They are, moreover, the periods most often represented in the concert
hall and recordings. One unifying feature for these epochs is the composers'
belief in the humanistic power underlying all musical creativity. The importance
of this idea will become more apparent as we progress. For now, let us say that it
is the substance that has contributed to extraordinary accomplishments in music
history. With these introductory thoughts in mind the present book will do
several things: suggest an aesthetic approach for greater musical enjoyment,
introduce the reader to leading composers and works, and help the listener to
identify memorable works in each of the historical periods.

Regarding the values of exploring our musical heritage, music historian
Donald Grout offers these thoughts:

> It is sad to think that so much beauty lies buried in the silence of the past,
> that all these things which so mightily pleased our forefathers have become
> things of yesterday. (*A History of Western Music*)

To open the door to these treasures—to remove them from their cloistered surroundings, to personify musically many great names such as Schubert, Mahler, and Beethoven, and to make music history more than a series of disconnected beads on a string—are some of the goals. The kind of "beauty" alluded to by professor Grout, and the kind toward which we will direct our efforts, is found in many different musical examples—large and small, profound as well as uncomplicated, emotional and intellectual. It is imbued in the melody, harmony and rhythm that characterize the significant works of music history. The periods chosen for this study, spanning several centuries, are perhaps, most representative of the artists' and musicians' search for beauty in its many forms. They are also most representative of the humanistic spirit that has motivated composers from J. S. Bach in the Baroque, to the present.

Restoring the Humanistic Spirit

Finding and renewing the musical charm and magic of yesterday should be a rewarding experience, especially in view of the large variety of music in our chosen historical periods. Such a quest is especially timely considering the confused, unsettled state of much new classical music. Current trends have made it increasingly difficult for the interested listener to encounter themes and subject matter possessing references to nature, beauty and human emotion. The notion that such values as greatness and beauty are no longer relevant needs to be discarded. Given our unstable times in the arts many seek out the order and stability offered by the "classics."

Many interested listeners want to know where are the Bachs' and Beethovens'?—those composers frequently referred to as "great." What they possessed, and what is increasingly difficult to find in the current musical scene, is creative imagination and invention rooted in humanism. The current situation in classical music has been commented upon by Jacques Barzun (*From Dawn to Decadence*), who states: "the lure of technology has displaced the tonally ordered intention of expressiveness." Musical thought, lacking a humanistic touch, becomes secondary to technical complexity and electronic wizardry. The "humanism," of which Barzun writes, has been gradually disappearing from the contemporary music scene. It is an integral part of our musical heritage, and, as we shall see, it is an essential key to musical understanding and enjoyment. Barzun's comments deserve further consideration.

For over 2000 years music making has been imbued with human emotion and action, a feature of music attractive to philosophers and historians since Plato. The whole gamut of music in history can be seen as a personification of human nature. On the small scale: melodies and rhythms mirror psychological properties such as sadness, reverence, anger, quietude and the joyful. On a large scale, in the symphonies and opera, music mirrors the exposition and development of character and action similar to what we find in heroic novels.

Christopher Small in *Musicking* writes: tensions, relaxations, climaxes and resolutions in music parallel human relationships. Moreover, the idea of story telling, so deep in our cultural tradition, seems to be echoed in the basic outlines of the symphony. For example, like the novel, there is a development of musical plot, the use of contrasting themes and climactic endings. More on this matter will be mentioned in later pages. With this long history of the literary-musical relationship, it is little wonder people attending the musical scene are drawn to the vivid settings and representations of the tragic, the comic and romantic—the themes of much great music. In short, without this connection to humanist experience, music would be lifeless and meaningless.

Expression and the Listener

How does *humanism* apply to this study? It has to do with the musical depiction or representation of some physical or psychological aspect of human nature. Essentially, it is the transference of such gestures—feelings, emotions—into meaningful tone patterns. When such patterns have meaning—they move or delight, or fascinate intellectually—we say they are "expressive."

The term "expression" is also used in conjunction with the performer who brings to life the musical notation on the printed page. This is done through interpretation and the use of what every pianist is taught—*expression*—that is, bringing out the subtleties of rhythm, melodic inflection and dynamics. Every time a violinist touches the bow to the strings, or the pianist touches the keys, the process of expression begins.

The reason for emphasizing expression and its role in listening, is simply this: it can, when understood, bring the music of the historical periods to life, thus removing the deadly "museum atmosphere." When the expressive touches of the composer are combined with an understanding of the cultural spirit of the period, the listener should begin to witness the surfacing of the "hidden beauty" of which Grout speaks. How do we reach this point in the musical experience and begin to enjoy some of the worthwhile, uncommon expressions which lift us up from the daily routine? What should be our approach?

For centuries music has been a dynamic cultural force for two reasons: its capability to move people emotionally, and its power to stimulate intellectual interest through its fascinating formal structure. For the listener this translates to enjoyment of "heart" and "mind." For example, when we hear a musical performance, oftentimes it is the emotional effect pulling for our attention. Emotion alone, however, is not enough to sustain enjoyment, for almost immediately the attentive listener will begin to sort out the cause or source of the emotion and contemplate the unfolding musical plot or production. This is where the "mind" becomes a powerful force for grasping the meaning of what we hear. There are many times, of course, when the "heart" or emotion is the dominant, controlling force in enjoyment. The following chapter, pertaining to the elements of music and aesthetic principles, will prepare the reader for this kind of listening experience.

A Starting Point: The Historical Periods

The intent of this book is to give the reader a broad view of noteworthy accomplishments in music history. Rather than following the all too often endless list of so-called "masterpieces" and biographies, an attempt will be made to look for some "signs of greatness." Where do we begin?—in the Gothic period? the Renaissance? Is one period greater than another? In contrast to some other fields where advancement and technical development are foremost, the arts move at a different pace. The history of the arts does not show scientific advancement or perfection of an art form from one period to another, but merely a series of movements, some stronger and more powerful, having deeper roots within the age and being more widely spread throughout the arts. After countless efforts by historians and critics in the process of cultural distillation (sorting out the major trends from the minor), each period stands as an entity, possessing its own unique artistic and intellectual spirit. This is essentially, what has happened in historians' naming of the various epochs such as "Baroque," and "Classical." It is these musical treasure-troves where we will concentrate our search.

Each period has added something to the evolution of Western music. For example, ancient Greece gave us basic music theory and poetic meters. The Baroque—a system of tonality (keys, scales) and the establishment of the orchestra. And the Classical—the development of the symphony. Such events collectively provided the momentum in the historical progression of this art form. An additional thought on greatness: The term can be applied to significant contributions made by a particular period of history. Clearly, the Baroque (roughly 1600-1750) represents a major turning point in the development of concert music in all of its forms, and thus is the lead-off period in this historical exploration.

Looking for Signs of Greatness

Why is it, as observers or participants we fervently pursue excellence in such fields as sports, music and theatre? Probably because we find enjoyment in being inspired or moved by the magic of outstanding achievement and skill, whether by an actor, musician or athletic star. We want to know "who" and "what" is worth following, we desire some "inside information" on the technique, and perhaps some knowledge of the "giants" in the field—those who set the bench marks and paved the way historically with outstanding accomplishments.

What really is greatness in classical music? It does not mean "bigger is better," (for instance, a concerto over a piano piece, or 100 symphonies over four symphonies). Music history has given us a wealth of great composers. It is impossible, of course, to place these in some sort of hierarchy, let alone find agreement as to what constitutes greatness. Some clues as to what to look for may be found in the history of musical criticism—in the views of knowledgable writers and music historians.

Another avenue for developing a helpful criteria is to be found in the relationship between literature, theatre and music. For example, what generally captivates us in certain literary works and films, are such things as the presence of style, the use of expressive dramatic technique, or an attention-getting story or plot. When we consider the successful works of composers through the ages, we find a similar set of aesthetic concerns presented in tonal form.

Since more will be said about these attributes later, they may be briefly summarized here: *style* refers to the "musical personality" of the composer; *technique*, to skill in handling the elements of music; *design*, to the structure or "plot"; and *expression*, to communicating ideas, feelings or emotions. When these are satisfactorily developed by the composer, we are probably in or near the realm of extraordinary musical creativity. In the course of these pages it is not the intent to give a detailed musicological examination of these signs of eminence, but rather to introduce them in connection with composers' creative profiles.

The Baroque Breakthrough

The reader may wonder why we begin with the Baroque instead of an earlier period. To explain, music in the early phases of history had a functional purpose: to mold character, to enhance the religious setting, to provide military signals and music for the dance. The turning point in musical creativity seems to center around the gradual shift to the principle of *aesthetic enjoyment*—the enjoyment of music as an art in itself. This ideal took a firm hold in the Renaissance. However, by the time of the Baroque, the movement increased in momentous proportions. It created an atmosphere powered by the truly significant works of Corelli, Vivaldi, Bach, Handel and many others. This aesthetic enjoyment evolved as society, increasingly aware of the value of the arts, became actively involved in music either as performers or as knowledgeable listeners.

A word about the role of the listener. As in the study of any art form, the participant is urged to become familiar with the basics of the language, become familiar with the territory, so to speak. As a preliminary preparation the next chapter, "The Composer's Workshop," provides an abbreviated tour through the musical process as seen through the skein of aesthetic principles. This discussion will underscore the dual features which often stand out as we listen to any style of music—the *expressive* (the feelingful, emotive side of music)—and the *formal* (the interesting way the music is put together, its organization).The focus is upon the perceptive listener, one who is interested in gaining some insight into musical workings and applying these concepts to the various periods and styles.

CHAPTER TWO

THE COMPOSER'S WORKSHOP

The arts appeal to the intellect and to the emotions.
Skillfully combined they give the highest pleasure.
Aristotle

AESTHETIC PRINCIPLES

Aesthetics and Music History

As a branch of philosophy aesthetics is concerned with "how" and "why" we enjoy the arts. Using these principles enlarges our consciousness of things we have taken for granted, and it also jolts our ingrained habits of observing and listening. As opposed to the theoretical approach of examining chords and keys (appropriate in an analytical context), the aesthetic approach can be most helpful. For instead of loading the listener with complex theory, the aim will be to determine what *makes a musical work memorable*. This is done in our pre-listening discussions of each musical work; specifically, by emphasizing those features having marked expressive qualities. Shortly, we will see how the composer creates expression in melody, rhythm, and harmony, the elements common to all music:.

In all of these matters we must pay homage to the Greek founders. In the writings of Plato (427-347 B.C.) and Aristotle (384-322 B.C.) we find the word *aesthetics* (aisthetikos), which refers to "things perceptible through the senses," in other words, those artistic endeavors such as music, painting, drama and sculpture in which human feeling and sensibility play a major role. The Athenians' aesthetic writings, which were fully realized in remarkable achievements in the visual and performing arts, became the philosophical superstructure for much of Western art. The thoughts culled from Aristotle's *Poetics* are still valid today. Consequently, some of these will serve as the rationale to be applied to listening and to the study of music history. Those of particular significance are given here:

- Art is an imitation of reality
- Unity of form should be a primary aim in art
- The inner significance of things should be represented in art

- Rhythm and melody imitate emotional states such as anger, gentleness
- The arts appeal to the intellect and to the emotions. Skillfully combined they give the highest pleasure

Capturing the Expressive

Acknowledging the philosophy of Aristotle, whose ideas have played an important part in Western aesthetic theory, our immediate attention is upon music's "expressive side"—that rhythm and melody imitate emotional states. This will be directed toward initial listening experiences. Following this we will apply Aristotle's "principle of unity of form" to listening and musical design.

Many consider expression as the intrinsic life of music. We may speak of some music as being softly subdued as in Brahms' Lullaby, or stormy and intense as in Tchaikovsky's Pathetique Symphony. Perceiving these moods or feelings, at what psychologists call the *affective level*, is often the beginning of a long relationship with this art. And, as we shall see, the inclusion of the "formal" or cognitive features involving melody, rhythm and harmony, add still greater enjoyment.

Many ways are available for enjoying music: as entertainment, religious enhancement, party atmosphere, and so on. The emphasis in this study is on the art of listening. It is an art because it is reliant on personal skills, aesthetic appreciation and perception. The acquisition of the "art" does not come automatically, cannot be gained by a flick of a switch. What follows are some suggestions for making this art a permanent part of one's pursuit of musical pleasure. It centers around expression which is the key to enjoying music of all periods and styles. Much of the art can be acquired through reading and listening. Following printed musical scores may help, but it is not the complete answer.

From the Mood-Feeling Snydrome to Something More Exciting

The art of listening begins with perceiving musical expression. It is defined as the mood or feeling the composer instills in the music. In some ways similar to the dynamic speaker who adds expression to the words of a printed text. Because so many semi or casual listeners consider emotion to be the central meaning in music (again, like focusing only upon the "sounds" of a dynamic speech) we will refer to this limiting practice as the "mood-feeling syndrome." Before going further with this first or primary level of expression, we should take a moment to review the psychological picture, specifically, how people react to music in general, which will help explain the popular appeal of the mood-feeling syndrome in listening. This will be followed by suggestions for building up from this stage to more exciting and challenging listening.

What intrigued the Greek scholars over 2000 years ago is still of major interest today among psychologists, namely, music's expressive power. Often a simple arrangement or grouping of tones will arouse an emotional or physical response. Why do some people experience anxiety in listening to certain types of music? Why do some musical pieces seem to be expressive of joy, others of mourning? Why is it some people's musical taste is for the ordered, logical pieces and others for more romantic, exciting works? In one way or another all of these questions center on emotion.

Many of us have felt the desire to tap a pencil or our foot in time with a rhythmic piece, or whistle or hum along with a popular tune. We have also felt our body and mind relax when a particular soft and pleasing passage is heard, or perhaps we have experienced a powerful spiritual uplift at the conclusion of a dramatic work. How are these emotional and physical reactions precipitated by musical happenings? Although difficult to put into words, we do know when something has pleased or perhaps disturbed us—has affected our personal "emotional barometer."

For instance, softly blended tones possess a soothing quality, whereas a totally different effect results from heavy ponderous sounds. A high shrill voice will often imply tension, or in quite the opposite manner, a softly modulated voice creates a feeling of relaxation. Some melodies remind us of joyful events or activities, others of serious tragic moments. Tonal complexity and disunity affect us the same way visual complexity and disunity: with feelings of tension and disorientation as the mind attempts to seek out familiar patterns and relationships. Many have experienced these and other effects in listening to music. They comprise the complex world of musical emotion.

Primary Perception

For the newcomer to music the general or primary perception is perhaps helpful as a starting point in trying to understand the meaning of music. The first consideration should be individual receptivity—an openness of mind and sensitivity to the sounds which emanate from music which we do not hear every day. The second: not all people respond the same way to music; many interpretations exist relative to the affective or expressive side of music. An illustration will indicate what we mean by the primary level of perception: In the concert hall the performer has begun playing a bright, scintilating piano sonata by the Baroque composer, Domenico Scarlatti. A lilting melody with its feeling of joy or sunny brightness catches our attention. Without having to resort to any printed information or musical score we have identified with the work, made a connection—principally through the emotional or intuitive mode of perception.

What causes this important connection? What causes our emotional response? Basically, pace of movement or tempo, melodic inflections up or down, choice of key, contrasts in consonance and dissonance, and so on. Needless to say, the major key, which is so prominent in Mozart, has a brightness and directness—qualities so highly loved by this composer. His upward reaching melodic movement is also a major contributing factor in this joyful expression. Again, as with so many musical patterns, we observe a relationship with humanistic movements and gestures. For example, our voices tend to reach higher, our physical movements and posture more upright when we are positive and outgoing. A typical classical symphony is driven forward by vibrant rhythm. In contrast, a typical romantic work, in a minor key, slow ponderous movement and in the low range, will obviously have a different effect on the listener. The presence of dissonant harmony may also contribute to heighten the emotional barometer.

Expressive Gestures

> Music is not really angry, joyful etc. Nevertheless,
> we construct thought-forms and give them reality
> as projections onto sounds. Jonathan Harvey

Many terms or mood-capturing phrases are used to describe emotion. Some may be helpful in forming an initial impression of a piece of music. The following are some examples of the common "stock gestures" which one will find in many music programs and record covers. Through the process of aculturization (radio, film, TV, soap opera) these have been part of the musical scene for years, if not centuries. Not all of the expressive types given here have the same meaning for everyone. Moreover, the expressive character of much music cannot be put into words. The following examples are merely illustrative for our introductory purposes. In all of these responses, empathic or intuitive, we find a connection with our memory bank of feelings, images, built up over the years of human experience. We draw upon these images, and in the process create metaphors for describing or formalizing our feelings which may arise in our aural experience.

A final thought regarding the first or primary level of listening: It takes time for the new initiate to learn that composers of the Classical period, for example, are not as likely to make the same emotional statement as representatives of the Romantic era. Each period has different uses of musical materials, different aesthetic objectives and different philosophies of music. As one writer commented: we must listen to eighteenth-century music with an eighteenth-century mind, ear and heart.

COMMON EXPRESSIVE GESTURES
(Extracted from record covers and concert program notes)

EXPRESSION	RELATED TERMS	DESCRIPTION	MUSICAL EXAMPLE
(1) Joy	Cheerful, happy, delightful	Bright sounding, quick-moving melody, usually in a major key.	Mozart: Cosi fan Tutti Overture
(2) Sentiment	Nostalgic, tender, dreamy	A languid, softly moving melodic line, inflected with light touches of dissonance.	Chopin: Etude in E Major
(3) Sadness	Mournful, solemn	Dirge-like patterns, Solemn, slowly descending tones at a low level of pitch. Frequently in a minor key.	Beethoven: Eroica Symphony, second movement
(4) Foreboding	Apprehensive, fearful, uneasy	An eerie calm caused by dissonant harmony "floating in air"—waiting for resolution; also by extremely soft sustained tones either very high or very low in pitch.	Mahler: Opening, first symphony
(5) Turbulence	Explosive, ferocity	Highest levels of volume, sudden harmonic changes, extremely powerful, jolting rhythm.	Berlioz: Symphonie Fantastique

Aristotle's thoughts on acquiring artistic pleasure through a combination of emotions and intellect form the basis for the following discussion. Beyond the primary level lies what we may refer to as the aesthetics of musical perception. It occurs when the listener begins to perceive musical happenings in an enlightened manner. Suddenly, perhaps, we experience wonder, amazement at the dazzingly manipulation of tones created by the composer and executed by the performer. Besides the pleasing emotional ambience, the listener may be aware of the subtle turning of a phrase, the power of a returning theme played by the full orchestra, the barely perceptible, almost soundless, ending chord of a romantic piano piece, or the soft muting of the violin strings. When these and other similar experiences are formalized—put into a frame of reference we can reflect upon—they appear under four facets of aesthetic enjoyment: expression, style, design and technique. In the course of this study we will touch upon these in our attempt to better understand the contributions of composers. They are, as we mentioned earlier, the makings for musical greatness. Brief definitions are necessary.

Expression

To summarize, expression has to do with the composer's use of certain melodic or rhythmic figures possessing emotional or intellectual import. Emotionally, they "move" us; intellectually, the figures or motives carry "mental import," in other words, they contain a cognitive character arresting the listener's interest in an intellectual manner. The humanistic sources for many expressive elements woven into the musical fabric, include the folk realm, nature, the military, religious ritual, popular dance figures and rhythms. The final type of expression comes through the performer, who adds life and character to the composer's musical score, governed, of course, by the styles and recognized performance practices of the period. The personal influence of the performer—applying nuances and shading, emphasis on certain notes, and other procedures—insures many new interpretations and audience appeal.

Style

We define style in music as the composer's distinctive unique manner of treating the musical elements. Sometimes the musical style matches the personality: Berlioz: fiery, explosive; Wagner: power and drama; Mozart: witty, charming. Style is like a "tonal signature"—the fingerprints which appear in every work. Knowing the style puts the person in touch with the composer. As Jonathan Harvey writes: "When we get to know a composer's works, we do not experience fragments, but a complex unified voice—in an almost "I"—"Thou" relationship." (*In Quest of the Spirit: Thoughts on Music*)

Design

Design is the form or structure, and the manner in which the structure makes sense by use of striking or interesting themes or motives followed by the listener as the work unfolds. All the passion in the world is aesthetically useless without the containment of form. Design can be very simple as in the ABA scheme of many folk and pop tunes or as complex as in the fugue form used by Bach and Handel in the Baroque.

Technique

This refers to the composer's ability to make use of such musical elements as melody, rhythm, harmony, medium and texture. The musical techniques—creating melody, harmony, keys, chords, writing for instruments—differ from one period to another. Some of the "greats" in history mastered the techniques pretty much on their own; some received a thorough formal music education; and some learned through close relationships with other composers.

Summary

In this chapter we discussed some of the characteristics of the informed listener, one who is able to enjoy the expressive qualities of a work and at the same time is aware of content, or musical information. The emotional aspect of music seems to have a cultural origin, specifically in musicians' ever-present quest for humanistically inspired tone patterns. Lastly, success in this venture depends on the listener's ability to respond to the musical stimuli and to adopt the aesthetic pace and process. Musical satisfaction is not measured quantitatively. Just as great art is an inextricable amalgam of technique and intuition, so too is appreciation at its higher levels. Aside from the skill and craftmanship we admire in the masterworks, it is, essentially, however, the apprehension of the inexplicable, the romantic and the dramatic which continually attract us—attributes that have drawn people to the arts since the earliest civilizations. Try as we may, we cannot uncover these qualities by detailed analysis of chord structures, in fact, the more intense our technical analysis the further they recede from our grasp. One of the goals will be to help the listener experience some of this magic.

AESTHETIC POWER: THE ELEMENTS OF MUSIC

The Tonal Spectrum

As indicated in the opening pages we will forego an intensive examination of the theory-side of music and instead concentrate on the heart of expression—the musical elements which are the source of aesthetic power. They include *melody, harmony, rhythm, form, dynamics, timbre* and *texture*. The aim is to show their role in shaping music which has emotional and cognitive meaning; in short, what it is that stands out in music—that gives it a sense of value for the listener. Before discussing and illustrating these let's look at the primary area in which all musical creativity occurs, namely *tonal space*.

The tonal space in which melody, harmony and rhythm move and interact, encompasses the lowest to the highest possible pitch used in musical performance, approximately a range of 90 tones. Note: The violinist may exceed the uppermost note in the accompanying chart by using *harmonics*. These are ultra-high pitches produced by lightly touching the violin string at specified points. The spectrum of tones, utilized by the full symphony orchestra, extends from the lowest pitched contrabass (the largest of the string instruments), to the uppermost range of the violin. Note: In the illustration below, the highest note "B" is the highest note playable on the modern piano. Similarly, the "A" is the lowest. The composer writes music symbols upon a staff of five lines. Piano music uses two sets of lines or clefs: treble for the uppermost set of lines, and bass clef for the lowest. Sometimes leger lines are added above and below the staff as in the following illustration covering the total range of tones.

The tonal spectrum is divided into four classifications of voices: *soprano, alto, tenor* and *bass*. This will be useful in discussing voices and instrumental ranges in subsequent pages.

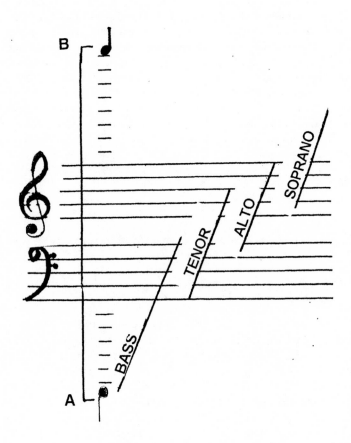

The Tonal Spectrum

Primacy of Melody

It is impossible to say which of the elements is most important; at times one or the other will dominate. Much of the music composed in our chosen periods, shows melody carrying a heavy aesthetic load—it is the framing idea around which a piece is composed, indeed, the germinating and controlling thought for whole movements and sometimes entire works. Melody is not only the chief substance holding everything together, but it is the element possessing the greatest staying power in our memory. Lastly, it is usually the identifying feature of a composer's style, a "tonal signature," as it were, which separates his or her work from all others.

Since it is often the cornerstone of a composition, melody might be considered the subject of the music. Like a literary theme or subject, it has meaningful content, aesthetically speaking, such as an abrupt turn, a skip upward or an arching line on which our mind fastens. A theme that makes a strong impression usually has a distinct aural form. Our intent is to conceptualize this form, to develop a mental image of the shape or contour and the manner in which tonal patterns more through musical space.

What we remember or recall are not individual tones, but rather a pattern or *gestalt* having two dimensions: linear and spatial. The linearity of a melody is similar to line in a drawing or painting. It may be smooth, moving primarily in conjunct fashion (as in the next example by the romantic composer Antonin Dvořák). Or the melody may be uneven with skips or leaps between the notes, or, disjunct style, as in the opening of Brahms' fourth symphony. Spatiality refers to the height and depth of the melody. Generally, folk tunes and many popular songs have a limited spatial movement, whereas classical music generally makes use of a greater tonal range.

Dvořák, Symphony No. 9, "New World" second movement opening

Brahms Symphony No. 4, first movement, opening

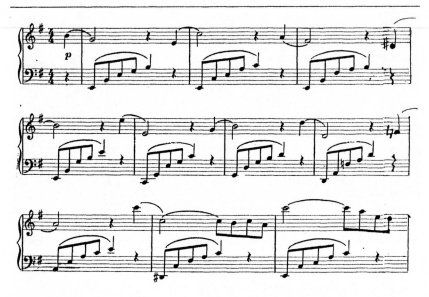

Rhythm

Rhythm is the heart of music. It generates forward motion, controls pace or speed of movement, and articulates the mass of sounds into recognizable patterns. Aside from melody, the most powerful, meaningful musical device is rhythm—the dynamic, driving force. Paradoxically, although it is seemingly the most elemental aspect of musical perception (we can feel it, and readily respond to it physically), it is the most complicated theoretically speaking because of the interworkings of its four components: pulse, meter, tempo and accent.

Listeners are perhaps most responsive to the sensation of beat or pulse, prompting us to move, sway, or tap our foot in time with the music. The strength of the sensation will vary from very little beat-feeling (non-pulsatile), to a strong emphasis (pulsatile). Tempo, the speed of the pulsating beat, ranging in concert music from extremely slow (largo) to very fast (presto), directly influences the psychological effect. A highly charged rhythm may be turned into a docile, gentle expression merely by slowing the pace of movement. The pace of music, as one might expect, has changed considerably over the ages, reflecting it seems the quickening pace of Western life in general—from the softer, flowing motion of the Renaissance, to the lightening speed and rhythmic complexity ushered in by the nineteenth-century romantics.

The mind cannot withstand unbroken, monotonous repetition in any form whether phone numbers or musical beats. This propensity to arrange everything in groups is reflected in the next element: meter. The musical appearance of this trait seems to antedate all intellectual activity as observed in extremely complex metrical patterns found among primitive cultures. In Western music, beats are organized into metrical groups of two, three, four, or six. They are notated by time signatures (2/4, 3/4, 4/4 etc.) appearing at the beginning of a musical piece. The top figure designates the number of beats per measure, the bottom number the type of note (quarter, eighth, etc.) which is to receive a beat or count.

Accents and Unaccents

The occurence of accents has much to do with musical propulsion we sense in varying degrees in all music. Forward motion, or impetus, is caused in part by the progression of tones (a kind of tonal gravity, the drawing or pulling of one tone to another). But for the most part this propulsion is caused by rhythmic patterns of stress and release, of accent and unaccent. The same principle prevails in certain types of poetry where repeated patterns of accented and unaccented syllables constitute a system of "poetic meters" devised by the ancient Greeks.

Musical rhythm has a similar scheme of stress-release, specifically alternating short and long notes. Beethoven, who has a penchant for the poetic meters, employs the iambic (short accent followed by long) in the Moonlight Sonata, third movement. The composer offers an example of dactyl meter (long and two short stresses) in his seventh symphony, second movement.

(Iambic), L. Beethoven Sonata No. 14 "Moonlight," third movement

---

(Dactyl), L. Beethoven Symphony No. 7, second movement

We must digress historically for a moment to show the impact of early dance rhythms and forms on instrumental music, an influence extending deep into much of the concert music of the Classical and Romantic periods. Although we can see sparodic development of dance forms in the Middle Ages, it was not until the sixteenth century when a large repertory for specified instruments began to appear in Europe. This trend, particularly evident in England during the latter decades (at the time of Henry VIII), was given impetus by the powerful surge of secularism, creating interest in popular dance forms in the court and village.

In the classical age of Mozart and Haydn, the dance spirit was infused in all forms of music. We find the distinct rhythms and meters of the contredanse (country dance), as well as the more polished and refined minuet (so prominent in the third movement of Haydn's and Mozart's symphonies), and beginning about 1800, the lively rustic flavor of the German folk ländler became a prominent feature in Beethoven's work. Beethoven, above all others, infused tremendous power in many of his dance-movements, which the above Symphony No. 7, stands as a supreme example. Later in the Romantic period (Chopin), more stylized dances were incorporated into formal concert music (such as the Polish mazurka, polonaise, and the Viennese waltz).

HARMONY

Essential Features

Whereas melody, comprising a successive placement of tones, is commonly regarded as the horizontal aspect of music, harmony, consisting of groups of tones (chords) sounded simultaneously, represents the vertical dimension. Developing much later than melody in the history of music, the crude beginnings of harmony did not appear until the ninth century. In the early 1700s, the principles of harmony, which governed music creativity for the next 200 years, were fully established by J.S. Bach, Georg Frideric Handel, and their contemporaries. This harmonic system came to be known as *tonality*, defined as the system of tonal gravitation to a central home-tone or tonic. This system is distinct from "atonality," a twentieth-century technique in which tones move freely without reference to a key-center.

Of all the elements, harmony is the most intricate and sophisticated, yielding aesthetic and intellectual qualities appealing to composers and audiences for centuries. If melody is the "subject" of music, harmony is the superstructure, the foundation. It furnishes the chordal support for melody and controls the flow of music from one key to another. Without harmony melody would be bare, austere. Oftentimes, harmony does, however, take a dominant role, its starkness and dissonance, or perhaps its unique indistinctness, becoming the center of musical interest. From the listener's point of view, the most pertinent questions to be considered are: How are chords formed? What makes certain chords "sound" different from others? And what do major and minor mean?

The Basis of Harmony

Classification of tonal combinations was made by the Greek theorists led by Pythagoras in the sixth century B.C. Using mathematical ratios applied to different lengths of sounding strings, they found the most perfect acoustic consonance was produced by the interval of an octave (eight steps) having a ratio of 2:1. For example, if two strings of equal length, density and tension are placed side by side and the second "stopped" at a point one-half of its length, the difference in pitch would be an octave. For the fifth (3:2) the second string would have vibration length of two-thirds of the first string. In addition to the octave the other consonant intervals included the fifth (3:2), and fourth (4:3). These intervals, with the much later additions (about 1350) of the third and the sixth, formed the theory of consonance that prevailed in music from the Renaissance up to the nineteenth century. The remaining second and seventh, were used but were carefully governed by the prevailing taste and compositional practices concerning consonance and dissonance

Intervals in the key of C

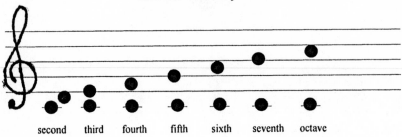

second   third   fourth   fifth   sixth   seventh   octave

How Chords are Formed

The simplest type of chord is the triad, made up of three different tones, each an interval of three steps apart. (An interval is the distance of pitch between two tones: C to D = a second; C to E = a third; C to G = a fifth, etc.)

I   II   III   IV   V   VI   VII   I

The tonic (I) is the chord of rest, usually the ending chord in traditional music. The other chords or triads represent a greater degree of activity or tension, and they, particularly the dominant (V), progress or gravitate to the tonic chord. The I, IV (subdominant), and V are the primary chords upon which much of our traditional music is based.

America with simple chord accompaniment

Following the Renaissance, composers of the Baroque era increasingly employed certain dissonant tones as regular components of chords, giving rise to the dominant seventh, the first of a variety of new colorful chords which came into common practice. The dominant seventh, which plays such an important role at closing cadences (V7 followed by I), is composed of the dominant triad, plus the seventh, which is seven notes above the fundamental (for example in the key of C: G B D F). The composers of the Classical period continued the Baroque practices, however, with considerable attention to subtlety and refinement of dissonance and reduced harmonic textures. In the Romantic era, harmonic dissonance in its many degrees of intensity was released in a variety of chords including all types of seventh chords (emphasis on the diminished form), and toward the end of the century the ninth, eleventh and thirteenth.

The Difference Between Major and Minor

Throughout the music of the classic and romantic eras we see constant reference to major and minor: Concerto in A Minor, Sonata in C Major and the like. What do these terms mean? These are the two fundamental tonalities in which a piece of music may be written. (The tonal system consists of twelve major keys and twelve minor keys.) We might regard each tonality as a color: major as a bright hue, minor as a dark hue; or the major as indicative of joy and cheerfulness, the minor as sombre. Although overworked, these distinctions will prove helpful in grasping musical style, for the major-minor duality is one of the strongest forces in developing aesthetic energy—the inner emotional power of music. The reason for the psychological impressions associated with these tonalities rests in the third and sixth tones of the scale: in the minor they are lowered (flatted), in the major they remain unaltered.

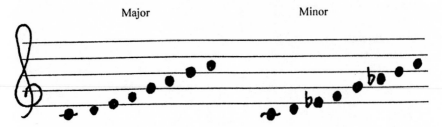

The difference in the two tonalities is made clear in the two versions of a familiar folk song, "Frère Jacques," presented (below) first in its traditional major key (D major), followed (in subsequent pages) by a distinctive treatment in the minor by the romantic, Gustav Mahler.

Musical Texture

The term "texture" is used to describe the manner in which tones are arranged in musical space. A single melody by itself, with no accompaniment is called *monophonic* texture. (Medieval chant is a good example.) *Homophonic* texture is achieved when chords are added as accompaniment to the melody. The chords may be in "block" form (tones of chord struck together, for example Chopin's Mazurka in F minor, op. 68). Or, in "broken" form (each tone sounded separately, for example Mozart's Piano Sonata in C major K. 545). When two or more melodies or themes are presented simultaneously the texture is called contrapuntal. A musical form which makes use of contrapuntal writing is the canon (or round) in which the theme is imitated in succession by the other parts, for example Mahler's Symphony No.1, part of which is printed below.

This Mahler example is an excellent illustration of contrapuntal texture. Following a two-measure timpani introduction, we first hear the main theme (the folk song Frère Jacques) in the contrabass. It is then echoed by other instruments in succession, creating a rich contrapuntal texture that becomes increasingly thicker as more instruments join in.

Mahler, Symphony No. 1, third movement
(Contrapuntal texture)

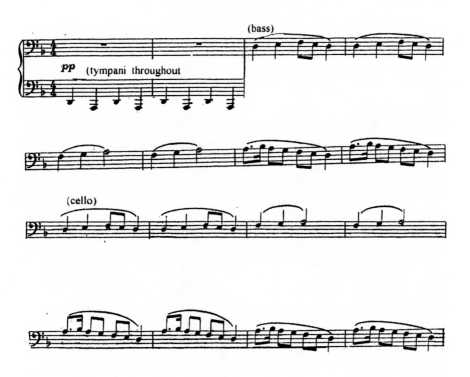

Incidentally, Mahler, who lived at the close of the Romantic Period, contributed greatly to the art of orchestration, that is, the technique of writing and scoring for instruments. The next example, Prelude in C Minor, is by Chopin, a leading figure of the early Romantic Period. His work in devising chromatically rich harmony paved the way for many composers who followed. Notice the depth of the harmony as well as the subtle dissonant effects.

Chopin Prelude in C Minor, Op. 28, No. 20
(Homophonic texture)

Mozart Sonata in C Major, K. 545, first movement
(Broken chord texture)

PRINCIPLES OF MUSICAL FORM

Introduction

A large orchestra is seated on stage warming up in preparation for the first work on the program, *Egmont Overture*, a dramatic and exhilarating composition by Beethoven. What will come out of this huge conglomertion? Will we find a thread of order—something we can "hold onto" or follow as the music unfolds? As the conductor brings the massive form to life we sense some kind of meaning here—the explosive force seems to be taking us somewhere. In short, there seems to be relationships and climactic points in much the same way an exciting story unravels.

The musician writing a new work is faced with two problems: how to produce an aesthetically appealing idea, and secondly, one which will be coherent and meaningful to the listener. Creative imagination will fulfill the first goal; the second, by skillful use of the principles of form. The word "form" is usually applied in two ways: "form in music" and "forms of music." The first refers to the inner musical workings and relationships, and the latter to the outer pattern or design—the molds like symphony, sonata, for holding musical thoughts.

From Motives to Symphony

The significance of formal design is most apparent in melody. The composer arranges his material syntactically—into meaningful relationships, similar to spoken language. Just as letters or words do not represent meaning until brought into relationship with other letters or words, musical meaning does not become possible until the tones are ordered into a definite pattern and the pattern or theme is related to another pattern. Below, is a general comparison of the rudimentary elements of form in verbal and musical expression.

VERBAL	MUSICAL
Letters	Tones
Alphabet	Musical Scales
Words	Motives (figures)
Phrase (a portion of a sentence)	Phrase (short passage, typically a few measures)
Punctuation	Cadence (a form of musical punctuation—see below)
Sentence (complete statement)	Melody (complete musical thought)

The comparison can be expanded upon, for in many ways the structural procedures in some music and drama are closely paralleled. This is particularly true when comparing a romantic orchestral work with a theatrical production of the same period.

DRAMA	SYMPHONIC MOVEMENT
The Beginning: characters are presented, plot is laid out.	Exposition: themes are announced.
The Middle: complication and tension builds.	Development: increasing musical tension through elaboration of themes and rhythms.
The End: resolution of plot.	Recapitulation: resolution of conflicting elements in grand climax.

In the composing process, musical form begins on a very small scale. Commencing with a chosen key and its scale, the composer selects a series of tones which are then grouped into small figures or motives (see "circled" tones in the Beethoven example below). These cell-like clusters are the intrinsic aesthetic features that give identity to the melody. However, before the melody is completed in its finished form, it is divided into melodic units called *phrases* thus allowing the melody to "breathe." A never-ending succession of tones, like continuous, unbroken series of words, is monotonous and unmeaningful to the listener. The phrases are separated by a kind of punctuation called *cadences*. For example, notice in the melody by Beethoven (below), a momentary pause occurs at the end of the first phrase (X). This is comparable to a comma in punctuation and is called a half cadence. Observe the definite close or stop at the end of the melody (XX). This effect is equivalent to a period, and is referred to as a complete cadence.

L. Beethoven, Andante F Major ("Andante favori")

X=End of first phrase. X X=Close of first theme.

A Higher Level of Musical Meaning

Thus far we have looked at musical meaning operating on the small scale— within a   section of a movement from Beethoven's Andante favori. To summarize, all listening whether on a small or large scale, we could say that the type of musical intellection required for serious listening is this: it is a process of following a discourse of tonal patterns (themes) arranged or presented discursively much like a story unfolds. Of course, not all music demands this kind of attention; the composer will occasionally concentrate on a purely colorful tonal display, rather than create interesting formal structures. As Jonathan Harvey writes: he will be less concerned with memory and form, but rather with the "now," with the color and flavor of the moment. The listening experience is not a matter of cold, logical analysis but rather one of following empathically the life of tonal ideas, as they grow, undergo tension and resolution, and reach their final goal. It may be helpful to outline a few of the fundamental ways in which thematic ideas may be treated in a composition; short descriptions are given below.

Thematic Juxtaposition

The idea of repetition and contrast is as old as primitive tribal calls. Musical forms most easily grasped consist of statement, digression and restatement, or, simply: A B A. this ternary form (and its companion, the binary form of A B) appears throughout music history. Over the centuries, the ternary and binary patterns have been the mainstay of songs (popular, folk and art). From its humble folk beginnings, the simple ternary pattern evolved into the sonata form, (later, see the Classical Period) becoming the most important method of musical organization in the late eighteenth century. Another popular mode of construction is the Rondo, which is usually found in the third movement of many classical sonatas and symphonies. It is identified by a recurring main theme interspersed between new or different material: A B A C A. This is the design Mozart uses in his Piano Sonata in C Major, K.545, third movement.

Thematic Variation

The repetition-contrast principle is also evident in the theme and variations technique: a recurring theme is subjected to a series of successive alterations, either in its melodic contour, rhythm or texture. The most basic method is to alter the melody, (via chromatics, or rhythm, for example), while still retaining the essential spirit. Other techniques include modification of the texture, (for example, from homophonic to contrapuntal); harmony (major to minor key); or orchestration (scoring the theme for a different group of instruments). The final movement of Beethoven's Eroica symphony and Brahms' Variations on a theme of Haydn, are excellent illustrations of the variation technique.

Thematic Imitation

In this technique one or more instruments or voices imitate the theme in succession. When a melody or theme is imitated exactly throughout the composition, it is called a *canon*. Its ancestors were the "rounds" which were popular in Europe in the medieval and Renaissance periods. Imitation may be partial, involving only a few initial tones (or "head-motives") of the principal theme. Frequently the imitation may begin with an exact mirroring but gradually thin-out or become absorbed in the general flow of musical ideas as in the second movement of Beethoven's first symphony.

Thematic Development

A more intricate and sophisticated method of expanding or evolving musical ideas is commonly found in the second section of the sonata form. In this portion, the "Development," the main theme, or themes, are embellished and worked over in various ways: presented in new keys (minor as opposed to major), given a new harmonic setting or possibly broken up into small fragments (called motives). In the Development section from Beethoven's fifth symphony (first movement), the composer develops the main theme, consisting of a four-note motive, by tossing it back and forth from one instrumental section to another.

THE FORMS OF MUSIC

Importance to the Listener

We will close this portion with a summary of the principal forms and some suggestions for making form an integral part of the listening experience. As with other personal listening achievements, such as being able to identify composers' and period styles, the comprehension of the larger forms also offers a high degree of satisfaction, specifically in knowing what generates these forms and the kind of musical information each has to offer. In striving for this goal, the listener may be somewhat bewildered when confronted with the many names of forms, and the generally confusing associated terms found on record jackets and in concert notes, such as "absolute" and "programmatic" music. The following should cast some light on these matters.

Abstract and Referential Forms

Musical forms differ as to the number of movements, sounding medium and the nature of musical thoughts or ideas communicated. For the most part we have stressed the dominance of *abstract* music where the focus is strictly on thematic workings as the principal type of conception. And yet another avenue of creativity appears throughout much of music history—the appeal of representing something *outside* of music. This *referential* vein of creativity focuses on musical thoughts suggestive of, or referenced to, people, places, events as well as literature, poetry and painting.

Abstract	*Referential*
Symphony	Art song
Sonata	Program symphony
Solo Concerto	Program overture
Double Concerto	Symphonic poem
String Quintet	Opera
String Trio	Oratorio
Piano Trio	Mass

It would be a simplification to say the abstract group represents the Classical period and the referential the Romantic. We will find, however, in the latter period composers searched for new sources of inspiration and ideas from a wide range of literature, poetry, philosophy and history. Incidentally, the term "program music" is often used to designate literary or story-based compositions, and "absolute" denotes abstract music.

Summary

The essential components of music consist of melody, harmony, rhythm, timbre, and form. Melody, representing the horizontal dimension of music, holds the paramount position for it is usually the central organizing idea. The listener distinquishes melodic ideas by their shape or gestalt: their angular or curving quality, their conjunct or disjunct form, and their range of movement. Rhythm, the life-blood of music, has four components: beat, meter, tempo and accent. Harmony, consisting of a group of tones sounded simultaneously, is the vertical aspect of music. Various types of chords are constructed on each of the steps of the scale. The harmonic vocabulary ranges from the simple triad to more complex chords of varying dissonance. Form has to do with shaping tones into recognizable designs, many of which have come down through history.

CHAPTER THREE

THE EARLY BAROQUE 1600-1685

POWER, SPLENDOR, DRAMA

The Baroque artist enters into the multiplicity of
phenomena...His compositions are dynamic and
open and tend to expand beyond their boundaries.
Germain Bazin, Art Historian

A Major Turning Point

Historians are often asked to name their favorite period of music. The
Baroque (1600-1750) frequently comes out high on the list for a number of
reasons. Around 1600 the entire field of music was about to explode with new
ideas and tremendous enthusiasm. New string instruments—the violin, viola,
cello and bass—created by Nicola Amati and Antonio Stradivari, were about to
revolutionize the entire art form. Music theory as we know it today—the system
or chords and keys—was about to open a totally different approach to musical
composition. Audiences now began to develop on a wide scale and to exert an
influence on musical taste. Finally, both religious and secular realms of music
undergo a revitalization with new forms and styles. In summary, this era marks
an extraordinary surge of creative activity, a renascence that is to be felt
throughout the world for the next 400 years.

Time-line Early Baroque Music

1600   Florentine Camerata, birth of opera.
       Euridice by Peri
       Beginnings of oratorio
1607   Monteverdi, opera, *Orfeo*
1637   Public opera theatres begin in Venice
1640   Polychoric style at St. Peter's by Benevoli
1642   Monteverdi opera, *Coronation of Poppea*
1664   Schütz: *Christmas Oratorio*
1680   Neapolitan opera dominant, A. Scarlatti
1689   Purcell: opera, *Dido and Aeneas*

As with all periods of art, the beginning of the Baroque is not clearly defined. Its ending is even less clear since it overlaps the next major trend in arts and ideas—the revival of classicism. In most periods we observe a certain clustering of ideas in intellectual and artistic thought or perhaps a series of social and political movements that provide the impetus to change. Prominent signs of the arrival of the Baroque include: a spirit of renewal within the Catholic Church stemming from the Counter Reformation in the sixteenth century; the founding of Catholic religious orders (such as the Society of Jesus by Ignatius Loyola), which fostered a great rebirth of Church art—an exhuberant, dynamic and ornamented style that flourished in the newly built Catholic churches springing up in Rome and elsewhere in Europe. These traits in art are also reflected in music—right up to the end of the period ending with Bach and Handel.

The word "baroque" is derived from the Portuguese *barroco,* meaning an irregularly shaped pearl. The term was applied in a deprecatory manner to Baroque art by later nineteenth-century critics who believed that the period was bizzare, grotesque, and overly ornate. The modern world has, of course, reversed this judgment, for highly valued today are the artworks of Bernini, Rubens, Caravaggio, Vermeer, Rembrandt, and the music of Corelli, Vivaldi, Scarlatti, Bach, Handel and many others who were discovered in the twentieth-century revival of the Baroque. A glance through the list of their works indicates a noticeable emphasis in two areas of artistic interest: sacred and secular, a basic separation of style which we will follow.

Announcing the Baroque: Drama in Sacred Art

The new outlook concerning the role of the arts in worship was one of the strongest forces in the shaping of the Baroque style. Essentially, it was the idea of reaching the spirit of the worshiper through dramatic sense impressions. The construction of the Church Il Gesu (the mother church of the new Jesuit Order founded by Loyola), in Rome, 1575, marked the change in policy regarding sacred art. The architecture and vestments of this, and many other churches that sprang up in many parts of Europe, became splendorous, ornate displays. Soon all the arts (music, architecture, sculpture, painting, and theater) were infused with the new spirit. In church architecture the various structural elements (twisting spirals, circles, and columns) and materials (plaster, granite, and marble) were multiplied and fused together. The eye of the worshiper was met with the rich ornate swelling and swirling movements of elements that moved upward in a mystical atmosphere.

About the time of the completion of the facade of the colossal St. Peter's in Rome (1612), the Catholic composers became the first to represent musically the new aesthetic, notably, Orazio Benevolo who created huge polychoric works (employing four or more separate choral groups) performed in the spacious St. Peter's in the 1640s. Located at different points in the vast edifice, the multichoral bodies sounded forth in a gigantic stereo effect.

On the Secular Side: An Overview

Secular music made significant strides during the Baroque, largely due to the shifting social structure which is identified by widespread absolutism and the rising bourgeois, or middle-class. The effect of absolutism upon the arts was particularly significant in France, where all the arts were given unparalleled royal patronage and where a wide variety of secular music (opera, ballet, and chamber music) flourished. With a newly acquired economic status, the middle class also shared in the expanding European culture. No longer was music solely the interest of the elite. Increasingly it became a public affair, as attested by the opening of public opera houses in Italy in the seventeenth century. And for the first time public taste played an important part in the shaping of musical style. This occurred in the field of opera, which underwent a gradual transformation from an esoteric art form (early 1600s) to a public-dominated expression at the end of the seventeenth century.

The works which opened the way for the development of opera were *Euridice* by Peri (1600), and *Orfeo* by Monteverdi (1607). Although initially not as grandiose and elaborate as early religious art, Baroque opera gradually became a stylistic counterpart to the "colossal Baroque," which was so dynamically and triumphantly expressed in the visual arts, originating chiefly in Rome.

Expression in Baroque Music and Art

A commonality of artistic traits would help us to understand what musicians were striving for in this period. Of the many characteristics three will serve our purpose as we commence this study: *power*, *drama* and *emotion*. They are represented tonally and visually in a number of ways: in the tragic Baroque operas *(Orfeo,* for example), in the thunderous, cascading movement of the organ toccatas and fantasias, in the exciting musical duels between soloists and full orchestra in the concertos, in the surging, ever driving bass in most instrumental music of the period, and in the deeply moving texts of the oratorios. Above all, a source for generating emotion is to be found in the dynamic opposition of musical elements, whether it be large group against small, high against low, soft against loud, or theme against countertheme, as in the great fugues by Bach.

One need not look far to observe the three qualities in the other arts of the Baroque: in the play of light and shadow in such realistic works as Caravaggio's *The Calling of St. Matthew,* Rubens' *The Lion Hunt,* and Bernini's sculpture *The Ecstasy of St. Teresa;* in the juxtaposition of many swirling, upward-moving architectural and sculptual elements inside many Baroque churches, such as St. Peter's in Rome, and the huge Benedictine church at Zweifalten, Germany; in the shadowy, mysterious atmosphere of Rembrandt's *The Night Watch;* and in his more deeply moving personality studies such as *The Supper at Emmaus,* which dramatize faith, pity, and suffering.

What to Expect in Baroque Music

Generally speaking, the Baroque is to be identified by the following characteristics: (1) a variety of forms which came into being at this time: concerto, concerto grosso, sonata, opera, oratorio, cantata and others described below, (2) kinetic, on-going rhythmic movement, (3) a continuous bass movement usually standing out in high relief in the musical texture, (4) use of the new major and minor keys to emphasize contrasting emotional moods and feelings.

In summary, the Baroque's inherent power, exuberance, and triumphant mood seem to have been nurtured by the restabilized Catholic Church in the late sixteenth century. The Baroque artists' and musicians' expressive language generally involves the statement of an idea in a spacious form, with power, force, and elaboration of detail. Although there are exceptions, we will usually find these to be present in most literature, music, painting, sculpture, and architecture of the Baroque. In the following pages we will see how these qualities evolved in the development of Baroque music.

It will be convenient to divide the music of the period into two segments: early Baroque (1600-1685), and late Baroque (1685-1750). The first part is principally identified by an extensive concentration in dramatic vocal music and the latter by the creation of the modern orchestra and its idioms as well as new chamber music forms.

EARLY BAROQUE MUSIC (1600-1685)

The Rise of Dramatic Vocal Music

The New Sound Ideal: Monody

In the closing years of the sixteenth century, the strong literary trend that had been gathering momentum in music since the early Renaissance, finally burst forth. The leaders of this movement were a circle of Renaissance humanists—poets, musicians, and scholars—known as the Florentine Camerata. This elite group of intellectuals, which met regularly at Count Bardi's home in Florence beginning about 1580, discussed theories of music, Greek drama, and formulated a new aesthetic ideal that greatly affected the course of Baroque music.

The new type of musical expression devised by the Camerata is called *monody,* from the Greek "monodia," to sing alone. Its principles were first presented by Vincenzo Galilei (father of the renowned astronomer) in *Discourses on Ancient Music and Good Singing,* written about 1580. Briefly summarized, these principles are as follows:

1. Music is to be subordinate to the words of the text.
2. Elaborate polyphony cannot express clearly the emotions of the text.
3. Therefore, a single vocal melody and chordal accompaniment is advocated

4. The vocal melody should be in the style of a speech-like recitation, that
   is, musical rhythm should imitate the natural inflections of the speaking   voice.
5. The singer should perform the melody with much expression and
   dramatic feeling.

The dawn of the seventeenth century, then, saw the coming of a new dramatic style of music, quite opposed to the thick contrapuntal textures of the Renaissance. For a time the art of counterpoint was set aside in favor of vertically arranged tones (homophonic texture), which could provide the expressive accompaniment necessary for the vocal soloist's declamation of a dramatic text. Later, toward the end of the seventeenth century, counterpoint was restored and remained as the mainstay of Baroque musical art.

To return to the beginnings of monody, we note that the Florentines favored an instrumental accompaniment that could provide a harmonic background for the soloist. Thus, instruments that could produce chords, such as the lute, harpsichord, and organ became the preferred types. The name given to this accompaniment was *basso continuo* (or continuous bass, so called because of its constant presence throughout the music). Moreover, by the beginning of the seventeenth century it became standard practice to include a cello or viola da gamba (sixteenth century predecessor of the modern viola). The music for the basso continuo usually consisted of a single melody in the bass clef with a series of number's below it. These indicated the various types of chords to be played above the given bass part.

Sonata da Chiesa in E Minor, Arcangelo Corelli

Thus, the harpsichord player was expected to "fill in" or to improvise over the bass melody. The other member of the basso continuo, the cello or viola da gamba, doubled the bass melody. The basso continuo idea was employed extensively throughout the Baroque, first used as the only accompaniment for the early operas and then later becoming the heart of every Baroque instrumental ensemble. Toward the end of the Baroque (c. 1740) when the new symphony form began to surpass the concerto form, the basso continuo gradually disappeared from musical practice.

Definitions of Vocal Music Forms

Among the members of the Florentine Camerata were several composers who applied the monodic principles to musical composition. From their experiments and those of their contemporaries, emerged the dramatic vocal genres of the Baroque: opera, cantata and oratorio. A brief description of these forms will be followed by a brief look at the development of opera—the dominant musical expression of the early Baroque.

Opera—Baroque opera may be defined as an elaborate theatrical presentation, that is, involving costumes and scenery, in which the entire text (called *libretto)* is set to music. Usually it is based upon a secular plot, which may be in the form of a tragedy *(opera seria)* or comedy *(opera buffo)*. Intrinsic features that gradually evolved in the early Baroque include the use of sung declamatory passages (called *recitative* and modeled after dramatic speech) and complete solo songs called *arias,* which are constructed on purely musical grounds, having distinct form, phrasing, and melodic contour. The instrumental accompaniment gradually developed from the simple basso continuo, used for the first operas, to a full orchestral group by the eighteenth century,

Oratorio—Although the oratorio is similar in some respects to the opera in its basic structure (chorus, soloists, and instrumental accompaniment), it differs in its use of religious subject matter (usually drawn from the Bible),a narrator who relates the unfolding story, and in its concert method of performance, that is, without stage scenery and costumes. This is the type of oratorio that is most often performed today. In general, the oratorio of the early Baroque period differs from the late in that the former type was performed in church as a religious drama with full staging and scenery, while the latter type (Handel), although continuing the sacred theme, was presented in a secular setting and without stage equipment and costumes.

Cantata—This vocal form, which first appeared as a *camera* (chamber) *cantata* for one or two voices and basso continuo, gradually developed into a substantial form by the late seventeenth century. Although the chamber cantata is much shorter than the opera, it is similar by nature of its secular and dramatic content—like a small scene extracted from an opera. Because of its sophisticated and more subtle intellectual character, and lack of theatricality (no costumes or staging), the chamber cantata was the chief interest of the discriminating elite rather than the masses in the public theater. The leading composer of cantatas during the early Baroque was Alessandro Scarlatti (1659-1725), who, composed in addition to numerous keyboard sonatas, approximately six hundred works in this form.

SEVENTEENTH-CENTURY OPERA:
BACKGROUND

By far the most important musical happening of the seventeenth century was the creation of opera. Little did the members of the Camerata realize that from their exclusive intellectual realm would arise a musical form that would become the dominant idiom of major European composers for a century and a half. It is interesting to note, too, that opera is the oldest of the large secular musical forms. The second-ranking form, the concerto, began about seventy years after opera (c. 1670) and the symphony came into being early in the next century (c. 1730). Several features pertaining to opera should be explained.

First, we must understand the inherent nature of opera and how this form differs from others. The major instrumental forms (symphony, concerto, string quartet, and so on) represent the private, more personal realm of creativity and are subject only to the composer's own aesthetic principles. Opera, on the other hand—due to its theatrical structure, subject matter, dual relationship of librettist and composer, and, above all, expense in staging—is a more self-conscious art form. It is thus more openly subject to the varied and changing tastes of its audience.

Another feature that has direct bearing on understanding opera of the Baroque, and for that matter of all periods, is the matter of text material. Opera must draw from human experience for its sustenance; consequently the subject matter generally reflects the life about it—the customs, habits, events, and language. Again, unlike the abstract aspects of the symphony and concerto, these intrinsic features have meaning only in terms of our understanding of the age. The witticisms, expressions of passion, comedy, and tragedy do not have the same meaning today. The operatic work, consequently, must be listened to against the backdrop of the period itself. Another basic problem: the conflict of reality with unreality.

For example, due to the medium, the story must be telescoped, resulting in distortion of time. Also, we find the unnatural convention of accompanying action, even in the most dire moments, by singing and the frequent extension or prolongation of the dramatic climax for purely musical reasons. One may wonder how the opera form ever developed with all of these complexities. And yet it is precisely because of its richness and complexity that many are attracted to it. On the one hand we note the double nature of the poetic text with its euphonic, sensual qualities of the sound of words and the appeal to the intellect through symbols, and, on the other, the double nature of the music, with its intensity of expression and an internal logic and order unparalleled by any of the other arts. It is this duality of expression of *tone* and *word* that continually challenged seventeenth-century opera composers.

The Development of Italian Opera

Claudio Monteverdi (1567-1643), unquestionably the leading composer of the early seventeenth century, was the first to explore the inherent dramatic and expressive power of the opera form. Although not a Florentine, (working mainly at Mantua and Venice), Monteverdi continued the same general style of the Florentines; however, his work is decidedly advanced in dramatic characterization, in emotional expression, and in musical construction. His first opera, *Orfeo* (1607), which is considered the first operatic masterpiece, is given an extraordinary depth of expression. This is particularly evident in the scene when Orfeo, having learned of his wife's death, expresses his profound grief and his determination to enter the terrible underworld and rescue Euridice. In this scene, in which Orfeo sings the recitative "Tu se' morta" (Thou art perished), strange, dissonant chords and an angular melodic line with chromatics, dramatically convey his intense sorrow and remorse.

Recitative, "Tu Se Morta" (Thou art perished) from *Orfeo*

Monteverdi's last great work, and according to many the most significant opera of the seventeenth century, *The L'Incoronazione di Poppea* was composed at the end of his long career as maestro di cappella at St. Mark's in Venice, in 1642. Although it does not have the elaborate choral and orchestral forces, this work ranks with his earlier *Orfeo* in its power and vividness of expression. Instead of using a plot based on a mythological subject, however, Monteverdi, as did his contemporaries at this time, now turned to historical subjects and settings, in this instance to Rome and the lascivious life of Nero. Monteverdi's skill in depicting characters as real people and his ability to mirror their inmost feelings musically, ranks him with the best of opera composers. Perhaps it is this single quality above all else—truth in the expression of emotion—that brings continual praise to the operas of Monteverdi, Puccini, Wagner, and others. This characteristic of greatness is the result of blending musical genius with a strong sense of the dramatic.

The Coming of Opera Seria and Opera Buffa

Italian musicians have always had a leaning toward lyrical expression, that is, a beautiful flowing melodic line with uncomplicated rhythm and clarity of form. These traits, which extend deep into Italian musical history, may account for the strong inclination in the mid-seventeenth century away from the pre-eminence of drama to a more lyric concept of opera—a trend that found its finest fulfillment in the Neapolitan School of opera composition. Developed mainly at Naples and championed by Alessandro Scarlatti, the Neapolitan School (or style) is noted for its beauty and elegance of melodic line rather than dramatic truth. In addition to the popularity of the lyrical style (which eventually develops into the famous Italian *bel canto* tradition of singing noted for its purity and simplicity), comical entertainment is introduced which leads to the establishment of *opera buffa*, or, comic opera.

Among the many composers associated with the Neapolitan style, Alessandro Scarlatti (1660-1730) must be cited. Contained in Scarlatti's and numerous other Italians' works are two types of opera: *opera seria*, a three-act form, usually based on history or legend; and *opera buffa*, a two-act form, noted for its liveliness, humor and scenes taken from everyday life. The comic form grew tremendously in popularity, gradually usurping the position occupied by opera seria.

In a typical Neapolitan opera, the dramatic and purely musical elements were placed in separate compartments. To illustrate, the story was related in the recitative or story-section, and then immediately following, an aria was sung in which the character would comment and reflect upon the previous action as set forth in the recitative. The central focus was upon the aria, usually in ABA form, in which the singer, on the last portion, was expected to improvise with amazing feats of vocal virtuosity. Out of these practices a highly artistic vocal technique became established (early eighteenth century) called *bel canto*. The ability to improvise was an important aspect of the bel canto style (as well as for the keyboard performers of this period). Over a groundwork of basic harmonies, the singer embellished the melody with all sorts of trills, turns, grace notes, frequently covering two octaves, and often vaulted wide leaps from high to low, as in the following excerpt sung by one of the leading divas, Lucrezia Agujari, in the presence of Mozart in 1770:

Passage reportedly sung by Lucrezia Agujari; note the extreme range,
the difficult intervalic leaps,and trills.

The Italian composers did much more. Opera buffa gave us a style of music
which was simple, direct and laid out in lilting repeated phrases—a trait that was
also carried over into the sinfonia (an overture) which preceded the opening act
of the opera. Made up of three parts, fast-slow-fast, the sinfonia's driving,
forceful rhythm, clarity of phrase structure, and homophonic texture became the
dominant characteristics of the classical symphony, which began to emerge
about 1740.

The Spread of Opera: France and England

As early as 1645 the French began to import Italian opera. However, they
did not adopt the new form until late in the century, probably due to their
preoccupation with their own cultural creations: the classical tragedy (Corneille
and Racine) and the ballet, which had begun in France in the fifteenth century.
The central figure in French opera, and indeed the supreme leader of
seventeenth-century French music, is Jean-Baptiste Lully. Of a humble Italian
background (born as Lulli in Florence, 1632), Lully traveled to Paris as a young
boy and became employed as a kitchen scullion. At the age of fourteen he joined
the king's famed *les vingt-quatre violons du roi* (the twenty-four violins of the
king). An exceptional violinist and a personal favorite of the young Louis XIV,
Lully became director of all royal musical activities, including chamber and
orchestral music, and, in 1672, the director of the new French opera established

in the royal palace. In this post, which he held until his death in 1687, Lully composed sixteen works in the opera form, or what the French called "tragédie lyrique" including *Thésée* (1675), *Phaëton* (1683), and *Armide* (1686).

French opera differs from Italian opera in many respects, most important of which, perhaps, is the style of recitative, which in French opera was modeled after the refined speech of professional French actors. This type of recitative, referred to as "rhetorical recitative" by some writers, follows precisely the accent length, and inflection of French syllables. This highly stylized and refined treatment of the text has a definite "classical" ring, so characteristic of French theater of this period. It is interesting to note that this vein of classicism (which antedates what is generally thought of as the classical period in the arts, 1750-1800) dates back to the early seventeenth century, when the French literary movement, with its emphasis on elegance, correctness of expression, and refinement, began to take shape.

Another powerful influence upon French culture, including musical art, was the founding of the French Academy (Académie Française) in 1634. Consisting of noted literary figures who ruled on practically all literary and artistic matters, this select body of connoisseurs greatly affected artistic directions in France from the seventeenth to the nineteenth century. The Académie favored moderation, conciseness, restraint, exquisiteness, and the importance of rule over individual taste—definite classicistic tendencies, which underlie French opera and keyboard music of this period.

The strong French interest in the dance is also important in relation to the opera and to other musical forms which appeared in the Baroque and later periods. Lully, who composed a large number of ballets *(ballet de cour),* included the ballet as an integral part in opera. Actually, ballet, the chief cultural contribution of seventeenth-century France, was the source of a number of dance forms which were later to have an important role in instrumental music. These include the *gavotte, bourrée, rigaudon,* and *minuet,* which are frequently found in the Baroque suite, played by solo harpsichord or orchestra. The minuet was eventually adopted as the third movement in the classical symphony.

Curiously, the opera furor did not affect England until the eighteenth century, when the Neapolitan-styled operas of the German-born Handel became the rage. Unfortunately, England's musical contribution in the seventeenth century—compared to her great achievements in the preceding period of the Renaissance—were very sparse. Aside from considerable chamber music (fantasias and ensemble sonatas or trio sonatas), little was done in dramatic vocal music, at least nothing that would compare with the Italian furor. The *masque,* a popular type of English court entertainment in the sixteenth and seventeenth centuries, was more of a spectacle than a drama. Elaborately staged and modeled after the French ballet de cour, it consisted of a succession of dances ranging from crude comic to the macabre, and danced by both professionals and members of the elite audience. The latter participants were called *masquers* (hence the name of this form), and usually wore exotic disguises. These dances were accompanied by voices and instruments and separated by spoken dialogue, recitative and solo songs. The most famous

English writer of masques was Ben Jonson *(The Vision of Delight,* 1617). Noted composers of masque music include William Lawes (1602-1645), Matthew Locke (1630-1677), and Henry Purcell (1659-1695). The latter composed the only true English opera of the seventeenth century. *Dido and Aeneas* (1689), of which the final aria, "When I am Laid in Earth," is widely celebrated. Purcell also wrote incidental music for various dramas, and a considerable amount of chamber music, for which he is most famous.

INSTRUMENTAL MUSIC OF THE SEVENTEENTH CENTURY

The Status of Instrumental Music

Opera and other forms of dramatic vocal music overshadowed instrumental music in the early Baroque. The developments that did occur in the instrumental idiom are to be found chiefly in music for solo instruments: organ music in Italy and Germany, and lute and harpsichord music in France. However, chamber music, and here we are referring to ensemble music for two or more instruments, did not dwindle during the early Baroque. The development here, although less than in solo instrumental music, was one of formal clarification. That is, the many names of various forms (such as sonata, canzona, ricercar), which were used at the beginning of the century to represent practically any musical design and combination of instruments, began to be thinned out into several fairly defined ensemble forms by 1650.

Two such forms, the *sonata da chiesa* (church sonata) and *sonata da camera* (chamber sonata) were cultivated by the Italians beginning in the last half of the century. Since these represent the achievements of Arcangelo Corelli, who announced the arrival of the great age of Italian instrumental music at the end of the seventeenth century, they will be discussed in subsequent pages, under the late Baroque.

Music for the Organ: Italy and Germany

The greatest period of organ music extends from the sixteenth-century Venetian masters at St. Mark's (Merulo and the Gabrielis) to the German musical genius, Johann Sebastian Bach, the culminator of the Baroque. The principal qualities of the Baroque—power, drama, boundlessness, ornateness, and breadth of expression—are perhaps most completely represented in the music for organ. To grasp this we must realize that the organ was a virtuoso instrument even as early as the Venetians, who used it to play all of the parts of a polyphonic composition. In a sense it was the most perfect of instruments, since it could, by itself, produce (1) the complete fabric of music, both contrapuntal and harmonic; (2) the complete musical range; (3) technical passages; and (4) dramatic shadings in volume and tone color. Thus the organ became the instrument of the virtuoso and a medium for brilliant technique and profound emotional expression. Occasionally technique outweighs the expressive in this period; however, in many of the works of the leaders—Frescobaldi, Buxtehude, Pachelbel, and Bach—the two aspects are aesthetically balanced.

The Venetians first realized many of the potentialities of the instrument and created some of the principal organ forms (ricercar, canzona, and toccata). However, the idiom was greatly advanced by the leading Italian organ composer and virtuoso of the early Baroque, Girolamo Frescobaldi (1583-1643), at St. Peter's in Rome during the first half of the century. His work represents the musical equivalent of the dynamic and boundless spirit that burgeoned forth in early Baroque art. His organ works seem to be musical representations of the mystical architectural dramas found in such churches as the Il Gesu and St. Ignazio in Rome. Contained in his Herculean toccatas is a driving, ever-reaching restlessness punctuated by strange dissonances and bold syncopations. And yet at other times, in typical Baroque fashion, a strange religious calm enhances the power and sweep of these architectural monuments of tone. Frescobaldi's stature rests chiefly on his extraordinary gift for treating musical ideas through such means as the theme and variation principle, and the use of such contrapuntal devices as diminution, augmentation, and imitation. (See Glossary). One of his favored forms was the *toccata,* a brilliant display piece, consisting of fast-moving scale and arpeggio figures. Its form is free (no set pattern), largely due to its rhapsodic nature that is given to sudden changes in mood and rhythmic restlessness.

In the north the great tradition of organ music was continued mainly by Buxtehude (1637-1707), organist at Lübeck, Germany (where the young Bach had traveled many miles to hear the great master), and Johann Pachelbel (1653-1706), the principal figure in the crystallization of the *fugue*—the most musically interesting and challenging form used by Baroque organ composers.

The basic features of the fugue (an example by Pachelbel follows) may be sketched briefly. It is a polyphonic composition in which one theme (called a *subject*) is first stated alone in one voice part in the tonic key and answered (imitated) in another key (dominant or subdominant) by a second part. Then other parts sound the subject or its answer in succession. When the various parts have stated either the subject or the answer, the first section (or *exposition)* is completed. Several other expositions may follow before the fugue's close. This type of fugue was perfected by J. S. Bach in the late Baroque.

Fugue by Johann Pachelbel

French Lute and Keyboard Music

In addition to the spectacular and elaborate opera and ballet, the French also concentrated on the miniature musical forms for the lute and harpsichord. In many respects these exquisite pieces heralded the approaching rococo period, which was to arise in France in the early eighteenth century. The lute of the sixteenth and seventeenth centuries had a pear-shaped body, a fretted fingerboard and eleven strings, five pairs of which were tuned in octaves or unison. It had a deep, rich tone, owing to its bass range and double stringing. Since the strings were paired rather than single (as on the modern guitar), the player had to pluck each string of the pair with extreme accuracy.

In seventeenth-century France, the lute was the instrument of the virtuoso, represented chiefly by Denis Gaultier (1597-1672). His major contributions to the lute repertoire are in a collection entitled *La Rhétorique de dieux* (The Rhetoric of the Gods), composed by Gaultier in the 1650s. This music consists of a series of popular dances (allemande, courante, pavan, and so forth). The following example is taken from this collection.

Denis Gaultier, Tombeau de Mademoiselle Gaultier

Idiomatic considerations, that is, the natural capabilities and limitations of instruments, have played a major part in the evolution of music written for specific types of instruments such as the lute, organ, and violin. For example, the organ became the preferred instrument for polyphonic textured music because of its keyboard structure and pedals, which permitted the playing of several different parts simultaneously. Also, the new violin, which was widely adopted by the Italians in the seventeenth century, was given two fundamental types of melodic material: (1) sustained, legato patterns suited to the violin's bowing technique and (2) characteristic fast-skipping movements easily performed by the violinist. The same is true of the lute. Its structure lends itself to a dominantly chord-structured music with a natural rhythmic pulse—in short, to the music of the dance. The dance origins of lute music extend back to the sixteenth century, when pairs of dances, notably the pavan-galliard combination were favored. These first lute pieces were very simple, consisting of a tune with chordal accompaniment. Later, lute music became more intricate, in addition to dance music, transcriptions of chansons were played.

Gradually, the harpsichord (called *clavecin* in French) attained considerable importance during the late seventeenth century and eventually surpassed the lute in popularity—probably because of the harpsichord's simpler, more modern notation and melodic and harmonic agility. The harpsichord differs from its successor, the piano of the late classical period, in several basic ways: the strings are plucked rather than struck, and its tone quality is very light. Interestingly, many of the melodic and harmonic patterns characteristic of lute music were absorbed into the new French harpsichord expression. The same type of stylized dance music, and even the characteristic lute technique (broken chords and ornamentation), were emulated by the leading French harpsichordist-composer of the period, Jacques Chambonnieres (c. 1602-1672). A contemporary of Gaultier, and musician to Louis XIII and XIV, Chambonnieres was the most brilliant harpsichord artist produced by seventeenth-century France. His work is contained in a collection called *Pieces de Clavessin.*

CHAPTER FOUR

THE LATE BAROQUE—AT THE ZENITH (1685-1750)

THE SUPREMACY OF ITALIAN INSTRUMENTAL MUSIC

The New Stringed Instruments

Following a period of heterogeneous activity in the early part of the Baroque, Italian ensemble and orchestral music burst forth in full grandeur—notably in the work of Corelli and Vivaldi who brought the development to its highest peak during the last quarter of the seventeenth century and early part of the eighteenth.

While a large number of concertos were written for the trumpet and other wind instruments, the dominant instruments of this great hour in music were the stringed instruments, the modern violin, viola, cello, and double bass. Many of the new stringed instruments that had now superseded the older Renaissance viols were made in the early Baroque by the Amati family, the first leading violin craftsmen; the art of violin-making reached its climax with Antonio Stradivari (1644-1737) in the early years of the eighteenth century.

Time-line: Late Baroque Music

1680   Start of Italian Golden Era of Instumental Music
          Corelli: 12 Trio Sonatas (da chiesa) pub. 1681
1685   Bach and Handel born
1721   Bach: Brandenburg Concerti
1722   Bach: Well Tempered Clavier (I)
1723   Bach: Cantata, *Christ lag in Todesbanden*
1724   Vivaldi: *The Four Seasons,* concerti
1740   Handel: 12 concerti grossi
1747   Bach: Mass in B Minor
1750   Death of Bach
1759   Death of Handel

The center for this amazing instrumental creativity was in the Italian city of Bologna, where during the last quarter of the century more sonatas and other instrumental music were composed than in any other city in Europe. Bologna has always had a strong musical culture; however, instrumental music was given impetus in 1657, when Maurizio Cazzati was appointed musical director of Bologna's Church of San Petronio. The huge edifice of San Petronio became the scene of widespread usage of ensemble music as a means for enriching the religious service. It became customary to perform a sonata or concerto during the various parts of the service, usually just before the Mass. Bologna's musical life was further enhanced by the abundant support of the wealthy class and especially by the founding in 1666 of the Accademia Filarmonica, a music academy that later became world famous.

It was this musically rich environment that Arcangelo Corelli (1653-1713) entered at the age of thirteen to begin his first study of the violin. Four years later he enrolled in the famed Accademia Filarmonica, where he studied violin and theoretical subjects in music. From 1685 until his death in 1713, Corelli was active in Rome, where he wrote a large number of sonatas and concertos under the patronage of Cardinal Pietro Ottoboni, an enthusiastic follower of the arts.

Forms and Styles

In looking over the list of Corelli's instrumental works, his chief musical forms are the *trio sonata, solo sonata* and *concerto grosso,* The trio sonata is so-named because of its three designated parts of two violins and continuo *(continuo* implying both a keyboard instrument and a low-pitched stringed instrument such as the cello). The solo sonata, which is for violin and continuo, was less common at this time; however, during the next period, the classical, it became a major musical form in the hands of Mozart and Beethoven. The concerto grosso, which was composed for a number of instruments, and so highly favored by the Baroque masters such as Corelli and Vivaldi, marks the beginning of orchestral music.

Corelli differentiated his trio sonatas by the terms "sonata da chiesa" (church sonata) and "sonata da camera" (chamber sonata). Although Corelli was by no means consistent in his treatment of these forms, certain prevailing characteristics may be noted. The sonata da chiesa was intended for church performance, as generally evidenced by its more serious tone and solemn adagio opening. It usually utilized polyphonic texture, and was divided into four separate movements having the tempos slow, fast, slow, and fast. The sonata da camera, which was designed for domestic performance due to its lighter mood, frequently consisted of a series of short movements based on the conventional dances of the period, such as the sarabande, allemande, gavott, and gigue.

Corelli's Sonata da Chiesa in E Minor

This sonata (Op. 3, no. 7), published in 1689, has in its first movement the characteristic majestic and reverent qualities common to many church sonatas.

Only twenty measures in length, the opening movement is based on a melodic idea which, after its abrupt upward step of a sixth, slowly drifts downward in conjunct motion. Alternately, the various string instruments (two violins and cello), supported by the organ, imitate this theme in close succession. Note the *figured bass* in the continuo. It may be recalled from earlier reading that these numbers constituted a kind of musical shorthand, and indicated the harmony or chords to be filled in by the keyboard player.

Sonata da Chiesa in E Minor by Arcangelo Corelli

ADVENT OF THE CONCERTO GROSSO

An outstanding feature of the Baroque style: pitting of one instrument or group against another in a kind of musical duel, is perhaps most clearly demonstrated in the new form—the *concerto grosso* (grand concerto)—introduced by the Bolognese composers at the end of the seventeenth century. Corelli's concerti exemplify an experimental stage of development since some have three, four, or more movements. The three-movement concerto eventually became established by Corelli's successor, Antonio Vivaldi. The basic idea of the concerto grosso is the contrasting of two bodies of instruments, the *concertino* (solo group of several players) and the *ripieno* (the accompanying full group). The final phase of the Baroque concerto was brought to fruition by Torelli (1658-1709) and particularly Vivaldi (1675-1741).

The life of the second leading figure of this period, Antonio Vivaldi (1675-1741), stands in contrast to that of Corelli, the musician of high Roman society. Educated in music and for the priesthood, Vivaldi, due to ill health, eventually turned completely to the music profession. His principal work was done in connection with the Conservatory of the Pieta in Venice, a convent-like institution for orphaned girls. For almost forty years (1704-1740) Vivaldi held the musical directorship of the conservatory, a post that included conducting, composing, and teaching. A flourishing program of music studies and concerts was carried on as an important part of the institution's educational curriculum. For the orchestra, numbering about thirty to forty players, Vivaldi composed a great quantity of music, particularly in the concerto form, which was performed at the school's public concerts and festivals. Clearly, his main contribution was the perfection of the Baroque concerto (over 400 works in this form).

His concertos follow the three-movement plan of fast, slow, fast. The bulk of these are, however, solo concertos in which one instrument (normally a stringed instrument) is juxtaposed against the full orchestra. These employ the concertino-ripieno division of the orchestra in which each of the two groups is assigned contrasting thematic material. (See diagram below.) Following the style of Corelli and other Bolognese composers, Vivaldi's themes gradually unfold in long, ever-moving, and ever-changing patterns. The Vivaldi orchestra is greatly expanded over the string-dominated group of Corelli. The strings are, of course, uppermost; however, other instruments are frequently called for, such as flutes, oboes, horns, and trumpets, providing a greatly enriched orchestral sound. Of the many concertos by Vivaldi, *The Four Seasons* (1725)—depicting musically fall, winter, spring, and summer—is perhaps the most famous. Interestingly, this is one of the first orchestral works to employ the *programmatic principle*—that is, basing the composition upon something outside of music—a concept common to the romantic era of the nineteenth century.

The Concerto Grosso in A minor (Op. 3, no. 8) provides a typical example of Vivaldi's treatment of this Baroque form. It has the usual three movements of fast, slow, fast, and makes use of the concertino-ripieno grouping in the first and last movements. The concertino group in this instance consists of two violins, which compete with the accompanying full group. A significant feature of many Vivaldi concerti is the *ritornello,* a recurring theme played by the ripieno (or tutti, meaning all together). Alternating with the ripieno theme are *episodes,* that is, sections in which the concertino plays contrasting material. These structural principles are shown in the following diagram of the opening of the first movement of Vivaldi's Concerto Grosso in A minor. (See diagram below)

RIPIENO	CONCERTINO	RIPIENO	CONCERTINO	RIPIENO
Ritornello I	Episode	Rit. II	Episode	Rit. III

Antonio Vivaldi, Concerto Grosso in A Minor

The Rise of the Keyboard Sonata: Scarlatti

The beginning of modern piano keyboard technique is to be traced to the Italian composer Domenico Scarlatti (1685-1757), son of the famous opera composer Alessandro Scarlatti. Unquestionably, Scarlatti ranks among the leading keyboard composers of music history: Bach, Beethoven, Mozart, Schumann, Chopin, and Brahms. Although an innovator of idiomatic techniques (crossing of hands, arpeggios, scale figures, repeated notes, and so on), which influenced generations of successors, Scarlatti's greatness lies in the especially distinctive style he consistently injected into the more than five hundred sonatas he composed for the harpsichord.

The formal pattern of these sonatas is quite simple: one short movement divided into two sections (A B), each set off by a definite cadence. These sonatas have a strong impelling movement and a clarity of texture (homophonic), in which emphasis is placed upon a scintillating, sparkling melodic line and supporting chords beneath. A few sonatas are written in a pensive, reflective mood; most are, however, lively and joyful. In many respects these sonatas foreshadow the growing classicistic trend, a trend particularly evident in their clarity or texture, clear-cut melodies divided into definite phrases, bright, outgoing mood, and over-all polish and refinement.

Domenico Scarlatti, Sonata in E

CULMINATION OF THE BAROQUE: BACH AND HANDEL

JOHANN SEBASTIAN BACH

Comparison: Bach and Handel

The music of the Baroque came to a grand climax with the contributions of Johann Sebastian Bach and George Frideric Handel. Both composers were born in the same year (1685) and died but a few years apart (Bach in 1750, Handel in 1759). Though both composers created in the eloquent and ornate musical language of the age, each is identified by a distinctive underlying artistic creed. For example, Handel, an extrovert and an international figure, was largely motivated by the public's demand for the colorful and extravagant Baroque opera and oratorio, which became so popular in England during the eighteenth century. Bach, on the other hand, a scholarly introvert who was motivated by deep religious feelings, dedicated his life to serving the Lutheran Church through his music. With the emergence of these two leading figures, the musical supremacy of Italy, which originated in the early Baroque was gradually usurped by a long line of German and Austrian composers.

In terms of sheer quantity alone, the creative output of Bach is staggering—well over a thousand works, covering all the major forms of the Baroque (except opera), both sacred and secular, vocal and instrumental. These range in scope from the brief chorales to the expansive and complex B minor Mass. In large measure, the choice of vocal or instrumental idioms and the actual genres were determined by the resources and requirements that existed in the various music positions Bach held during the fifty years of his creative life.

Some writers, notably Hans David and Arthur Mendel (*The Bach Reader*), have pointed out that perhaps Bach's greatness can be attributed to the rich musical ancestry from which he stemmed. Born in Eisenach, Germany, in 1685, J. S. Bach represented the culmination of many generations of musicians who had lived in Germany since the sixteenth century. The lineage began with Veit Bach (c. 1580-1619) and ended with Johann Christian, the last of Johann Sebastian Bach's musician sons, who died in 1782. One child from the large family, Regina Suzanna (1742-1809), lived into the nineteenth century. Paul Bach, born 1878, continued the lineage into the twentieth century.

Following the death of both parents before his tenth birthday, young Sebastian came under the care of his older brother, Johann Christoph Bach, an organist who had studied with the renowned Pachelbel. The musical environment of his brother's household, and particularly his instruction in harpsichord and organ, provided a suitable foundation for the budding musician, who was eventually to become the outstanding organist and composer of the eighteenth century.

In his fifteenth year, J. S. Bach won a scholarship to St. Michael's School in Lüneberg. Here the maturing youth encountered a cosmopolitan atmosphere and received excellent academic instruction, which included Latin, Greek, religion, rhetoric, logic, and, of course, music. The scholarship, which covered tuition, room and board, stipulated that Bach participate in the school's choir, which performed at the principal church services of the institution, funerals, weddings, and civic processionals. Bach's musical horizons were further expanded by his listening to the playing of the noted organist Georg Böhm at St. John's Church in Lüneberg and to the French-style chamber and keyboard music at the nearby French court at Celle. It was during his Lüneberg experience that Bach began composing his earliest works, the organ preludes and variations.

Arnstadt

Shortly after his graduation from St. Michael's School, Bach obtained his first important musical position, as church organist and choir director at Arnstadt, where he remained from 1703 to 1707. The first of his more than 200 church cantatas were composed here (notably *Denn du wirst meine Seele* (Suffer not Thou my soul), as well as several organ fugues and preludes. It was during this period that Bach traveled on foot to Lübeck, about 200 miles distant, to hear the renowned organist Dietrich Buxtehude. He remained over the allotted time, and on return was reprimanded by his superiors. And thus began a series of skirmishes with church authorities; such disagreements plagued Bach the rest of his life. Moreover, his newly composed organ compositions (showing heavy traces of Buxtehude's influence) were criticized for their dazzling cadenzas, dissonant harmonic progressions, and chromaticisms. The church fathers were evidently pleased to learn that the young genius had decided to accept the organ post at St. Blasius' Church in Mühlhausen, where Bach remained only a short time (1707-1708). During this period he married a distant cousin, Maria Barbara Bach, and began to compose in earnest. He completed, among other sacred works, the famous chorale prelude *Ein' feste Burg ist unser Gott* (A Mighty Fortress Is Our God), which was composed for the Reformation Festival in 1708.

Weimar

At Weimar, 1708-1717, Bach was employed in the court of Duke Wilhelm Ernst, as chapel organist and chamber musician. This proved to be a pleasant position in many ways. Not only was his income doubled over his previous post, but, more importantly, the strong Lutheran environment was conducive to Bach's deeply religious musical conceptions. Duke Wilhelm, a man of firm religious convictions, had a particular interest in organ music. And thus it was here that Bach composed most of his great organ compositions, such as the Toccata and Fugue in D minor, the "Little" Fugue in G minor, and the gigantic Passacaglia in C minor. It was also at Weimar that Bach's second son was born, Carl Philipp Emanuel, the most famous musician of the Bach offspring.

Cöthen

For some strange and unknown reason. Bach chose the position as *Kapellmeister* (court musical director) at the castle at Cöthen under Prince Leopold. The Cöthen directorship afforded no opportunity for Bach to further his church music career, since Prince Leopold, a devout Calvinist, showed little interest in elaborate church music. Hence, between the years 1717-1723, Bach devoted his efforts to composing secular music, specifically chamber music and solo works, including such well-known examples as the two- and three-part inventions (for clavier), the three sonatas and three partitas for unaccompanied violin, the six suites for unaccompanied cello (the violin and cello pieces were written for the key players in Bach's chamber orchestra), the six trio sonatas, the English and French Suites for clavier, six concertos (the famed Brandenburg Concertos) and the first part of the collection of clavier preludes and fugues entitled *The Well-Tempered Clavier*.

Shortly after the death of his first wife, Maria Barbara (1720), Bach married Anna Magdalena, who bore him seven children. This marriage also produced several sons of exceptional musical talent: Johann Christoph Friedrich and notably Johann Christian, who, with his older brother Carl Philipp, contributed to the rise of the classic style in the mid-eighteenth century.

Oddly enough. Bach's employment at Cöthen was evidently terminated as a result of a change in the artistic life of the palace. The prince's wife, who was apparently resentful of Leopold's extensive preoccupation with music, instigated a general decline of musical activity in the palace. Thus, it was during this time of enforced inactivity that Bach composed the first part of the *Well-Tempered Clavier* (1722). Ironically, soon after Bach accepted the new position at Leipzig, the prince's wife died.

Leipzig

Bach was thirty-eight when he accepted the highly prestigious position as cantor (musical director) at St. Thomas' Church in Leipzig. His predecessor was Johann Kuhnau, who had adapted the sonata idea to the harpsichord. In the staunch Protestant city of about 30,000, Bach was in charge of music at two large Lutheran churches (St. Thomas' and St. Nicholas') which required much of his time and creative energy. On an alternating basis, the new cantor provided the music for the main Sunday church service at each church. The service, extending from seven to eleven o'clock A.M., usually required a cantata, a motet, several chorales, and the Kyrie and Gloria of the Lutheran Missa Brevis (short mass). In addition to furnishing all of this music for each Sunday service, he had to provide choral music for numerous special programs such as at Christmas and Easter, Passion music for Good Friday (he wrote three large works of this type), and funerals. For a time, Bach helped supervise the children living in the school at St. Thomas' and also taught Latin and the Catechism.

The Leipzig cantorship was, to say the least, much more complicated than his relatively peaceful position at Cöthen. His output at Leipzig was amazingly great, especially in view of the many duties that consumed his time. Instead of chamber music, Bach was concentrating on sacred idioms; thus, most of his greatest choral works were created at this point in his life. These choral works include over two hundred cantatas (among them the famous *Christ lag in Todesbanden* of 1724), the B minor mass, and the three extant Passions *(*St. John, St. Matthew, and St. Mark).

Bach's tenure at Leipzig was fraught with tension as a result of constant friction between himself and church officials. The final phase of this long series of conflicts was attained when Johann August Ernesti became rector. Ernesti was completely unsympathetic to Bach's needs and to church music in general. Thus, working conditions became increasingly intolerable, reaching a climax in 1738, when Bach completely turned away from sacred choral music and devoted his genius to highly personal and abstract instrumental creations, including the last part of *The Well-Tempered Clavier, A Musical Offering* (dedicated to Frederick the Great) the *Goldberg Variations,* and *The Art of the Fugue,* which was left uncompleted at the time of Bach's death in 1750. Ironically, both Bach and Handel had eye disorders that were treated by the same oculist, Sir John Taylor. The operations were unsuccessful and both composers spent their last days in darkness.

Prelude and Fugue No. 1 in C Major

Among the best known works by J. S. Bach is the *Das Wohltemperierte Clavier* (The Well-Tempered Clavier*),* consisting of a series of forty-eight preludes and fugues. In using the general keyboard classification of "clavier," Bach undoubtedly intended that the works be played on either the clavichord or harpsichord. (The strings of the harpsichord are plucked; those of the clavichord are struck by hammers). The title of the collection refers to a "well-tuned" instrument. However, some writers believe that the title alludes to the modern "tempered" system of tuning, in which each of the twelve semitones within the octave are tuned equally, thus permitting use of all the major and minor keys. Although Bach did not "invent" equal or tempered tuning, his *Well-Tempered Clavier* marks the establishment of the complete major and minor key system early in the eighteenth century.

The Prelude and Fugue No. 1 is representative of the technique and style employed by Bach in this collection. The prelude, a short introductory piece in a free improvisatory style, is based on a melody presented in the form of a broken chord pattern (notes of the chord sounded in succession instead of simultaneously). This pattern is woven through various related keys and various dissonant chord combinations, which provide a steady rise and fall in tension, gradually reaching its dissonantal peak in the closing measures.

Prelude No. 1, *Well-Tempered Clavier*

The fugues of *The Well-Tempered Clavier,* as with others in the large body of contrapuntal works by Bach, do not follow a set pattern. As a general rule they are between fifty and seventy-five measures in length and are built around a brief melodic idea (called the subject), which is imitated in succession by the various voice parts (usually four). The accompanying fugue for the Prelude No. 1 is based on a clearly marked subject of two measures' length. Like many of the Bach subjects, it has a lilting rhythmic vitality and a distinctive beginning of long note values. The subject gradually gains increased motion through a series of quick-moving notes of smaller duration:

Subject from Fugue No. 1, *Well-Tempered Clavier*

The *subject* of this particular fugue (No. 1 in C major) is first presented in the alto part (in the tonic key of C), and the answer is stated by the soprano part in measure two. Note: The *answer* is the subject imitated at a different pitch level, usually in a key a fifth higher (the dominant) or fourth higher (the subdominant key), as in this example. As the fugue unfolds, the various parts sound either the subject or answer in succession. (Note the appearance of the subject and answer in the following example below). Quite frequently, as in this example, Bach's fugues end in a climactic fashion, punctuated by a long sustained tone, called a *pedal tone,* held by the bass part during the last few measures. Above the pedal tone the upper parts clash in strong dissonant fashion as they seek their final goal—the closing cadence.

Opening, Fugue No. 1 in C Major, *Well-Tempered Clavier*

Cantata: Ein' feste Burg ist unser Gott

The reader may recall from the readings in the early Baroque, that the first cantatas dated from the early seventeenth century and were chiefly secular-styled compositions performed by a solo voice and continuo in small, intimate surroundings. During the late seventeenth century, the sacred cantata rose to prominence in Germany and reached its apex in the work of J. S. Bach, who composed over two hundred during his Leipzig period (1723-1750). These vocal forms were employed as an integral part in the Lutheran liturgy and generally were referred to as *Hauptstücke* (principal works), which were performed prior to the sermon at the Sunday service. Interestingly, Bach also composed twenty-four secular cantatas, which were written for special occasions, such as civic and university ceremonies, birthdays, weddings, and the like.

Bach's sacred cantatas do not follow a set pattern. However, many of these works are identified by (1) a number of sections or movements such as arias (solo vocal passages), recitatives (sung declamatory passages, in a speechlike style), duets and choruses; (2) a continuous narrative text of a religious nature; and (3) instrumental accompaniment. Many of the Bach cantatas are of small proportions, for a vocal solo or duet with only a continuo accompaniment.

However, for special events such as Christmas, Easter, and Ascension Sunday, he composed many larger works requiring full choir, soloists, and orchestra. Moreover, the particular Sunday of the Church year called for a particular type of text, which also accounts for the wide variety of expressions found in these works.

One distinguishing feature quite commonly observed in these works is the employment of a chorale tune that serves as a musical foundation for the entire composition. This melody is generally woven through all the divisions of the cantata, serving to unify its complex contrapuntal texture. Usually it is restated in full force in the four-part harmonization that brings the cantata to a close with a feeling of power and majesty. Sometimes the theme is developed in the various movements of the cantata through fugal treatment or through the theme and variations technique, as in the famous cantata *Ein' feste Burg ist unser Gott.* This cantata, appearing as No. 80 in the series of cantatas published by the Bach-Gesellschaft, was written for the bicentennial celebration of the Augsburg Confession. It represents the festive type of cantata, as indicated by its large structure and performing body: it consists of an eight-movement plan, with vocal soloists, chorus, and an orchestra of three trumpets, timpani, three oboes, two oboes d'amore (a sweet-sounding oboe, pitched a third lower than our modern oboe), two oboes da caccia (curved shape, pitched lower than modern oboe), organ, and a string section of violins, violas, cellos, and basses. It should be borne in mind, however, that the orchestra used by Bach at Leipzig was generally under twenty players. Bach arranged this cantata into the following form:

1. Full choir and orchestra; the choral melody is developed in fugal style
2. Aria for bass and soprano (with oboe, violins, violas, and continuo)
3. Bass recitative
4. Soprano aria
5. Chorus (orchestra and choir)
6. Tenor recitative
7. Alto and tenor duet
8. Chorale

J. S.Bach, Cantata Ein' feste Burg ist unser Gott, Part 1
Full choir and orchestra

Brandenburg Concerto No. 2 in F Major

Bach composed a set of six concerti grossi, which were dedicated to the Margrave of Brandenburg in 1721. As with many of his other compositions, such as the cantatas and the *Well-Tempered Clavier,* Bach provides each concerto with its own distinctive musical character, either as to instrumentation, form, or treatment of the solo instrumental group. With the exception of

Concerto No. 1, he follows the Vivaldi concerto grosso form: three-movement plan of fast, slow, fast and the division of the orchestra into concertino (solo group) and ripieno (the accompanying main instrumental body). However, these groups are not always separated into distinct bodies but are frequently mixed together in a contrapuntal web of sound. An interesting feature is to be noted regarding the use of the harpsichord in the Concerto No. 5. Here Bach relieved the instrument of its perfunctory duty of supplying the harmonic foundation and gave it extended solo- like passages. The technical skill demanded of the harpsichordist and of the other instrumentalists, in this and other concertos (notably the second, with its difficult trumpet part), clearly stamp these works as virtuosic.

The second Brandenburg Concerto is particularly noteworthy for it unusual concertino group, which is composed of wind instruments: the high-pitched trumpet (or clarino), recorder, oboe, and violin. The ripieno group consists of the customary strings and continuo. Following the pattern typical of many Baroque concertos, the work begins with a statement of the principal theme by the full orchestra. In the first solo entrance of the concertino, only one instrument is presented; then, in successive entrances, two concertino instruments are paired. Later, all four concertino instruments are pitted against the ripieno.

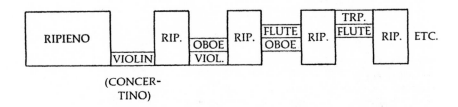

(CONCER-
TINO)

Structural Plan, opening of Second Brandenburg Concerto in F Major

The second movement, marked "Andante," and scored for only flute, oboe, violin, cello, and continuo, is based on a fugal development of the main theme. In the last movement (Allegro Assai), the full instrumentation of ripieno and concertino reappears. (See diagram below). The principal theme (having the same driving force of the theme of the first movement) is given a fugal treatment by the instruments of the concertino, while the ripieno serves to form a kind of backdrop for the imitative dialogue in the concertino section.

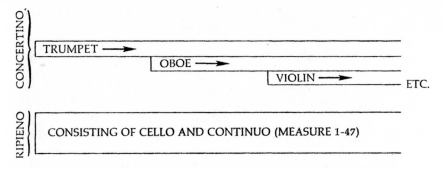

Structural Plan, opening, Last Movement, Brandenburg Concerto in F

The B Minor Mass

The culmination of Bach's work in the choral idiom was reached with his setting of the Ordinary of the Mass, completed about 1747 or 1749. Bach's interest in the mass form stemmed from the Lutheran practice of using the Kyrie and the Gloria in the worship service. This abbreviated form of the mass was performed at the principal Sunday service and on festival days. In 1733 Bach sent the Kyrie and Gloria of the B minor Mass to Frederick Augustus (the Catholic king of Poland) in an attempt to gain a court title, which was awarded three years later. The other movements of the gigantic work, the Credo, Sanctus, and the Agnus Dei, date from various periods of the composer's life. Each of the five parts of the Ordinary is divided into separate movements. For example, the Gloria and Credo have eight separate divisions or movements. In addition to a five-part chorus, the work requires vocal solos, duets, and an orchestra of trumpets, flutes, oboes, bassoon, timpani, strings, and organ. Understandably, the mass is too extensive for either the Catholic or the Lutheran Church, and thus, like Beethoven's *Missa Solemnis* and Mozart's *Requiem Mass*, it is normally heard in a concert setting.

Opening of the Gloria section, B Minor Mass, J.S. Bach

GEORGE FRIDERIC HANDEL

The life and work of the figure who personified the magniloquent aspects of the Baroque, stands in strong relief to his contemporary, J. S. Bach. In many respects both the music and career of Handel represent the summation of the more objective manifestations of the Baroque spirit, whereas Bach, on the other hand, represented the culmination of the more subjective artistic traits of that era of opulence and grandeur. Handel's dramatic and colorful flair appealed to the masses, and, in contrast to Bach, his popularity remained undiminished for a long while after his death. Bach's subtle artistry did not speak directly to the masses, consequently, lacking theatrical appeal. Bach's influence worked at a different pace and on a different level. It was only gradually, particularly after the revival of his works by Mendelssohn early in the nineteenth century, that his greatness was acknowledged by practically every musician, composer and devotee of musical art. Handel, on the other hand, reaching out as he did to the masses, played an important role in the development of English musical culture during the first half of the eighteenth century.

Handel's early music education, consisting of the customary subjects of counterpoint, organ, and harpsichord, was acquired under Friedrich Wilhelm Zachow in Handel's native town of Halle in Saxony. After one year at the University of Halle, he went to Hamburg and performed in an opera orchestra as a second violinist. This close contact with Italian-styled opera, which was sweeping all of Europe by the opening of the eighteenth century, influenced Handel's esthetic outlook at an early age, for we note that at nineteen he wrote his first work, the opera *Almira* (1705). And even at this date he showed a penchant for the Baroque "grand manner," which was to win for him the following of many opera lovers. In Italy, from 1706 to 1710, through his associations with the leading contemporary Italian composers (Corelli, Alessandro and Domenico Scarlatti), Handel thoroughly assimilated the Italian style of opera established by Alessandro Scarlatti and the orchestral technique developed by Corelli. The opera *Rodrigo* (Florence, 1708) and especially *Agrippina* (Venice 1709) marked his arrival as an opera composer.

With his name established in the operatic field on the Continent, Handel moved to London, where in 1710 he completed the widely celebrated *Rinaldo*. Shortly after, he and several members of English society formed an opera company called The Royal Academy of Music. This venture provided Handel with an opportunity to compose more than thirty operas. However, the company began to lose money and by 1728 the English taste shifted its focus from Italian to English opera, as attested by the acclaim of the middle class for John Gay's *The Beggar's Opera*, which parodied the Italian operatic style of Handel and his contemporaries. The desire of the English for works in their native language, and particularly the satirical writings of the music critics Addison and Steele (in *The Spectator)*, contributed to the demise of the musical expression that had brought so much fame to Handel. When the Academy failed, Handel devoted his talents to composing oratorios, which are, in effect, Handelian operas minus staging, costuming, and acting. Although produced in public theaters, these twenty-six works were based on religious subject matter generally drawn from Biblical passages. These include the oratorios *Israel in Egypt, Samson, Esther, Joseph, Joshua,* and *The Messiah.* Handel's creative output in the orchestral field was considerably less than in the vocal. Noteworthy are the twelve concerti grossi. Opus 6 (1740), three sets of six organ concerti (Opp. 4, 7), the *Water Music Suite* (c. 1717) consisting of twenty-five pieces, mostly popular airs and dances and scored for large orchestra; and the *Royal Fireworks Music* (1749) in five movements: Overture, Siciliana, Allegro, and Minuet I, II, scored for a large wind band.

G. F. Handel, "Comfort Ye" from the Messiah

Summary

    In looking back over the Baroque three major movements seem to stand out above all else: the rise of opera, the establishment of the orchestra and its concerto forms, and the great period of Lutheran music brought to fruition by Bach. Essentially, the Baroque was an expression of two cultures: the Italian with its color and vivacity, and the German with its more serious, logical undertone. Both cultures were successively fused in the music of J.S. Bach the towering giant of the Baroque.

CHAPTER FIVE

THE CLASSICAL ERA 1750-1800

THE SOCIAL AND INTELLECTUAL CLIMATE

> Then beauty of style, harmony, grace and
> good rhythm depend on simplicity—I
> mean the true simplicity of a rightly and
> nobly ordered mind and character.
> Plato

Overview

Following the climatic work of Bach and Handel, musical style again altered its path. The change was essentially from the Baroque grandeur to the classic style, characterized by clarity, balance, and simplicity. These traits gradually came to the foreground after 1740 in Germany and Austria—the center of classicism in music—and were most fully exemplified in the music of the leading classicists, Franz Joseph Haydn (1732-1809), Wolfgang Amadeus Mozart (1756-1791), and in the early works of Ludwig van Beethoven (1770-1827). As with all periods, the boundaries of the classical period (sometimes called the neoclassical era) are arbitrary. The new style-movement was foreshadowed in the music of the preclassicists: Bach's famous sons, Carl Philipp Emanuel (1714-1788), Johann Christian (1735-1782) and the German contemporaries (Monn, 1717-1750, Wagenseil, 1715-1777, and Stamitz, 1717-1757).

The ending date of the period is also arbitrary; however, the death of Haydn in 1809 may be thought of as the concluding point. Beethoven's earliest works (his first and second symphonies, for example) are generally regarded as classical in style. His Third Symphony (1803) marks his departure into the romantic style of the nineteenth century, which we will take up in the next chaper. The classical period is chiefly one of unprecedented creativity in the instrumental idiom. The bulk of the music was composed in the new forms of symphony, piano sonata, and string quartet, as well as in the established concerto form. Sacred music continued, but was diminished over the Baroque era. Opera maintained its popularity in Italy. In Germany, interest in the new symphonic idea became a high priority among composers. The genius Mozart, who created in all of the forms of the period, stands as the musical giant of the age in terms of both quantity and quality of music. Of the other leading figures, Haydn is best known for his summation of the symphonic form (he composed approximately one hundred and four works in this genre), and Beethoven for his earliest symphonies, piano sonatas, and string quartets, which are in the "classic" style. His "romantic" phase (from 1803) will be taken up in the next chapter, under nineteenth-century romanticism.

The Crosscurrents in Eighteenth-Century Music

Musically speaking, the eighteenth century was far from being the quiet, reserved age we somehow associate with the rise of classicism. Despite the dominant rational tone that is often cited in arts and letters, there were several distinctive stylistic currents in music: (1) the Baroque was drawing to a close about 1750; (2) the rococo was the dominant expression in France during the reign of Louis XV (1715-1774); (3) the *empfindsamer Stil* (sensitive style) surfaced in Germany about 1740; and (4) the period concluded with classicism as the prevailing mode in the last half of the century. Clearly, the"galant aesthetic" is in the cultural air—an emphasis on articulated melody that is elegant, simple and pleasing, traits which were rooted in the intermezzo sections of the new Italian (Neapolitan) opera. (Intermezzi were theatrical entertainments presented between acts of serious opera.) The galant, with its simplicity and grace of melodic movement and light chordal accompaniment represents a turning away from the complex contrapuntal style of J.S. Bach. The galant is so wide spread it should be regarded as a common musical convention that came to be employed in all musical forms of the era: opera, symphony, and sonata.

Time-Line: Classicism

1720's	Symphony (sinfonia) emerges
	Sammartini, Italy
1740's	C.P.E. Bach, "sensitive style," northern Germany
1732	Haydn born
1756	Mozart born
1761	Haydn begins employment with Esterhaży family
1762	Mozart (6 yrs) begins European tour
1765	Mozart (age 9) Symphony No. 1
1770	Beethoven born
1787	Mozart: opera, Don Giovanni
1788	Mozart: last 3 symphonies No. 39, 40, 41
1791	Death of Mozart

Social and Intellectual Movements Underscoring the Classic Temper

The most progressive and widespread musical activity in the classical era was centered in Italy, Germany and Austria, the latter countries took the lead in the development of the symphony and sonata, the dominant forms. Why did Germany and Austria become the center of the classical movement in music? Although space limits the discussion of this important question, several contributing factors may be briefly touched upon. One dominant factor behind the flourishing musical culture in eighteenth-century Germany was the presence of an active patronage of the arts by both private and public interests. It may be recalled that, prior to the Baroque, the arts were supported chiefly by either the Church or the private benefactor—the princely court or wealthy family such as the Medici in the Renaissance. In the Baroque, beginning with the rise of public opera theaters in Italy, music increasingly became the concern of the middle class as well as the elite. And in the classical period, the composer found a large, receptive audience in both the private and public areas of music.

Wealthy patrons commissioned the writing of symphonies, sonatas, and chamber music for specific events, concerts, and festivities. And, on the other hand, the middle class clamored for both instruments (such as the popular harpsichord) and the new galant-styled music suitable "for the connoisseur and dilettante"—words that frequently appear on the cover pages of printed keyboard sonatas of this age. Family music-making was also in vogue in Germany, where string quartet playing became a favorite pastime of many cultured families. Perhaps the strongest impetus to public patronage of the arts was provided by the series of concerts offered to the public such as the *Concerts spirituels* in Paris in 1725 and *Liebhaberkonzerte* in Berlin in 1770. Also for the first time, the publication of music took on considerable economic importance for the composer. One of the largest publishers in the music world today, Breitkopf and Härtel, was established at this time (mid-eighteenth century). Among the first major compositions printed by this firm were works by C. P. E. Bach, son of J.S. Bach, and Leopold Mozart, father of the leading classicist.

Germany was not yet a national state. It consisted of numerous principalities such as Saxony, Prussia, and Bavaria. Moreover, each principality had its own highly developed court orchestra, opera, and chamber ensemble. Prominent among these cultural centers was the royal court at Potsdam in Prussia, where Frederick the Great developed a flourishing musical culture and where C. P. E. Bach established himself as a leading German composer. Another important center was Mannheim, where in the 1740s, one of the finest orchestras came into existence under the leadership of Johann Stamitz. From this orchestra emerged the orchestral techniques that were eventually to become the trademarks of every classical symphony. Vienna, the capitol of German musical classicism, was the spiritual home of the greats of the period—Haydn, Mozart, Beethoven, and numerous other composers whose works are now being uncovered through musical research.

Intellectual Trends—The Age of Reason

The eighteenth century is perhaps best known as the age of reason, or the Enlightenment, when intellectual consciousness prevailed in all matters— political, social, religious, scientific, and artistic. Reason became a religion; it stood as "the highest authority, as the universal arbiter in all matters." The leading figures in the Age of Reason included: Voltaire, who probed intellectually, and with a biting satirical pen, the social problems and ills of the Enlightenment *(Candide,* 1759); Pope, who mirrored the scientific temper of the day in a highly logical, measured, and restrained poetic style *(Rape of the Lock,* 1712); and Rameau, who applied rational thought to music and formulated the theory behind the modern major and minor key system *(Treatise on Harmony,* 1722).

PRELUDE TO CLASSICISM: ROCOCO ELEGANCE

The Rococo

Before dealing directly with the Classical period, some mention must be given to the rococo period and its relationship to the emerging major styles. For the setting of the rococo we turn to France of the early eighteenth century (the reign or Louis XV, 1715-1774), and to the prevailing aesthetic ideals of the painters, writers, and composers.

The classicistic vein, we found, was firmly entrenched in the arts of France during the seventeenth century: in the paintings of Poussin and Le Nain, in the operas of Lully, and in the plays of Corneille and Racine. It was the French artists' intent to avoid excessive display of physical action, to preserve dignity and decorum, and to create in a highly refined style. The French arts truly reflected the highly cultivated society of Louis XIV—a society in which the French language was purified and made clear, conversation made a fine art, and wit esteemed above all else.

This trend subsided shortly after the death of Louis XIV (1715). With the ascension of Louis XV to the throne, there was a change from large to small, from the formal to the intimate and playful—a movement away from the rational to the sentimental, an interest in making sentiment the criterion for artistic judgment. Instead of *raison* and *hon sens, charme* and *esprit* were the catchwords of the literary salons around 1720. In the words of Friedlander, "this artistic mentality did not wish to live in the rarified atmosphere of reason and morality, but at the same time had no desire to descend into the depths of emotion. It attempted rather to capture the attractive surface of reality." This, in essence, seems to capture the culture of the rococo in which refinement, elegance, and taste for the sensuously superficial prevailed.

The leading representative in rococo painting was Jean Watteau (1684-1721), whose art covered the walls of the new locale of French society—the fashionable Parisian *hôtels* with their intimate, playful surroundings. In this make-believe world Watteau painted such works as *Embarkation for Cythera,* and *The Champs Elysées,* in which ethereal, feminine, wispy forms and infinite fantasylike space replace Baroque power, drama, massiveness, and rhetoric.

These same characteristics are found in rococo music, led by François Couperin, "Le Grand" (1668-1733), who was the court composer to Louis XV. The musical style, like the paintings of Watteau, Boucher, and Fragonard, is characterized by its emphasis on much decoration in the melodic line, pleasantness (almost neutral in feeling), grace, and elegance of expression. It is music written for the casual entertainment of the aristocracy—as atmosphere. And thus, surface treatment, manifested in numerous types of trills, grace notes, and turns (see the following example), replaces the more serious and profound treatment of musical ideas so common among the Baroque composers.

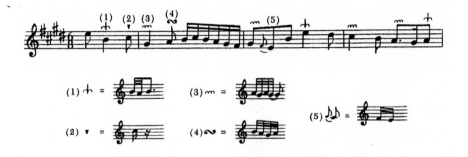

Couperin's Pièces de Clavecin. Illustration of various types of ornamentation.

F. Couperin, "La Galante," from Pièces de Clavecin

Fanciful titles such as *La Galante* and *La Voluptueuse,* among others, were commonly provided these dainty, thinly polyphonic pieces, which were normally written in the preferred form of the rococo, the suite (or *ordre)* for harpsichord. These ordres are much like the Baroque suite in that they are made up of a series of dance movements; however, they frequently contain many more dances than the usual Baroque suite of the allemande-sarabande-courante-gigue plan. Interestingly, one highly favored dance found in the ordre—the minuet—was eventually adopted by the German classicists and became an integral part of the symphony and piano sonata.

Further illustration of the rococo, and indeed its central focus, is to be found in French interior decoration—in the numerous Parisian hotels, where the walls, panels, doorways, and ceilings are richly overladen with scrolls and a shell design (or *rocaille,* the origin of the word *rococo).*

Concluding our discussion of the rococo, the words of historian Paul Henry

Lang are most fitting: "this style did not need bold creative architects, powerful dramatists, and robust musicians; it addressed itself to the decorator" who worked with small forms, avoided the philosophical probing of emotion, and communicated to the elite of society.

THE CLASSICAL TEMPER IN THE ARTS

Formative Influences

Classicism gradually supplanted the rococo style in the latter half of the eighteenth century, after the rococo had spent its energy. As a style period it may be described as a time when the aesthetic concepts of ancient Greece and Rome were renewed in the fields of painting, architecture, sculpture, music, and literature. Several possible influences can be mentioned: the discoveries of ancient Herculaneum and Pompeii (1763), the writings of Wincklemann *(History of the Art of Antiquity, 1764)*, and the reassertion of the power of reason which had been growing steadily in Europe since the late seventeenth century. Artists, composers and writers turned to the ancient civilizations for inspiration and direction. They did not actually imitate the Greek achievements but rather attempted to capture the essence or distinctive qualities found in their fine arts. These qualities include clarity, balance, logical order, simplicity, refinement, control, and restraint; quite opposed to the grandiose and rhetorical style of the Baroque and the purely decorative and ethereal make-believe world of the rococo.

The Classical period did not, of course, suddenly come to fruition in the middle of the century. The establishment of classicism in music was relatively late in the period (Haydn and Mozart about 1770), and in painting very late in the century (David in the 1780s). Literature was the first of the arts to thoroughly assimilate the rational temper. The classical literary style began to be perfected as early as the age of Louis XIV, whose court cultivated a pure, correct, and logical diction. Louis' Académie—the selected group of artists and writers who governed French literary and artistic taste—attempted to establish a highly refined type of French as the norm or standard for good writing.

By 1700, under the influence of science, the growth of a reading public, and particularly the French Académie, English writers underwent a change in literary style: from the majestic, emotional, ornate style of the Baroque (Milton) to order, simplicity, lucidity, and precision (Pope). Moreover, if the general tone of the literature or journalism of the English masses was one of clarity, brevity, and directness, that of the elite was perfection and absolute refinement of expression. To the literary classicists like Pope, Collins, and Gray, "polish," not "fire," became the artistic credo. Pope's work in particular represents the epitome of classicism, for we find in his poetry an emphasis on correctness of style, restraint, balanced phrases, clarity of structure, a bright, witty effect, and a polished "gentleman's" English. Most emphatically, personal idiosyncracy is subordinated to the universal norm—that of the refined language of society.

Perhaps the creed of classicism is best summarized in a passage from Pope's *Essay on Criticism* (1711):

> Tis more to guide, than spur the muse's steed;
> Restrain his fury, than provoke his speed;
> The winged courser, like a gen'rous horse
> shows most true mettle when you check his
> course.

Jacques Louis David (1748-1825) is the leader of the classic or neo-classic movement in French painting. One of his most famous paintings is the *Oath of the Horatii* (1784). In following the trend of glorifying the distinctive traits of the ancient Greek and Roman civilizations, such as virtue, self-control, dignity and manly strength, David chose as his subject a Roman father pledging his three sons to take up arms against the enemies of Rome.

This painting mirrors many of the traits that we associate with neo-classicism: (1) clarity and simplicity—lines are sharply drawn and uncluttered; (2) balance—the focal point is the swords, which are balanced on the left by the father and three sons and on the right by the weeping wife—moreover, the three columns provide a "balanced" background; (3) strength and solidity of form—shown in angular lines, body posture, and muscular features; (4) restraint of emotion—rational control over the emotions. and (5) idealism and refinement—"ideal" human figures with their perfect physical proportions.

Approached in a very generalized way, many of the preceding traits will be found in the works of Haydn and Mozart and in the early works of Beethoven. For example, the classic composer frequently stresses *simplicity* and *clarity* in melody and orchestration, *Control* or *restraint* is exhibited in the composer's holding in check the amount and use of dissonance. *Balance* and *order* are found in the arrangement of the melodies (very often in two phrases); in the constant return to the main key center (the tonic), and most importantly in the use of the large symmetrical plan of the sonata form: exposition (A), development (B), and recapitulation (A). To this list of basic characteristics we might add *universality of expression*, meaning that the main composers all wrote in the same accepted musical forms (symphony, piano sonata) and adhered for the most part to a common musical language made up of a widely used system or chords, keys, and instruments. Moreover, like the literary classicism of Pope and others, musical classicism often exudes "bright," "witty" manner, as demonstrated in the lively tempos (in opening and closing movements), the scintillating rhythmic patterns, and use of the joyful-sounding major key.

THE INFLUENCE OF THE MIDDLE CLASS

For the composers born into emerging classical spirit, the older style of the senior composers, represented by J. S. Bach, was considered outmoded, too contrapuntal, and too complex for the "modern" German composers and listeners of the era. Their taste was definitely for the less complicated "natural" modes of musical expression favored by the bourgeoisie, symbolized in the widespread popularity of the "galant"manner of musical composition with its light hearted feeling and simplicity of structure which gradually permeated most all keyboard sonatas and symphonies of this time. Interestingly, this trend was given impetus by the amateur keyboard players who favored the relatively easy-going of the galant-styled pieces. (The love of the pianoforte was soon to explode accross Europe and England as we look ahead and see the coming of such piano makers as Johann Stein and others in the 1770's.)

Another aspect of the bourgeoisie influence is "sentimentalism"—a strong wave of melancholy and passion which appeared in numerous literary works by such writers as Richardson (*Pamela* 1740), and Goethe (*The Sorrows of Werther* 1774). The pouring-out of one's heart also appears in music, specifically in the work of C.P.E. Bach in northern Germany (about 1740) known as the *empfindsamer Stil*, or sensitive style. His expressive style is unlike that of his father, posessing marked sentimental qualities—much use of chromaticism, impetuous shifts in tempo, volume and mood, and what the historian Donald Grout calls the *melodic sigh*: an accented dissonance resolving on a weak beat. Quite naturally there is a mingling of the rococo spirit in these works—he was employed in the court of Frederick the Great at Potsadm, where rococo taste ruled in the arts. However, in C.P.E. Bach's music, the French style of grace and elegance, is subordinated to the strong evocations of sentiment and nostalgia.

C.P.E. Bach, Sonata in B Minor (III)

The Keyboard. Sonata

The two most important forms of the classical period need be discussed, namely the keyboard sonata and the symphony. Following the achievements of

Scarlatti, who established many of the fundamental keyboard techniques and classical clarity of melody and texture, the keyboard sonata gradually acquired its rudimentary pattern of several movements, notably in the music of C. P. E. Bach. The keyboard sonata of the classic era proper—that of Haydn and Mozart—is usually in three movements, each having a different tempo and theme. Quite frequently the first and last movements are based on a particular structural plan called the *sonata form.* Thus, the word *sonata* may refer to a particular genre (piano sonata), or it may refer to a specific way of organizing the musical ideas within a movement.

Although there are a variety of ways for organizing the inner workings of the sonata form, the most general features found in the classical period are these: an opening statement, called the *exposition* presents two or more themes sounded in succession.This is often followed by a *development* in which these themes or parts (called motives) are elaborated upon, that is, presented in a new harmonic setting, or in a minor key as opposed to a major, or perhaps given a contrapuntal treatment, using imitation and other devices. The third and last section of the sonata form is called the *recapitulation,* where the exposition section is repeated in its entirety or in shortened form.

EXPOSITION	*DEVELOPMENT*	*RECAPITULATION*
(usually two themes are stated, the first in the tonic key, second in the dominant)	(theme or themes are elaborated, broken up, combined, given new keys, etc.)	(repetition of exposition)

The Classical Symphony

The symphony follows the same plan as the keyboard sonata described above, except, of course, that it is in four movements, played by an orchestra rather than the harpsichord or the piano, which, incidentally, became a favorite instrument in the classical era. Moreover, the string quartet is generally based on the same plan as the keyboard sonata and symphony,.

THE CLASSICAL SYMPHONY
(general features)

First Movement
    Tempo and character: lively (allegro),usually duple meter
    Form: frequently in sonata form
Second Movement
    Tempo and character: usually slow (andante) and lyrical
    Form: sonata form, song form (A B A), theme and variations,
    or rondo
Third Movement
    Tempo and character: stately minuet dance style (early classicism),
    much quicker in late period; triple meter. Form: A B A
Fourth Movement
    Tempo and character: fast and gay, duple meter common
    Form: frequently in sonata form, sometimes in rondo form

Summary

Concomitant with the culmination of the Baroque in the early part of the eighteenth century, the French composers introduced an ornate, elegant style, best described as the *rococo*—the musical equivalent of the delicate, decorative, and intimate designs found in French paintings and interiors. In many ways its rational character (complex ornamentation, restraint of feeling, and required precision in execution), was a prelude to the classical period, which emerged about mid-century. About this time, several German composers, working in the galant mode of melody-centered, light homophonic textures (now the rage in all musical circles), incorporated a deeply sentimental and at times emotional expression known as the *empfindsamer stil*, which was adapted to the new sonata and symphony. This early phase of classicism was completed by C. P. E. Bach, J. C. Bach, and Johann Stamitz, The next discussion will trace the final phase of the movement in the music of Haydn and Mozart.

JOSEPH HAYDN

Life Sketch

An outline of the major aspects of Haydn's life frequently draws a comparison with Haydn's compatriot of the classic age, Mozart. The two composers are poles apart in terms of family background, early childhood, music education, and personality. However, both used the same classic musical language—the neat phrases, clear-cut rhythms, cadences, and the same forms. However, the distinctive personal traits—the bold, happy, outgoing side of Haydn's nature and the highly refined, more sensitive nature of Mozart—are perceptible in their respective music.

Franz Joseph Haydn was born in 1732, at Rohrau, a little village in the eastern part of Austria, near the Hungarian border. In contrast to the auspicious beginnings of his contemporary, Mozart, who grew up in a culturally rich environment, Joseph Haydn was born of a modest family background. And in contrast to Mozart's protected and carefully nurtured youth, Haydn almost from the very beginning had to rely on his own resourcefulness. At the age of six he was sent to live with his uncle, Johann Mathias Franck, a school principal and musician in Hainberg. Again, in contrast to Mozart, Haydn's musical education was fragmentary and, for the most part, self-acquired. The young Haydn obtained, apparently, only general musical instruction (some training in clavier, violin, and singing) from his uncle, who was burdened with many responsibilities in the village school. Curiously, Haydn never became an outstanding performer on any instrument; even in his late youth he was only moderately proficient on his favorite instrument, the violin. Mozart, on the other hand, was an artist-pianist of international repute. However, even though Haydn lacked the precocity of Mozart, he must have acquired (mainly on his own) considerable skill in harpsichord and violin, for we note that during his early adult years in Vienna he taught harpsichord, played the violin in chamber ensembles, and later regularly conducted orchestral performances from the harpsichord.

At the age of eight the young Haydn entered the *kantorei* (school for boy choristors) at St. Stephen's Cathedral in Vienna, remaining here until his voice changed completely at the age of seventeen. Aside from extensive choral singing experience, little formal music education was offered; such instruction would have, undoubtedly, given the world a glimpse of Haydn's budding genius well before his late twenties (in contrast to Mozart, who had created his first nine symphonies by the age of twelve).

Following his dismissal from St. Stephen's, the teen-aged youth took up residence in Vienna and began to eke out his own existence by playing in Viennese street serenades and by giving private instruction in harpsichord. It was also at this time that Haydn made an intensive study of the sonatas and symphonies of C. P. E. Bach and received his first real formal instruction in counterpoint from Nicola Porpora. Gradually, the struggling musician began to make a name for himself. Through his teaching and chamber music performances in wealthy Viennese circles, Haydn's musicianship was recognized by the elite patrons of the arts. In 1759 he accepted the post of music director and chamber composer to Count von Morzin in Vienna. During his short stay, to 1760, Haydn acquired a foretaste of the work he would follow the remainder of his life: he conducted an orchestra of twenty-five, wrote several string quartets, and composed his first symphony (1759).

For almost the next thirty years (1761-1790), Haydn was in the service of the Esterházys, one of the wealthiest Hungarian noble families. The castle of Esterháza, located about eighty miles from Vienna and modeled after the court at Versailles, was a sumptuous edifice that had two theaters (one for opera and one for marionettes) and two large concert halls. Haydn, as the absolute personification of the eighteenth century royal court composer and musician, was assigned a number of duties: conductor of an orchestra of twenty-five players, coach and conductor for all operatic productions, and composer. His weekly schedule was a busy one for in addition to rehearsing the orchestra, he conducted two opera performances and two full orchestral concerts, and still found time to carry out a very fruitful schedule of composing. During his lifetime he amassed over a hundred symphonies, eighty-three string quartets, fifty-two keyboard sonatas, twenty-three operas, four oratorios, concertos, and over a hundred and fifty works (mostly in string-trio form) for the prince's favorite instrument, the baryton (member of the sevententh century viol family, similar to the viola da gamba, with the addition of twelve resonating strings beneath the fingerboard).

Between the years 1791 and 1795, Haydn devoted his efforts to a series of London appearances. Under the aegis of the impressario Johann Salomon, Haydn conducted orchestral concerts and wrote his last twelve symphonies (Nos. 93-104) referred to as his "London" Symphonies. He was widely acclaimed by Londoners who bestowed many honors on the renowned Haydn— culminating in an honorary doctor's degree conferred at Oxford in July, 1791 (for which occasion Haydn dedicated his Symphony No. 92, the "Oxford"

Symphony). Following his London sojourns he resumed his position with the Esterházy family and wrote his last major compositions: two oratorios. *The Creation* and *The Seasons,* his last string quartets (Op. 76, Op. 77), and a magnificent concerto for keyed trumpet and orchestra (1796).

Some Characteristics of Style

Haydn's creative genius touched many musical idioms: symphony, opera, string quartet, piano sonata, concerto, oratorio, and even the mass. However, the achievements that won him international fame in his day, and a permanent position in our own time, lay in the symphony—the form that sustained his interest for practically a lifetime. Confronted with his enormous creativity in the symphonic medium (104 works), the modern listener, anxious to sample some of Haydn's greatness, may be somewhat bewildered by the range and scope of Haydn's gigantic symphonic treasure. Therefore, our focus at this introductory level will be upon a general view of his style periods and selected examples from each.

Haydn's composing career is usually divided into three phases: the first (rococo, 1759-1770), the second (emerging classicism and "sturm und drang") 1770-1782), and the third (age of maturity, 1782-1803). The early-period symphonies (Nos. 1 to early 40s) exemplify Haydn's strong interest in the rococo style. Not only do some of these works bear descriptive French titles ("Le Matin," "Le Midi," "Le Soir") typical of the French rococo, but also there is a preference for the divertimento-like structures (light, entertaining chamber pieces, similar to the French ordres), lightness of texture, and an over-all playful, delicate effect quite unlike the mature Haydn of the later classical style.

In the center of the small orchestra of about twenty-five is the harpsichord, whose soft, delicate plucking sounds tend to give a courtly aristocratic atmosphere to this music—ironically so, since we will find that, in his later work, Haydn, perhaps more than any other composer of his day, most fully demonstrated the Enlightenment's ideals. For we find him at the later date turning away from the aristocratic rococo and seeking his musical ideas in the world about him, in nature, Viennese street songs, folk dances, hymns, and Gregorian chant.

A typical work from Haydn's *rococo* period is the Symphony No. 22, subtitled "The Philosopher" composed in the early days of his Esterházy employment (1764). Here, in the movement selected (Minuet), the cultural accents of the rococo—the subtle gestures and mannerisms that we find in interior decoration and painting—are replicated in Haydn's rhythm which is relatively slow, stately, and in the melodic line played by a cor anglais (English horn) which has a touch of grace, revealing aristocratic bearing and elegance.

The number of instruments used by Haydn at this time was about twenty-five. This work, Symphony No. 22, is unusual in that it calls for two English horns, instruments which will figure prominently in the Romantic era. Other instruments employed in this symphony include: violins I, II, viola, cellos, basses, bassoon, French horns, harpsichord.

J. Haydn, Symphony No. 22, "The Philosopher" (Minuet)

An Early Haydn String Quartet

Although Haydn is incorrectly called the "father of the string quartet," he did more than any other composer to draw the elements together into a standardized form. Most of Haydn's earliest quartets are typical of the composer's pleasant and elegant rococo phase—entertaining, salon-music, loosely strung together with short pieces rather than complete movements that we later see. However, beginning with the six quartets (Op. 3) composed between 1755-1766, the standard string quartet form comes definitely to the fore. We note the usual four-movement plan (Fast—Slow—Minuet—Fast) and the rudimentary outlines of the sonata form in the first movement. The fifth quartet in this series (subtitled the "Serenade" because of the song-like melody in the second movement) was probably composed early in the Esterházy period. (Some historians believe this quartet was composed by Hoffstteter.) The first movement (opening measures given below) has a clearly marked sonata form.

Joseph Haydn, String Quartet Op. 3, No. 5

Sturm und Drang (Storm and Stress)

Concerning the second period (1770-1782), particularly the symphonies numbered 44-49, Haydn, undoubtedly heavily influenced by the stronger wave of emotionalism sweeping literature and art, abandoned the ephemeral galant aesthetic for the philosophy of the *empfindsamer Stil:* the idea of C. P. E. Bach that "music should not only entertain and delight but have a deeper meaning." Consequently, many of the symphonies of this period (referred to as his Sturm und Drang phase) are imbued with a greater feeling of emotion achieved through use of minor keys, wider melodic skips, and sudden changes or fluctuations in tempo and dynamics. Uppermost are the classicistic traits: the establishment of the outer framework or mold of the four-movement idea of the symphony, including the development section in the first movement; down-to-earth humor in the final movement; and, above all, chiseled-out themes with clear-cut phrases, sharply defined contours, and striking rhythmic patterns. With the final passing of rococo traces, the harpsichord is no longer an essential instrument in the orchestra, for the light, delicate sounds of the instrument are not attuned to the classicistic creed of clarity, strength, and economy of means. Moreover, the function of the harpsichord—to lend harmonic support to the ensemble—is now taken over by the horns, which are frequently given sustained chords.

Classical Fulfillment

Haydn's drive toward the classical traits of clarity, strength, balance and refinement, became fully realized about 1780—marking the start of his last period of writing. The chief characteristic of this final phase of his symphonic style was his intensive application of the development principle, that is, the working out or elaboration of musical ideas in the section immediately following the exposition portion of the first movement. The thorough treatment of the development section was heralded by Haydn in 1781, in his "Russian" String Quartets, which he himself declared as being written in "quite a new and special way." This portion of the first movement in his string quartets and symphonies had been, up to now, merely a brief episode or digression before going on to the concluding recapitulation section. Haydn's essential contribution to music was simply this: he made the development section an area of intense dramatic action and the main center of interest of the classical sonata form— indeed, as the testing ground of the composer's musicianship.

Haydn's interest in the development principle, tightness of form, and dual themes of the first movement is well established by the time of the so-called "Paris" Symphonies, which were commissioned for Paris concerts of 1785-1786. These symphonies are as follows:

Symphony No. 82 in C major ("L'Ours"—"The Bear")
Symphony No. 83 in G minor ("La Poule"—"The Hen")
Symphony No. 84 in E flat major
Symphony No. 85 in B flat major ("La Reine"—"The Queen")
Symphony No. 86 in D major
Symphony No. 87 in A major

In 1796 Haydn composed his Trumpet Concerto which was an experiment in "modernizing" the old Baroque instrument—from its limited pattern of a few notes to an instrument capable of playing a complete scale. Haydn's friend, Anton Weidinger, devised this instrument (fitted with keys similar to those on the modern saxophone) which enabled the player to fill in the gaps of the harmonic series, thus opening the way for scale-like melodic passages as in the concerto for trumpet that follows.

J. Haydn, Trumpet Concerto in Eb, first page conductor's score

Some writers have set off the London Symphonies, numbered 93-104, as the summit of Haydn's creative work. However, it is perhaps more meaningful to the general reader (and more accurate, musicologically speaking) to regard this phaseas the logical continuation of his classic style, begun in the 1780s. Indeed, the "London" Symphonies, aside from stronger traces of romanticism, do not differ drastically from the "Paris" Symphonies. These final statements of the symphonist show Haydn as the supreme master of the idiom and its techniques, which took a lifetime to develop.

A representative work from the final period is the Symphony No. 104 in D major. This composition follows the customary plan of four movements: Allegro (with a slow introduction), Andante, Minuetto, and Allegro Spirituoso. Although the classicistic clarity of texture predominates, there is a "thicker" and heavier orchestral sound (foreshadowing romanticism), due to increased use of brass and woodwinds on a more independent basis. Up to now these sections were entirely subordinate to the strings. The sonata form is used in the first and last movements, and the symphony is greatly expanded over earlier works. Of considerable importance is his use of the Austrian *Ländler,* a heavy-footed folk dance that is frequently incorporated in the minuet movements of his later symphonies. Definitely, the minuet is now devoid of the traces of the polite, elegant rococo of the French court. Interestingly, Haydn's successor, Beethoven, further alters the minuet—seemingly in defiant contempt for the aristocratic connotations of the minuet—by turning it into a rollicking, dynamic movement called a *scherzo* (Italian, meaning a musical joke or jest). Haydn's work was emulated by many, notably the young Mozart, who, by the age of thirty, completed the equivalent of Haydn's lifetime endeavor.

J. Haydn, Syphony 104, III (Menuetto)

WOLFGANG MOZART

Mozart's Position in the Classical Period

Much has been written about the musical genius of the eighteenth century, Wolfgang Amadeus Mozart. In many respects he stands in the same light as J. S. Bach—both represented the musical apex of the epoch, and both summarized the main trends and styles of the period in highest musical terms. Rather than uproot previous modes of creativity, the two composers refined and perfected the inner content of the established forms of the period. Interestingly, Beethoven, another member of the esteemed society of musical excellence and Mozart's heir, was a revolutionist who, after a short "classical" phase, ushered in a new romantic expression. His early work will be discussed following this appraisal of Mozart.

Mozart's life work may be divided into three periods: the so-called "wunderkind" years (1756-1773) of amazing musical precocity; the middle period (1773-1781), the era of a surfacing distinctive personal style; and the late period (1781-1791), the time of prodigious creativity and, ironically, a time of serious financial problems and professional frustration.

Wunderkind Years 1756-1773

Born into a musically rich and economically secure family in Salzburg in 1756, Mozart, under his father's guidance, became by the age of six a clavier virtuoso and by twelve a budding composer. This astounding early record was due in large measure to the nurturing of the boy's musical genius by his father, Leopold, a well-known composer, conductor, and teacher in Salzburg. After discovering the three-year-old Wolfgang "picking out" thirds at the keyboard, Father Mozart began teaching him some pieces on the clavier. The extraordinary talents of the youth were soon made known to the world in a number of journeys, during which Leopold had his son (and occasionally his daughter) play before nobility in Europe and England.

These tours began in 1762, when the six-year-old Mozart and his talented sister Maria Anna spent most of the year in Munich and Vienna. Later (1763-1766), a tour covering more than three years encompassed Paris, London, and various German and Dutch cities. It was during this time, specifically in London in 1764, that Mozart was introduced to the music of Johann Christian Bach (the second leading musical son of Johann Sebastian Bach), which had a profound effect on the development of Mozart's early instrumental style. The last series of noted trips was taken to Italy between 1769 and 1773.

The first compositions (of a total of more than six-hundred completed in his lifetime) were written in Mozart's sixth year. An ingratiating (incomplete) andante in B flat, (K. 9b), composed in the following year (see next example), shows the boy to be very adept with chromatic harmony and also capable of expressing poignant feelings characteristic of the mature composer.

Andante in Bb K. 9b (incomplete).Composed by Mozart at age seven.

(Note: The "K." refers to the catalogue designation made by L. von Köchel, who first codified Mozart's compositions.)

The phenomenal achievements of the youth are well known, including his polylingual ability, unusual performing skills, which placed him before leading rulers and courts of Europe, and his grasp of the symphonic techniques. He completed his first symphony by age nine, and, amazingly, eight more symphonies and his first opera, *La Finta Semplice,* by this twelfth birthday.

Stylistically, the early instrumental music of Mozart is a combination of several musical currents or strains, principally the *style galant* and a bright, energetic, scintillating style called *opera buffa,* which was characteristic of the Italian comic opera of this time and which was the principal mode of the Italian *sinfonia* composers, chiefly Giovanni Sammartini.

The young genius Mozart probably assimilated the opera buffa style during his year's stay in London, beginning in April of 1764. Here the boy undoubtedly heard the symphonies of the native English composers, William Boyce and

Thomas Arne. However, it was Johann Christian Bach who exerted the strongest influence on the lad.

The classic mode we noted evolving earlier among the Italian opera composers and the Mannheimers, quickly spread through Europe. By the time Mozart visited London in 1764, the classic spirit had already been imported, largely through the work of Johann Christian Bach, official composer for the King's Theater in Haymarket. J.C. Bach's smooth, scintillating "classic" expression was acquired through his extensive association with Italian musical culture prior to his royal appointment in London.

Karl Geiringer, the noted musicologist, has written that

> Johann Christian had the pleasure of arranging for the appearance at Buckham House of that unique youthful prodigy, Wolfgang Amadeus Mozart, age 8. John [Johann] Bach was fascinated by Wolfgang, they became great friends and liked doing stunts together before an enraptured audience. He would for instance, have Wolfgang on his lap while they played the harpsichord together, alternating after every bar; or they would compose a fugue. Bach starting, Mozart completing it. For the child genius this association with John Bach was of the greatest artistic significance, and his compositions clearly show the tremendous influence the mature composer exercised on him.

Middle Years (1773-1782)

A decided change occurred in Mozart's music about 1773, from the Italian buffa to a style more expressive and personal. The new style arising from this transformation is noticeable in both his chamber works and symphonies. It possesses the more serious overtones so characteristic of the German and Austrian temperament.

Six of Mozart's quartets (K. 168-173), all written in the late summer of 1773, were created under the magic spell of the musical crossroads of Europe—Vienna. And, more importantly, they show the influence of the famed musician from Esterháza, Franz Joseph Haydn, whose newly composed quartets (Opp. 17 and 20, 1771 and 1772) greatly excited the youth from Salzburg. In essence, it was a "new" Haydn who inspired him, for, as Einstein writes: "Haydn, approaching his fortieth birthday, was tired of the galant style; he felt the necessity of deepening his work, of infusing it with greater seriousness, greater intimacy."

Thus, feeling and passion replace *galanterie* in the Mozart gems of that eventful summer of 1773, but perhaps what most impresses the listener is their greater use of polyphonic textures, imitation, and fugue. The change is also noticeable in three important symphonies completed at this time: Symphony in C, K. 162 (1773), Symphony in G minor, K. 183 (1773), and Symphony in A, K. 201 (1774). In these, the sweetness of Italian buffa is replaced by rhythmic agitation, extreme contrasts of dynamics, sharp accents and a finer development of the thematic material.

Late Period (1781-1791)

Following the Mannheim and Paris tours taken with his mother from 1777 to 1779, Mozart settled in Vienna, where he remained, except for several brief periods of travel, for the rest of his short life. The latter years were fraught with disappointment and struggle. He continually sought important musical positions (such as the *Kapellmeister* position with King Frederick II of Prussia), but these attempts were completely in vain. In order to make ends meet financially he taught clavier and composition to wealthy patrons of the arts.

These activities were necessary even though he won many triumphs in concertizing and in his opera performances (four of his greatest operas were composed during this period). Perhaps much of Mozart's trouble stemmed from his lack of ability to manage his personal matters; moreover, his wife Constanze (whom he married during the Vienna years) was equally inept as a family manager. Further complication arose from Mozart's lack of diplomacy and an arrogant mannerism that prevented him from attaining the positions that he desired.

An example from the mature phase of his work in the operatic form is *Don Giovanni*, composed in 1787. One of the highlights of this opera occurs in Act One in which the famous "catalog" aria is sung by the hero, Don Giovanni.

> Don Giovanni and Leporello meet a lady who seems to be in distress but when Don Giovanni offers his assistance, he discovers that she is Donna Elvira, whom he had deserted some years before, and she has been voicing her desire for vengeance on the Don himself. Making feeble apologies, the Don slips away, leaving Leporello to console the lady. This is done in a very odd way: Leporello reads to her a list of the Don's conquests. It includes no fewer than two thousand sixty-five ladies—Italians, German, French, Spanish, tall ones, short ones, blondes, brunettes. As Leporello sings this famous "Catalogue Song" he brings out a huge notebook, which unfolds and stretches halfway across the stage.

Mozart, *Don Giovanni*, Act I

Incredible as it may seem, Mozart created more than two hundred of his most significant works in this period of hardship a partial listing follows:

Symphony No. 35 in D ("Haffner") (1782)
Symphony No. 36 in C ("Linz") (1783)
Symphony No. 38 in D ("Prague") (1786)
Symphony No. 39 in E flat (1788)
Symphony No. 40 in G minor (1788)
Symphony No. 41 in C ("Jupiter") (1788)
Marriage of Figaro, opera (1786)
Don Giovanni, opera (1787)
Cosi fan tutti, opera (1790)
The Magic Flute, opera (1791)
17 piano concerti (1782-1791)
Requiem (1791)

Summary

Mozart explored every musical idiom of his day—attaining brilliant success in every form that he touched. The essence of his musical style, the indefinable quality or "tone" we immediately detect as Mozartian, was already present in his earliest works. His relationship with Haydn, beginning indirectly through his hearing of the Haydn quartets in the summer of 1773, was a deciding factor in the shaping of Mozart's mature style which was subsequently exhibited in the quartets and symphonies. On the other hand, Haydn was influenced by the genius of Mozart, as can be observed in the more lyric melodic style, greater refinement, fullness of sonority, and compactness of form in Haydn's later works. Both Haydn and Mozart built their symphonic style on the foundations furnished by the Italian *sinfonia* composers and the German musicians at Mannheim and Vienna.

Mozart's contributions to opera are numerous: he was the first to successfully use the symphony orchestra to enhance the vocal elements in opera. Although he did not reject the Neapolitan style (as did his contemporary Gluck), he perfected the materials and concepts such as the opera seria and opera buffa forms, the aria, and the recitative; and, more importantly, he, like Monteverdi a century earlier, gave his operas real characters, possessing feelings and emotions. Again, like Monteverdi, he found a balance between the dramatic and the musical.

LUDWIG VAN BEETHOVEN

Early Beginnings

The turning point from eighteenth-century classicism to the romanticism of the nineteenth century is generally cited in the music of Ludwig van Beethoven. Born in 1770, at a time when musical classicism was in full force in the music of Mozart and Haydn, and indeed when the classical spirit was fully manifested in all of the arts, it was inevitable that the first creative urges of Beethoven would be in the measured and controlled classicistic vein. Although some music historians have divided Beethoven's life into several periods, for our purposes a simple division of early and late, or classical and romantic, will suffice. The so-called classical phase extends from the time of his first works (notably the first two symphonies and string quartets (Op. 18) up to 1803, the year when Beethoven completed his monumental Third Symphony (the "Eroica") and which is a landmark in the coming of romanticism in music. Our discussion at this juncture will pertain only to the highlights of his early life and work. His romantic style will be dealt with at the beginning of the next chapter, "The Romantic Age."

Beethoven was born in Bonn in 1770—the year that the fourteen-year-old Mozart was making his first sojourn to Italy and the year that Haydn completed his tenth year of employment in the Court of Esterházy. The story of Beethoven's rise to greatness despite tremendous physical and environmental handicaps is truly a phenomenon in music history. For example, Beethoven's family background was quite the opposite of Mozart's. His father was not a well-known, established musician as was young Wolfgang's (Father Beethoven was employed as a singer in the electoral court). Nor was there the careful guidance and cultural upbringing (Beethoven's father was, apparently, a coarse, unruly fellow with an intemperate liking for alcohol), nor was there the careful nurturing of musicianship. In fact, in many ways there is a close parallel between the early years of Haydn and those of Beethoven.

Actually, aside from some instruction in clavier and violin provided by his father, Beethoven was largely self-taught up to the age of eleven (1781), when he received lessons in composition from Christian Neefe, an organist and composer. Even Beethoven's formal education was terminated in his eleventh year. From about 1782 to 1792 he was employed as a musician (accompanist, organist, and violinist) in the Electoral Court. And outside of a few lessons with Haydn in Vienna in 1792, and a year of counterpoint with Johann Georg Albrechtsberger, Beethoven, like Haydn, acquired his performance and compositional skills through intensive personal effort.

In Vienna, in 1792, he entered the realm of professional music as a pianist, playing extensively in wealthy circles and making a name as a composer as well. Royalties from his music, fees for performances, and commissions from wealthy benefactors permitted Beethoven to live very comfortably as a professional musician; in fact, he was the first major composer to attain complete economic status. (Although Mozart's final period was one of personal frustration, recent findings show him to be fairly well-off financially but inept at money-management.)

In 1798 Beethoven discovered that he was beginning to lose his hearing. By 1802 the affliction had worsened considerably, to the extent that he was compelled to write, in most moving terms, an account of his incurable malady. This letter, known as the "Heiligenstadt testament," was addressed to his brothers and was to be read after Beethoven's death. This condition grew steadily worse, and by 1820 deafness was practically total—a time when Beethoven composed his last five great piano sonatas, the *Missa Solemnis,* the "Diabelli" Variations, and the last work, the Ninth Symphony, completed in 1824.

The music composed up to 1802-03—that is up to the Heiligenstadt document—follows the styles and formal outlines of Haydn and Mozart. The Symphony No. 1 in C major, for example, has the customary four-movement plan, sonata form in the opening and closing movements, "classic" sounding themes, and clarity of orchestral texture. However, there are some signs of Beethoven's own personal stamp: a heavy, boisterous quality in the fast movements, sudden crescendos, a lively third movement (formerly a sedate minuet, now a vigorous scherzo; Haydn, of course, also quickened the tempo of this movement in his latter period). And, above all, there is the ever-present emphasis on rhythmic drive and power, which although still somewhat tame, is so characteristic of almost all of his music.

The Second Symphony (in D major), although classically structured in themes and over-all design, possesses a greater feeling of breadth and scope. Beethoven seems to paint, orchestrally speaking, in long, sweeping strokes; moreover, this symphony has more of the dramatic flair and excitement that becomes so firmly ingrained in Beethoven's style, beginning with the Third Symphony, completed in 1803.

Summary

It seems that every epoch has its ebb and flow, when the common musical language of the era is fully explored and brought to perfection by a select few, and when a new mode of musical thought or style gradually emerges from the old expression to become the interest and challenge of the new generation of composers. In this regard, Beethoven may be considered the innovator, the stimulus, or the prime mover behind the rise of a new musical expression called *romanticism*—taken up next.

CHAPTER SIX

EARLY ROMANTICISM 1800-1850

THE SETTING: A NEW SENSIBILITY

> Music is the most romantic or all the arts—one might
> almost say, the only genuinely romantic one—for its
> sole subject is the infinite.   E. T. A. Hoffmann

Introduction: Proclaiming the Revolutionary in Music

By 1800, the whole of Europe was caught up in *romanticism*—an artistic trend that had been gaining in poetry, painting and literature in the late eighteenth century. In music, we saw signs as early as the sensitive style of C.P. Bach and then in the Sturm und Drang phase of Haydn. The full power began to be felt around the turn of the century with the musical front runner Ludwig van Beethoven.

The new era was proclaimed by Beethoven on April 7, 1805, the date of the first public performance of his Third Symphony (subtitled the "Eroica"). Like so many pioneering works, the "Eroica" at its first public performance met with unfavorable reaction. The halls of the Vienna Theater, which had echoed the balanced, restrained phrases, and elegant style of classicism, now resounded with power, fire, and demonic energy. From reports we learn that the audience was shocked and astounded by the hammer-stroke opening chords, the dynamic shifting and thrusting of accents, and the breathtaking pace of the final movement. Critics referred to the composition as being "daring," "wild," and "lacking unity." History has taught us that not only was the work misunderstood, but that it was the first major composition to "point the way" into the nineteenth century. Ironically, the path music was to follow is indicated in the very words of Beethoven's critics—a revolutionary new direction in which fantasy, imagination, freedom of form, daring invention, and virtuosity would become the chief elements of expression of practically every nineteenth-century composer.

The musicians of the first generation of romanticists, like their counterparts of the early Baroque, wanted to part ways with the old, to break tradition, and to experiment and find new ways for treating musical materials and forms. Occasionally, this romantic tendency is to be seen in certain moments in classicism, for example in Haydn's *Sturm und Drang* period, in the brooding melancholy of Mozart's Piano Fantasia in C minor in 1785. However, the power of spontaneous emotion was finally unleashed by Beethoven.

Perspective: Major Trends and Leading Figures

Because of the vastness of the romantic era, our aim will be to cover only the principal players who were closely aligned to the romantic movement centered in Germany and Austria. Moreover, rather than explore all of their music, we shall limit our discussion to biographical summaries, principles of style, and illustrative examples that most clearly embody the romantic spirit. Although there were many individual styles during the romantic age, four tendencies or phases are to be noted: the *heroic,* under Beethoven (1770-1827); the *poetic,* represented by the young romantics Franz Schubert (1797-1827), Robert Schumann (1810-1856), Frederic Chopin (1810-1849), and Felix Mendelssohn (1809-1847), the *programmatic* of Berlioz and Liszt, and lastly, *late romantic,* Richard Wagner (1813-1883), Anton Bruckner (1824-1896), and Gustav Mahler (1860-1911).

Time-Line: Early Romanticism

1802   Beethoven: *Heiligenstat Testament*
1803   "Eroica" symphony
1804   *Appassionata* piano sonata
1808   "Pastoral" symphony (No. 6)
1809   "Emperor Piano Concerto" (No. 5)
1810   *Egmont Overture*
1815   Schubert: *Erlkönig* art song (at age 18)
1822   Schubert: Symphony in B minor, "Unfinished"
1824   Beethoven: Symphony No. 9
1827   Death of Beethoven
1830   Berlioz: *Symphonie Fantastique*
1840   Songs of Schumann: *Dichterliebe*
1848   Liszt: *Les Preludes*

The Romantic Mind

The youthful artistic attitude that favors experimentation, adventure, and unbridled spontaneous inspiration, is an ever-present state of mind that cannot be confined to a single epoch. How that love of adventure and experimentation is reflected artistically in the various "romantic" cycles of Western art, differs of course. Some of the characteristics which seem to be fairly constant are these: (1) an intense interest in expressing personal feelings and emotions in the most poignant and dramatic way, (2) a love of nature, ranging from peaceful, pastoral scenes to depiction of nature's violent and destructive forces, (3) a longing for past ages, and (4) a desire to know the mysteries of life. Due to social and intellectual changes and other factors, the romantic spirit may be present in stronger degrees at given moments in history. It would seem, too, that various social tensions give rise to peaks in emotional expression in the arts, such as the Greek Hellenistic period, the Mannerist movement of the sixteenth century, and the Baroque and romantic eras.

Moreover, shorter, more incisive waves of romantic effusion are to be noted even in times when classicistic calm and balance generally prevail. For example, the "romantic" side of Leonardo da Vinci, according to Eric Newton, is to be seen "as an example of romanticism struggling to express itself in an unromantic age." The same can be said of Haydn and his storm and stress phase of creativity.

The Classic and the Romantic Compared

Even in an age of intense passion there are continuing strains of the rational or classical mentality; that is, there are those who believe that the rules of composition are to be followed and that formal balance dictates content. Traditionally, two outstanding composers of this period, Mendelssohn and Brahms have been given a "classical" label. Though they lean heavily in that direction, there are many romantic traits which we will come across as we listen. The true romanticists, such as Schumann, Berlioz, and Wagner, differ from the classicists chiefly in their greater pursuit of aesthetic energy—balancing and unbalancing forces—not only through new tonal combinations but also in their use of words or text to amplify expression.

The element of conflict, so important to the romantic, is, however, also important to the classicist who acknowledges the constant struggle between forces that threaten balance or equilibrium. Eric Newton (*The Romantic Rebellion*), writes: the classic temperament delights in the equilibrium that results from the conflict of opposites. The romantic, on the other hand, focuses attention not on the balanced state of affairs, but on the struggle, the tension, and the pulling of forces. However, in the pursuit of the unusual and the bizarre, the romantic artist or musician must eventually grapple with one of the most difficult problems: to seek order out of chaos, to make the irrational intelligible to the listener.

Pre-romanticism: Sources of the Movement

As with all periods, we must begin by looking for distinctive signs or landmarks which provide a perspective leading into the period. Without a doubt the most important of these is what Arnold Hauser (*The Social History of Art*) calls the "dissolution of courtly art," and the development of "bourgeois subjectivism," the former referring to the style set by the French courts (refined, aristocratic, and rational), the latter to the taste of the middle class (sensualistic, natural, and spontaneous), which, during the course of the eighteenth century, gradually superceded the courtly art.

Bourgeois subjectivism, then, constituted the cultural setting out of which the romantic movement emerged. The rapidly changing taste for the naturalistic and sentimental rather than the refined and elegant was felt in all of the arts of the eighteenth century: in the music of C. P. E. Bach (in his *empfindsamer* or sensitive, style), in the French paintings of Greuze and Chardin, in the pastoral, picturesque writings of the English author Thomson (*The Seasons*), and in the novels of Richardson (*Clarissa*), to name but a few examples. Moreover, it was Rousseau, who gave form and direction to the already existing tendencies to "legitimize and encourage a display of feeling." His *Confessions* stands as an important testimony of the romantic mind. Rousseau, perhaps more than any other preromantic, gave the strongest voice in the revolt against the ethical and aesthetic standards of the rococo. The cry was later echoed by Beethoven, who rebelled not only against the servant status of the court musicians of Haydn's and Mozart's time, but also against the overly comfortable, pleasant, and elegant qualities of the court expression. For Beethoven, born in the midst of bourgeois subjectivism, naturalism and emotionalism were the true inner urges, which were finally unleashed after a brief experience with the courtly style.

The Requirements of Romantic Music

Our preliminary examination discloses several other interesting aspects of the elusive phenomenon known as romanticism. One concerns the frame of mind of the listener, his preparation and mental orientation. For example, the very nature of the romantic's emotional approach to his art points up the futility of seeking an understanding of this music on purely rational grounds, that is, to approach it with the same set of expectations one would have in listening to a classical symphony. In classicism, the experienced listener is generally very conscious of the formalistic elements of music: the theme and its contour, its repetition, its variation, the balancing of A section by B, and the symmetry of form achieved by repetition of A after B (A B A). In romanticism, the composer focuses our attention on sound itself, and frequently sound for the sake of sound, for the haunting, moody connotations it evokes on the part of the listener. The formal elements are of course still there, but they are frequently subordinated to the expressive.

Perhaps the best way to describe it is to say that romanticism requires a complete personal involvement—a sinking of one's self into the work of art— and then only is it possible to fully appreciate the romantic's message to its fullest. For, as Marcel Brion (*Art of the Romantic Era*) writes, "one cannot reach the substance of romanticism by dialectical routes; only an immediate and total communion reveals that deep reality which reason alone will never uncover."

THE HEROIC PHASE: BEETHOVEN

Eclipse of Classicism

As we have already noted, some music historians regard Beethoven as the first real romantic composer, while others think of him as the last member of the distinguished line of classicists, as the apex in the final statement of musical classicism. Both points of view must be acknowledged, since we find that even in his most dramatic and powerful works there is a sense of form and balance, that is, a definite compulsion to restore order after turbulence. Of one thing there is little doubt: Beethoven fully personified, in musical terms, the creative spirit of romanticism. This is shown in his revolutionary attitude toward his art and profession, in his interest in nature as a source of inspiration and consolation, and in his desire to exalt the mysterious and the extraordinary.

Third Symphony—the "Eroica"

Historically, the "Eroica" appeared at a unique time and place, a knowledge of which may help us to understand the significance of the "Eroica's" musical style. This symphony was created when classicism was at its apex and romanticism was bursting forth in Europe. It also was the time of explosive French Revolution and the Napoleonic era. The dynamic expressions in many paintings of this era (*May 3* by Goya, *Liberty Leading the People* by Delacroix) are also mirrored in Beethoven's work from this period. His Eroica Symphony stands as a testament of the times. Concerned with the oppressive tendencies of the aristocratic classes, Beethoven originally dedicated the Eroica to Napoleon, whom Beethoven regarded as a liberator of the common man. However, upon learning that Napoleon declared himself Emperor in 1804, Beethoven tore up the dedicatory page of the score and simply titled the work *Sinfonia Eroica* (heroic symphony).

Moreover, the Eroica emerged from a culture that had produced its greatest dramatists, Schiller and Goethe. Their works, like Beethoven's, disclose an underlying two-sided creative spirit that, on the one hand, exalts freedom of expression and, on the other, shows a devotion to inner logic and order. Moreover, there is a certain "heroic" quality evident in the works of Beethoven and his literary colleagues. This quality, which is identified by dramatic conflicts, great breadth, and climactic endings, is exemplified in all of the Beethoven symphonies, and in Schiller's historical dramas *The Robbers* (1781) and *Wallenstein* (1799), and in Goethe's *Faust* (Part One, 1808).

The composer's title of the Third Symphony, "heroic," is particularly fitting. Perhaps the most important mark of the heroic is the principle of conflict and resolution, which Beethoven works out on a massive scale. Here, *conflict* is associated with the intensive development section, and *resolution* with the climactic ending, in which a feeling of balance and equilibrium is restored. In relation to Beethoven's previous symphonies, the composition is of increased size and has a wider range and depth of feeling. Beethoven, through his artistic manipulation of tonal materials, created in the "Eroica" an intensity of feeling quite unknown to his classic predecessors.

For example, after the surging, joyful first movement, Beethoven presents a slow, mournful funeral march, which, despite its solemn, grave procession, builds (in a fuguelike section) to a great peak of exhilaration that overpowers the initial state of depression experienced at the beginning of the movement. A complete reversal of mood is provided in the spirited third movement (a scherzo in place of a staid minuet), and finally the symphony is climaxed with the terrific pace and relentless rhythmic charge of the fourth movement.

On a smaller plane of expression, Beethoven frequently startles us with such devices as the two sharp, stabbing chords in the opening measures, the sudden unexpected change in meter from triple to duple (near the close of the third movement), and the dramatic sounding of the eight hammerlike dissonant chords about midway in the first movement. The sudden dynamic shifts loud to soft and vice versa, unexpected rests, feverish tempos, shifts in meter, and deliberate use of bold dissonance, all show Beethoven's great zeal to push asunder the boundaries of classicism. A brief synopsis of the "Eroica" follows:

The jubilant first movement (in classical sonata form) opens with two hammerlike chords followed by the main theme in the cellos.

Opening Theme, "Eroica" Symphony

This melody and the succession of other themes, which come and go with great rapidity, are not, however, complete melodies in the style of Haydn or Mozart, but fragments that eventually become wielded into a gigantic whole. The second movement, in the style of a funeral march, is based on a large rondo form, the main theme of which is first stated in the strings. An interesting feature is a fuguelike passage *(fugato)*, which appears about midway in the movement. The third movement (Allegro Vivace), a very fast scherzo, begins with soft staccato notes in the strings, accompanied by a gradual buildup in momentum and power. The trio, or B section (the scherzo, like the minuet, has an A B A form) features three horns in a brilliant display. The breathtaking final movement, which opens with a fast flourish, is based on a theme-and-variations plan. The main theme, a simple folklike tune, is sounded first by strings in pizzicato style, followed by a series of nine variations and a short coda.

The Sixth Symphony—the "Pastoral"

The Sixth Symphony (1808), although much more reserved than the preceding symphonies, represents another landmark in the romantic movement. In this composition Beethoven inaugurated a new concept that was eventually to become the hallmark of later romanticism: that of adapting a program or story to the classic symphonic form. The "program" in the sixth consists of Beethoven's impressions of nature.

The reader may recall that music based upon an extramusical idea, that is, on something outside of the music (a poem, story, nature scene, historical event, a philosophical idea) is referred to as *programmatic music.* On the other hand, music that is devoid or such connotations—that is pure sound alone such as in the classical symphony or sonata—is called *absolute music.*

Beethoven, we learn from his writings, had a true romantic love for nature. He wrote: "No one loves country lire as I do. It is as if every tree and every bush could understand my mute inquiries and respond to them." And twelve years prior to his death, he proclaimed "Almighty God, in the woods I am blessed. Happy everyone in the woods. Every tree speaks through thee. 0 God! what glory in the woodland! On the heights is peace—peace to serve him." And in 1817, nine years after the "Pastoral" Symphony, he wrote to a friend in Baden, "When you wander through the mysterious forests of pine, remember that Beethoven often made poetry there—or, as they say, "composed."

In typical romantic fashion, nature became a great source of inspiration to Beethoven. Its mysterious, ever-changing moods, its unpredictable, terrifying force and boundlessness, were idealized in musical terms. Just how much nature's moods and actions became objectified in Beethoven's music will, of course, remain unknown. However, certain definite signs of his intentions are most strongly manifested in his Sixth Symphony. For on the title page he wrote: *"Sinfonia pastorella* (pastoral symphony) or recollections of life in the country." Each of the five movements is provided with a title that gives the listener a clue as to its meaning:

> First movement: Pleasant, cheerful feelings aroused on arriving in
>   the country
> Second Movement: Scene by the brook
> Third movement: Happy gathering of villagers
> Fourth movement: Thunderstorm
> Fifth movement: Shepherd's song offering thanksgiving to
>   the Almighty after the storm

Of prime importance in relating Beethoven to the romantic movement is the question of how the composer achieved his idealized, abstract conception of nature through the use of musical symbols. In this work Beethoven paved the way for one aspect of the romantic musicians' creed, that is, the attempt to suggest and in some cases actually depict objects in reality. Music, of course, cannot accurately depict, but it can suggest or evoke certain images in the mind of the listener. Over the centuries, especially since the Renaissance, there has been a gradual expansion of the sources of musical imagery (military, religious, folk, nature, love). These are the wellsprings of musical art, serving directly or indirectly as a point of departure, an inspiration, or a kind of catalytic agent in the creative process. A simple folk dance rhythm, for example, becomes in Beethoven's Seventh Symphony an all-consuming aesthetic principle around which the entire symphony is based. Thus musical imagery operates two ways: intrinsically, as inner inspiration for the composer, and extrinsically, for the listener, who may relate the image to something in his or her experience and identify it for what it is (folk song, folk dance, religious subject, military expression, and so forth).

Clearly, imagery derived from folk experiences and from nature served as inspiration for Beethoven in the writing of his Sixth Symphony. Some of the devices used to represent or suggest the mental pictures include a drone bass (in the opening movement), which is characteristic of folk dance music; its accompanying melody has a lilting vocal style typical of folk tunes. Also, it has been suggested that the melodic idea that follows has a birdlike quality.

Opening Theme, "Pastoral" Symphony

The second movement's rippling undercurrent, consisting of triplets in the lower strings, is undoubtedly supposed to convey a pleasant, murmuring brook. The pastoral scene further unfolds with very real imitations of bird song. The flute trills in the manner of the nightingale, while the clarinet plays two downward notes of the cuckoo and the oboe supplies the high monotone of the quail. The third movement (Allegro) captures the festive setting of a country dance. Its triple meter, brusque leaping melodic line, and lively tempo clearly signify Beethoven's intent. The gaiety is soon interrupted by a dramatic storm complete with bursts of thunder (timpani) and whistling wind (high piccolos and strings).

Principal Theme and Countertheme, Opening
Second Movement, "Pastoral" Symphony

Perhaps, however, what insures the Pastoral's continued presence in the concert hall is its essentially abstract nature. That is, the composer has suggested scenes to us but states that these are only reflections and not an attempt to depict nature in an exact way. Thus, verbal meanings have not been permitted to dominate the musical progression; the scene and peasant activities are only implied, allowing various interpretations.

The Ninth Symphony

As with many of Beethoven's works, the last symphony, in D minor (the "Choral"), required many years to germinate. The powerful work probably began to evolve as early as 1792, when the composer was taken with the idea of making a musical setting of Schiller's poem, "Ode to Joy." Beethoven's notebook sketches of 1814-1815 reveal the melodic germs that were to serve as the foundation for this gigantic musical edifice. In 1817 he set to work in earnest, eventually completing the symphony early in 1824. Its premiere performance, in Vienna on May 7, 1824, was enthusiastically received.

The Ninth rests on a different plane from all the previous symphonies. Whereas the mightiest of these—the Third and the Fifth—represent the ultimate in the conflict of titanic forces within the framework of the classical symphony, the Ninth completely sweeps away all the traces of the classical structure. And perhaps even more striking is its philosophical content—a concept that is to play an increasing role in the unfolding romantic movement. Let us briefly examine these two aspects—that is, the structural and the philosophical bases of the Ninth Symphony—and show their relationship to the romantic movement.

Structurally, the Ninth differs dramatically, not only from the symphonies of Haydn and Mozart, but from Beethoven's earlier works as well. There is the conventional symphonic plan of four movements, but these are quite unlike their classic predecessors. For example, there are extreme contrasts in tempo within the individual movement (particularly the fourth, which has nine successive changes in tempo). The movements are not arranged in the conventional classical pattern of fast (Allegro), slow (Andante), minuet (Moderate), and Allegro ending. In place of a slow, meditative second, Beethoven wrote a very fast, exhilarating movement marked "Molto Vivace." And in the third movement, instead of the classic minuet or a rollicking Beethoven scherzo, we hear a serene adagio.

As with earlier symphonies, Beethoven worked with motives rather than complete themes. These motivic figures are to be heard as unifying elements in all movements of the Ninth Symphony. Characteristically, these thematic germs are distinctive "leaping" figures of large intervals. To illustrate, the opening of the first movement is based on a downward leap of a fourth heard, in the violins; the motive that follows is based on a three-note motto with a jarring up-and-down octave leap. Beethoven's earlier departure from classical thematic structure (notably in the "Eroica") is now carried to its fullest extent with these abstract motives, which generate and propel the musical flow in each movement.

Principal Theme, Symphony No. 9

The most unusual aspect of the symphony is the choral finale in the fourth movement. It is unusual because of its unprecedented use of a large chorus and vocal soloists and because of the philosophical message conveyed in a text based on Schiller's "Ode to Joy. There has been much debate about the fourth movement, specifically over its organic connection with the three preceding instrumental movements and its extremely difficult vocal solo parts, which go beyond normal voice range and technique.

Aside from these matters, there is little doubt that Beethoven wanted to communicate his personal philosophy of life in highest musical terms. Employing verses from Schiller's poem, he proclaimed joy as the power to unite men. Through tumultuous waves of orchestral and choral sonorities, and soaring, mystical choral parts in which the voices are treated like instruments, Beethoven seems to shout to the heavens in his joyful affirmation of the Divine Creator. Interspersed are two strange celestial interludes, whose reverent atmosphere is perhaps even more overpowering than the dynamic symphony's Herculean conclusion. A translation of the opening of Schiller's poem (Ode to Joy, 1785), from which Beethoven selected his text for the choral part (Baritone Solo, Quartet and Chorus), is as follows:

> O friends, not these strains—rather let us sing
> more pleasing songs, and more joyous.
> Joy, thou gleaming spark divine,
> Daughter of Elysium,
> Drunk with ardor, we draw near,
> Goddess, to thy shrine.
> Thy magic unites again
> What custom sternly drew apart;
> All mankind become brothers
> Beneath thy gentle hovering wing

Summary

Beethoven passed through several stages in the evolution of his musical style. The first (1795-1802) is identified by its classical tendencies, such as clear textures and melodic outlines, balance, and rational control. Representative examples from the first period include the first two symphonies, first three piano concertos, three string trios (Op. 1, 1795), six string quartets (Op. 18, 1798-1800), and the first seventeen of his thirty-two piano sonatas.

The second period (1803-1816), dating from the early stages of his affliction, represents a dramatic shift to the romantic style, with its greater emotion, unexpected changes in dynamics and tempo, an expanded and intensified development section, and emphasis upon drama and suspense. The main works of the period include the Third through the Eighth Symphonies, the "Waldstein" and "Appassionata" piano sonatas. Piano Concertos No. 4 in G and No. 5 in E flat (the "Emperor"), the *Egmont Overture,* and the "Rasumovsky" String Quartets (Op. 59).

In the third and final period (1817-1827), Beethoven's style became increasingly abstract, impersonal, and introspective. This turning inward of musical style was undoubtedly precipitated by Beethoven's deafness, which was virtually total by 1820, causing him to forgo normal social contacts and to withdraw into his own world. The works of the period, characterized by their intricate manipulation of thematic material, flexible form, contrapuntal textures, and an intense emotional level, include the *Missa Solemnis* (1822), the Ninth Symphony (1824), and the last string quartets. Thus, as with Bach, Beethoven turned to his most profound expression in his last years. And, again like Bach, these later works require repeated listening and considerable study for comprehension.

FROM THE HEROIC TO THE POETIC

> There is a pleasure in the pathless woods,
> There is a rapture on the lonely shore,
> There is society, where none intrudes,
> By the deep Sea, and music in its roar:
> I love not man the less but nature more,
> From these our interviews, in which I steal
> From all I may be, or have been before,
> To mingle with the Universe, and feel
> What I can ne'er express, yet cannot all conceal.
>
> Byron

The marked change in the early decades of the nineteenth century, from the heroic to the poetic, stands out as the first major transformation of the romantic spirit. One of the main contributing factors behind this change was the dissolution of the boundaries that had separated the arts of the eighteenth century. Around 1800, poets, philosophers, painters, and musicians sought a new focus—a union of all the arts in which each reflected the spirit of the other. For example, lyric poetry strove for the mysterious, magical, and sensuous qualities of music. As Alfred Einstein relates, "Not only in Germany but also in England and France, the Romantic poets strove to create a new verbal music .... The more musical a poem, the surer seemed its advance into new unexplored regions of feeling."

Moreover, artists attached literary significance to their paintings, such as Delacroix's *The Death of Sardanapalus,* inspired by Byron's drama. The famous German painter Otto Runge compared the similarity between colors and tones. William Blake, the poet, musician, and painter, fully exemplified the trend toward a fusion of the arts. It is little wonder then that musicians attempted to capture the essence of the other arts—namely the *pictorial* and *literary* qualities. Pictorial quality refers to "picturelike" musical expressions, that is, musical pieces derived from or suggestive of scenes of nature or everyday happenings. Such expressions abound in Schumann's piano pieces, for example, *Kinderscenen* (Scenes of Childhood), *Album für die Jugend* (Album for the Young), *Carnaval, Waldscenen* (Forest Scenes). Literary quality refers to musical expressions derived from or inspired by literature or poetry. This type is, of course, the essence of the art song *(lied)*, which flourished in the hands of Schubert and Schumann. Undoubtedly, the intense interest in fusing the arts tended to draw young composers away from the large-scale symphonic conception to the small-scale, poetic conception, but the significant achievements of Beethoven were also a contributing factor.

Many of the younger composers, working in the constant shadow of Beethoven's greatness, realized their inability to rise above the musical titan. Some continued to write in the same classical forms of symphony and sonata, but, the truly creative musicians, instilled with the romantic passion for experimentation and invention, turned in the opposite direction from Beethoven's dynamic, heroic style of romanticism, to miniature, intimate means of musical expression. The new aesthetic values rested, not upon breadth and power, but upon subtle musical nuances and interplay of feelings and moods.

Where the first great romantic dealt with the more objective states of emotion, such as joy, robust humor, sorrow, and the demonic, the young romantics delved further into the soul, revealing an infinite variety of moods and feelings expressing childhood reveries, amorous love, and picturesque scenes. Because their work stressed, for the most part, a lyrical, subjective expression in which fleeting mood pictures replaced the more powerful, large scale structures, we may characterize much of their music as *poetic,* in contrast to the *architectonic* style of Beethoven.

Inspired by the fresh, spontaneous poetic spirit, the new composers, like their fellow romantics in art and literature, breathed a new life into their art. These highly imaginative musicians aspired to communicate, not through the syntactical tonal relationships of the classicists, but rather through *feelings.* Their aim: to delight listeners, to stir them with sheer sensuous sounds, and to relate these sounds to literary and pictorial ideas. Such was the artistic bent of Schubert and Schumann.

The third composer to be discussed in the following pages, Frédéric Chopin, was least inclined toward the creation of pictorial or literary musical ideas. Instead, he devised still another kind of tonal art, one closely akin to the music of Schubert and Schumann. His piano nocturnes and preludes constitute a kind of wordless poetry, that is, abstract mood pictures or tone paintings in which the emphasis is on the communication of feelings and emotions, rather than on concrete thematic ideas.

FRANZ SCHUBERT

They say that beauty of the most important kind need not emerge
from some profundity but can just as easily float along the surface.
Bernard Holland, Music Critic

Life Sketch

The circle of musicians who set the tone of romanticism during the early
decades of the nineteenth century were all born about the same time: Schubert in
1797, Mendelssohn in 1809, and Chopin and Schumann in 1810. All but one,
Chopin, were of Germanic heritage, and, although musical romanticism touched
many countries, it was chiefly an Austro-German movement from beginning to
end. It is also interesting that each of the above illustrious figures made a
distinctive contribution to the romantic movement: Schubert, the development
of the German *lied;* Chopin, the style and character of early romantic piano
music; Mendelssohn, orchestral "landscapes," and Schumann, the
psychologically based art song and piano piece.

Franz Schubert was unquestionably the master composer of nineteenth-
century songs (*lieder*). He was born in a suburb of Vienna in 1797, at a time
when Beethoven was just beginning to make his mark in the Viennese music
world. The close proximity of the eminent Beethoven undoubtedly exerted a
powerful influence on Schubert. For we shall see that the great song composer
stands, stylistically speaking, at the point where classicism and romanticism
converge, and that the two opposing tendencies are perhaps more clearly
represented in him than in any other member of the first generation of
romanticists.

In some respects Schubert resembles Chopin: both were caught up in the
poetic spirit, which they adapted to music—Schubert to the song form and
Chopin to the piano piece. However, the family background, personality, and
musical achievements of the two composers rest on completely different ground.
Schubert's youth, for example, was quite unlike that of Chopin, who grew up in
a comfortable home and in a highly cultured cosmopolitan atmosphere, in which
refinement and social graces were naturally acquired. Actually, Schubert's early
childhood seems to resemble Haydn's, whereas Chopin's bears a striking
relationship to Mozart's. It is also noteworthy that the cultural background of
these composers tends to be mirrored in their musical style: down-to-earth,
folklike touches pervade many of Schubert's lieder, and, quite expectedly, an
over-all refined, delicate, and polished quality is ingrained in Chopin's piano
compositions.

Father Schubert eked out an existence as a parish schoolteacher, a job that
carried no salary but room and board and a pittance tuition from each pupil.
Although Franz Schubert grew up in a less socially stimulating environment
than his contemporary Chopin, he was given some music instruction from his
father and from the local parish organist, Michael Holzer. Family string-quartet

playing also formed an important part in the music education of the young boy, who aspired to a musical career. However, the elder Schubert made it quite clear that Franz should follow his footsteps in the field of teaching.

At the age of eleven (1808), young Schubert embarked on the same educational path as did Haydn almost seventy years earlier. A vacancy in the court chapel choir at the Imperial *Konvikt* (seminary) in Vienna led Schubert to try out for the position. Gifted with a splendid voice and an advanced knowledge of music, he won with little difficulty. Here, in addition to regular academic subjects, he was permitted to receive special music instruction from the famous Italian Antonio Salieri, who also at one time had instructed Beethoven. Perhaps the most important musical events at the *Konvikt* occurred in connection with the small school orchestra, which played the standard "classic" repertoire and afforded Schubert an opportunity to perform as a violinist and to try his hand at conducting.

In 1813, the sixteen-year-oid Schubert left the seminary and subsequently enrolled at St. Anna Training College to prepare for teaching. Ironically, after one year at the college he became a teacher in his father's parish school, where he remained from 1814 to 1817. Odd as it may seem, the three-year stay was extremely fruitful from the standpoint of productivity. On top of his six hours' daily teaching of the three R's to elementary-age children, Schubert poured out an incredible amount of music, most of which constitutes a treasure of romanticism.

Beginning his surge of creativity in 1814 at the age of seventeen, he composed such noted examples as the Second Symphony in B flat, the Mass in F, and the famous art song, "Gretchen am Spinnrad" (Gretchen at the Spinning Wheel). Set to a text from Goethe's *Faust,* this composition with its beautiful and imaginative setting both tonally and textually, announced a new era in German song. 1815 was a most productive year: six operas, two masses, his third symphony (in D major), three sonatas, and one hundred and forty-four songs, including the well-known "Erlkönig," based on a poem by Goethe. In the following year (1816) he composed the fourth and fifth symphonies and over a hundred songs, including "Der Wanderer."

Outside of some summer teaching in 1818 artd 1824 at the estate of Count John Esterházy in western Hungary, Schubert did not have regular employment the remainder of his short life. He led, for the most part, a kind of cultured-Bohemian life until his death in 1828. Fortunately the forlorn economic existence during these years was brightened by his association with a warm circle of intellectual friends who organized a "reading society" composed of writers, artists, and dilettantes such as the lawyer-poet Johann Mayrhofer, the singer Franz von Schobert (who offered Schubert considerable assistance in this difficult period), and the famous artist Moritz von Schwind, among others. The group held frequent gatherings called "Schubertiads," consisting of literary discussions, readings of the works of such poets as Tieck, Kleist, Heine, and Goethe, and musical performances by Schubert. The members of Schubert's circle were not true Bohemians in the usual sense of the word. They were educated, cultured men who were rebelling against the decayed Viennese society and the sentimental taste of the bourgeoisie.

Constantly striving for financial stability, Schubert wrote a number of unsuccessful operas and made several attempts to procure a conducting position. It was not until 1821 that some of his music began to be published, and then only by private subscription. Perhaps it was due to Schubert's retiring personality and dislike for appearances in formal society that recognition of him as a great song composer did not extend much beyond private circles of intellectuals.

Unfortunately, he died at thirty-one—before he could experience the recognition that was heaped upon him later in the nineteenth century. It is doubtful if Schubert ever heard his two finest symphonic works. The Symphony No. 9 in C major, for example, was "discovered" by Robert Schumann in 1838, ten years after it was completed, and the world renowned Symphony in B minor, the "Unfinished" (1822), was not given its first performance until 1865.

Schubert's Romantic Nature: The Art Song

Earlier, it was stated that Schubert stood at a point where classicism and romanticism converged. When we glance over the total output of this prodigious artist, the two-sided creative nature becomes evident, at least in outward respects. On the one hand, we note his classic leaning in regard to choice of forms: he wrote nine symphonies, twenty-two piano sonatas, and fifteen string quartets. But on the other hand, many of the six hundred art songs and a vast number of small pieces for piano not only show the romantic concern for the miniature, but especially the melancholy, the dreamy, and the sentimental. This is particularly true of the eight *impromptus* and the six *moments musicaux,* which are actually brief "mood pieces" in which one mood (joy, sorrow, for example) is presented in concentrated form.

The early symphonies are to be admired for their youthful freshness and obvious mirroring of Mozart and Beethoven. The Symphony No. 8 in B minor, the "Unfinished," composed in 1822, provides by far the most rewarding music experience for the listener. To be sure there are classic traits, such as a clarity of melodic line and texture, and use of strict sonata form. But what strikes the listener, especially in the first movement, is the prevailing dark moodiness, the many dynamic changes, and the power of expression so characteristic of Beethoven.

Schubert's musical significance extends to many other forms such as the String Quartet in D minor, the Mass in G, and the "Trout" Quintet. However, his real romantic contributions, and for that matter his distinctive personal quality and originality, lie in the art-song form. In contrast to his symphonies and sonatas, he demonstrated complete mastery of the song form right from his very first creative attempts.

The art song may be defined as a musical setting of a lyric poem for voice and piano. The form originated during the classic era, but, it was not fully developed and widely used until the nineteenth century. Its brevity, literary basis, and unrestricted form became an excellent vehicle for the romantic's spontaneous flow of feelings. The essential features of the form include a solo vocal part, an accompaniment (normally piano), a text drawn from a lyric poem and emphasis on one mood. Generally, there is no preconceived formal design, since the art song form is determined by the content of the poem. Some art songs follow the *strophic* form, in which each verse is sung to the same melody and accompaniment. Others, like most of the Schubert songs, are in *through-composed* form, in which the music changes with the meaning of the text, as in "Der Erlkönig." (Elf King). Schubert drew his texts most often from Goethe, adapting over seventy of his poems; other texts include works by Ossian, Klopstock, Heine, Mayrhofer, Schiller (over forty texts), and Shakespeare.

"The Trout," Art Song by Franz Schubert (1817)

Der Erlkönig, composed in Schubert's early youth, stands as a characteristic expression of the early romantic interest in strangeness and wonder. Based on Goethe's narrative, the work is a miniature drama centered around three figures, each of whose character is clearly portrayed in musical terms. The setting is a dark, dismal night. A father is madly galloping on horseback through a dark forest, holding a sick child in his arms. Suddenly, the terrified youngster sees the Erlking, spirit of death, approaching through the mist. The father tries to persuade the child to ignore the evil spirit, who then tries to coax the infant away. Enraged that he will not go with him, the Erlking grasps the arm of the child, who utters a cry of anguish. In a state of shock the father dashes homeward with the boy in his arms. Suddenly, abrupt silence discloses that death has triumphed.

In this medium, Schubert is undeniably the master. Strange, dissonant chords and bass tones depict the mystery and darkness of night. Different pitch levels assigned to each of the three figures delineates their character: high range, the child; middle, the Erlking; and bass, the father. And on a deeper level, successive, ascending key modulations enhance the child's increasing feeling of terror. The piano accompaniment has several important functions in Schubert's songs: to support the solo voice, to create and maintain the desired mood, and to provide "imagery" through characteristic rhythmic and melodic figures, such as the galloping effect provided by the triplet rhythm in "Der Erlkönig," the spinning wheel motion in "Gretchen am Spinnrad," and the swimming of fish in "Die Forelle" (The Trout).

Schubert's successor in the art-song field, Robert Schumann, carried these techniques to a deeper, psychological level some twelve years after Schubert died. However, before turning to the leading champion of romanticism we will briefly discuss the work of Frédéric Chopin, who successfully transplanted the poetic ideals of early romanticism to the piano idiom.

FRÉDÉRIC CHOPIN

Life Sketch

Chopin's most significant contribution to the romantic movement was his invention of the idiomatic piano style. This fact is attested by a long list of imitators extending into the twentieth century. It is not in terms of the Beethovenian scope and depth that we value much of Chopin's music, but rather in his unique handling of the miniature forms for piano such as the prelude, mazurka, waltz and nocturne. The early background of Chopin reads much like that of Mozart. Nicholas Chopin, the father of Frédéric, attained to considerable distinction as a professor of French at the Warsaw Lyceum. Under the careful guidance and cultural nurturing of his parents, young Chopin formed the good manners and refinement characteristic of the Polish nobility. His lifelong relationship with the aristocracy began at the age of eight, when he played the solo part in a piano concerto presented for charity by the Polish elite.

In 1831 he moved to Paris, where he performed in wealthy circles and mingled with ambassadors, princes, and ministers. Here, his rise to fame was primarily in the fashionable world of the salon, beginning in the home of the Paris Rothschilds, who introduced him to the aristocratic world. In contrast to many musicians, who were still treated as servants, Chopin was acknowledged not only as a superb virtuoso but as a gentleman of distinction, a role he played exceedingly well, with carriage, manservant, and clothing from exclusive shops. In this fashionable social whirl he gave lessons to the families of the nobility and performed at private concerts (one in 1841 brought him 6000 francs).

After making several appearances before the general public (and after critical rebuffs), Chopin was convinced that his intimate playing style was unsuited for large public hall concerts. Thus, his last public appearance in Paris was made in 1835. Undoubtedly these events contributed to his increasing interest in publishing his earlier .music and creating anew. His music began to be published in 1832, commencing with the sets of mazurkas (Opp. 6 and 7) and followed by numerous works in 1833 and 1834. Chopin's music was favorably received by critics in France and in Germany, where the budding music critic Robert Schumann heartily hailed Chopin in the *Neue Zeitschrift für Musik* (New Music Journal*)*, which appeared in 1834.

Chopin's life shifted completely when, in 1836, Franz Liszt introduced him to the French novelist George Sand (Mme. Dudevant). This famous literary figure was indeed a personification of romantic fiction, as Herbert Hughes writes: "A voluptuary without vice, who could take delight in recording her erotic impressions; a woman in whom the qualities of compassion, of hypocrisy, of pure motherliness and of the vampire were grotesquely mixed."

In the tempestuous romance that followed, a great amount of piano music was created, mostly during his visits to Mme. Sand's chateau at Nahant. She encouraged him to create and took care of the frail and sensitive artist during his frequent periods of illness. During the last three years of his life very little serious creativity was undertaken, mainly due to the grave state of his health. Most of his time was taken up with his teaching; however, in 1847 he again performed in Paris (for the first time in five years), and in 1848 he made two visits to London, playing before the queen and other notables of English society. As with many of the early romantics, his life ended before his fortieth birthday.

Musical Style

In regard to Chopin's musical contributions in the piano idiom, it might be said that he created a new idiom, a kind of musical poetry set in the keyboard style. Of his more than two hundred piano compositions, there are only a few traditional forms, such as his three sonatas and two concertos. The rest are Chopinesque innovations such as *etudes, scherzos, ballades, preludes, nocturnes, mazurkas,* and *polonaises.* (These compositions for piano fall under a category of nineteenth century music labeled "character pieces," designed to express a mood or programmatic idea, or to emphasize a particular technique as in the etudes.)

These compositions are analogous to Schubert's songs: in addition to stressing one mood or feeling, they are generally short, intimate, homophonic, strongly lyrical, and of free form. That is, they do not follow any preconceived established pattern, but rather the form grows out of the musical content, in a free-folding, spontaneous fashion. The occasional overshadowing of the virtuosic over the expressive side of music indicates the chief difference between the music of Schubert and Schumann on the one hand and Chopin on the other. Many of Schubert's and Schumann's compositions (especially the songs and piano pieces) have a simple, folklike quality, and are rooted quite frequently in German folklore. In contrast, Chopin's music is highly idealistic, and largely removed from the mainstream of life. However, he frequently uses native Polish elements, which he transforms into abstract designs, such as the basic rhythm of the mazurka. The etudes are chiefly didactic in nature, built as they are around one particular technical element, such as an arpeggio, a scale, or perhaps a chord figure. The most expressive, and therefore the most valuable pieces to the listener, are the nocturnes, ballades, and especially the twenty-four preludes, which demonstrate Chopin's true originality in mood painting.

F. Chopin, Mazurka Op. 17 No. 4 in A Minor

In conclusion, Chopin's invention of a new piano idiom led him to one of the most important contributions to romantic music—that of its harmonic basis. The harmonic language of Chopin and that of succeeding romantics is identified by a thicker chord texture and a more colorful harmony resulting from use of many chromatics, numerous key modulations, and greater dissonant level, as exhibited in the following prelude:

F. Chopin, Prelude No. 20 in C Minor

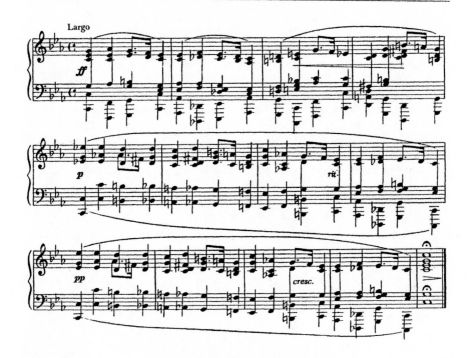

ROBERT SCHUMANN

Romantic Position

With the name of Robert Schumann (1810-1856), the third figure in the eminent group of early romanticists, we approach the climax of the poetic phase of the movement. In his early work we find many of the characteristics of young romanticism brought into full display in their many forms and colors. Everywhere in his music there is the feeling of experimentation, spontaneity of expression, and a constant reflection of inner emotions and desires. Revealed in his emotional outpourings is the full spectrum of romanticism: images of early childhood, sentimental declarations of love, and expressions of moodiness, despair, melancholy, and the tragic—one might say he is the most romantic of the romantics.

Why is Schumann often considered the most romantic of the romantics? His all-seeking, reaching, romantic temper led him to experiment in all the forms, to champion against musical philistines (the uncultured and unenlightened) through his writings on music, and above all attempt to make his music a mirror of his inner and outer life. This point is particularly basic to grasping a full appreciation of his music. Life and music are perhaps more closely interrelated in Schumann than in any other romantic figure; hence his compositions seem to be more personally "inscribed" than those of his fellow composers. For example, after listening to his piano pieces and songs, we somehow seem to sense the warmth and compassion of Schumann the person, the human, rather than Schumann the technician or virtuoso. The personal presence, is of course, an undefinable, intangible element. However, Schumann's use of the musical language as a vehicle for conveying feelings and moods takes the listener into the realm of the heart and into nocturnal shadows.

Life Sketch

The three leading "poetic" musicians of early romanticism, Chopin, Schubert, and Schumann, have many characteristics in common. They were all born about the same time, they lived short lives, composed in the same poetic vein, and were of highly sensitive, temperamental dispositions, and all began creating their major works early in life: Schubert at seventeen and Schumann and Chopin at twenty. However, it is amazing that Schumann is the only one whose creative pattern is closely aligned to his life experiences. In the case of Schubert, for example, outside of isolated pieces that seem to have some bearing on external happenings, there is little of the life-art relationship that we find in Schumann. There is even less evidence in Chopin, the most abstract and idealistic of the three composers. A brief overview of Schumann's life will bear out this striking characteristic of his art.

Schumann was born into a middle-class family in Zwickau, Germany, in 1810. His father, a bookseller and printer, was apparently a man who had worked hard to establish his business and who took great pride in his cultural tastes. Naturally, as Schumann grew he was greatly influenced by his father's musical and artistic leanings. To say the least, the environment was highly conducive to the development of respect and appreciation for the fine arts and humanities. His father's abundant supply of books, and especially the works of the German romantic poet Jean Paul Richter, was undoubtedly a decisive factor in shaping Schumann's artistic nature. Later, as Schumann became a composer of songs, he frequently used the emotional poetry of Jean Paul in addition to works of Heine and Goethe.

Two years after the death of his father the eighteen-year-old was sent to Leipzig University to seek a law degree. During the following two years of study his mind was definitely not upon jurisprudence, since we learn that the hours supposedly spent in law lectures were actually secret periods of piano practice and "poetic communions" with the works of Jean Paul and Heinrich Heine. Also, during his university days he met Leipzig's leading piano teacher, Friedrich Wieck, and undertook a serious study of piano with the renowned man. Little did Schumann realize the complicated relationship that would later develop between himself and Wieck's daughter then nine years of age. Already at this early age, Clara showed the remarkable piano skill and virtuosity that would eventually establish her name in the leading concert halls of Europe.

Schumann's short period of university study ended in 1830, when he finally completely ended his legal explorations and turned completely to music.However, the irresoluteness of his decision to become a success did not hold up against his constant romantic inclination to want to try everything in music, which eventually included performance, composition, journalism, and conducting. His ambition for a performing career was aborted in 1832. In an attempt to obtain a "shortcut" to pianistic technique he contrived a mechanical device for the fourth finger that permanently crippled his right hand. Since a concert career was now impossible, he turned to his true "calling," composing, which he actually had already begun two years earlier with his first opus, the "Abegg" Variations for piano, published in 1831.

The following ten-year period of composing became a decade of intense piano creativity; indeed, it was a time in which he wrote his most significant works in this vein. These are chiefly character pieces with quaint titles, such as his Opus 1 ("Abegg" Variations), Opus 2 *(Papillons (*Butterflies*),* and Opus 9 *(Carnaval)*

Like Schubert, Schumann also enjoyed the companionship of intellectual friends—poets, writers, and musicians whose never-ending discussions in the famous Leipzig *Kaffeebaum* covered all the principal artistic problems and controversies of the day. Uppermost was their concern for the inroads made by the philistines in German culture, foremost of which was the public's demand for keyboard "acrobats" who played "from the fingers rather than the heart."

As a result of these artistic gatherings, Schumann and a group of friends (including Wieck, who became a director) formed a new music journal, the *Neue Zeitschrift für Musik,* which presented its first issue in April, 1834. Soon after, the editorship was given to Schumann, who for the next ten years contributed many imaginative and inspiring articles, which unquestionably did much to strengthen German musical culture.

In an attempt to counter the philistine movement, he created an imaginary society, the *Davidsbündler* (David's League), a band of progressive-minded artists (who were actually his close collaborators under strange pseudonyms). It is also in these series of Davidsbündler articles that we learn of Schumann's schizoid personality (first disclosed in his letter to his mother in 1832). In adopting the pseudonym of "Eusebius," Schumann expressed his introverted and dreamy nature, and, conversely, in "Florestan" the extroverted, forceful, and masterly side of his personality is revealed. And as we will see, this dualism was carried beyond his journalism into his piano works, *Carnaval* and the *Davidsbündler Dances.*

The year 1840, like 1830, was a turning point in the composer's life. After four years of struggling for Friedrich Wieck's permission to marry Clara, Schumann obtained a court order allowing the couple to carry out their long-awaited plans. The marriage gave Schumann a new lease on life; it opened up a whole new vein of creativity, which suddenly poured out in a grand effusion of songs. More than a hundred of his two hundred and fifty songs were composed in the great "song year" of 1840. Clara occupied an important position in relation to these and other works, for/ as he related in true romantic fashion, she was frequently the inner stimulus for these works. Then, almost as quickly and unexpectedly as he entered upon song composing, he advanced into the larger, more complex forms of symphony and chamber music.

In 1844 there was also a turning point. After Clara's Russian concert tour in that year, Schumann had a breakdown in his health. He thus relinquished the editorship of the journal and departed for a restful sojourn in Dresden. Residing here from 1845 to 1850, he next moved to Dusseldorf, where he was musical director from 1850 to 1853. A series of very trying experiences as orchestral conductor in Dusseldorf, combined with increasing emotional disturbance, provoked a complete mental disintegration, which occurred in 1854. Two years later, Clara, with her close companion Brahms at her side, laid Schumann to rest in Bonn.

Characteristics of Style: Piano Music

Ranking among the greatest treasures of piano music are the many miniature pieces composed by the youthful romanticist Schumann. After reading over the events of his life it is understandable that the piano should occupy his first creative thoughts. Denied a pianist's career, he turned immediately to the keyboard idiom, completing approximately twenty-six works in the first creative period (1830-1840).

Stylistically, all of these pieces share a unique group of characteristics. They are relatively short, spontaneous "mood pictures" rather than large-scale dramatic dialogues. Tightly knit in structure, their unity is achieved through the repetition of a rhythmic figure, an arpeggio or perhaps a series of octaves in the bass, as in "Nordisches Lied" (Northern Song). Above all, we note an improvisational quality, that is, as if they were composed on the spur of the moment or suddenly created in a burst of passionate inspiration. Like Schubert, Schumann did not gradually develop this unique language over a period of years, but spoke at once in his early years with sureness of his objective and artistry. His later works, the sonatas for piano and the symphonies, do not have the youthful spontaneity and imagination that have given his piano pieces a permanent position in the concert repertory.

In seeking the meaning of Schumann's quaint expressions in the piano idiom, it is necessary to change our focus from the customary external point of view—that is, the music itself—to include the internal—the composer—as well. The inner and outer world are more clearly interrelated in Schumann's music than in that of any other major composer. This unusual approach to musical composition is manifested in two basic ways: (1) in the musical characterization of his double personality, and (2) in the use of some extramusical idea, such as a name or place that serves to spark his creative imagination. Several excellent examples of this unusual approach to creativity are to be found in his piano music.

Carnaval (Op. 9), composed in 1834-1835 and perhaps Schumann's most famous piano composition, is made up of a series of twenty short pieces, each provided with a descriptive title such as "Chiarina," "Estrella," "Pierrot," "Florestan," and "Eusebius."

"Florestan" and "Eusebius," of course, represent Schumann's two-sided personality: Florestan, the outgoing, gregarious Schumann, and Eusebius, the dreamy and introspective artist. It is noteworthy that this dual nature is also exemplified in Schumann's *Davidsbündler Dances* for piano, and even in his orchestral works, in the form of sudden impulsive shifting from the moody Eusebius to the stormy Florestan. His use of various names in *Carnaval* serve as outside or external sources of inspiration. In actuality, they are a kind of musical characterization: Chiarina is Clara Wieck, Estrella is Ernestine von Fricken. Chopin and the violin virtuoso Paganini are inimitably portrayed through certain musical traits generally associated with each artist.

Schumann's use of external ideas (extramusical ideas) for musical inspiration is best exemplified in the *Carnaval's* four-note pattern (A Eb C B), which is woven through all twenty pieces. The motto is derived from the German town, *Asch,* the birthplace of Ernestine von Fricken, Schumann's first romantic interest. Translating "Asch" into notes, S is Eb in German, and H is B-natural. Schumann also used the extramusical principle in his first piano work, the "Abegg" Variations; the name Abegg is apparently derived from another early acquaintance, Meta Abegg. Other examples of the Schumannesque technic include G A D E in *Armes Waisenkind* and B A C H in the six fugues (Op. 60) for organ.

The Art Song

Music historian Joan Chissell states that just as the nineteenth-century romantic poets such as Heine and Eichendorff could crystalize a mood or emotion into several lines of poetry, Schumann likewise could give us unusual expressions in both the piano piece and art song. The song form of Schubert was followed in various settings—the poems of Heine, Eichendorff, and others which were treated in unusual psychological mood pictures. These cover a wide variety of moods or emotions, delicate and dreamy as in *"Mondnacht"* (Moon Night), passionate expression of love in the *Dichterliebe* (Poet's Love) Song Cycle, and the patriotic "Die beiden Grenadiere" (Two Grenadiers), or despair and sorrow as in, again, the *Dichterliebe.* Most of the Schumann songs closely follow the mood of the poem; thus, the *through-composed form* prevails for most of the two hundred and fifty songs. The piano part in his songs has a more important role than in the Schubert compositions; in fact, here the piano part is in many instances of greater importance than the vocal part, particularly in the postludes, when the pianist closes with a solo passage quite frequently more expressive than the vocal melody.

Orchestral Music

Many of the later works of Schumann are in such classical forms as the symphony, string quartet, and string quintet. As we have said, these do not have the spontaneity and the lyrical quality of his songs and piano pieces. In striving for an architectonic expression, similar to the classics, Schumann encountered considerable difficulty in extending his lyrical ideas over great lengths of musical canvas. Lacking the developmental power of Beethoven, he often strung together a series of ideas that did not have sustaining values. In short, the lyrical element, which is rightfully at home in the small forms, prevails.

Of the four symphonies, the first (the "Spring" Symphony) is most frequently performed. The fourth, the Symphony in D minor, is particularly significant from the standpoint of structure. Its continuous one-movement form is the predecessor of the programmatic *symphonic poem,* which becomes established shortly by Franz Liszt and is widely used throughout the remainder of the romantic era. In conclusion, Schumann's temperament was ideally suited to the romantic forms of art song and piano piece. He employed the song form of Schubert, giving it, however, a new psychological interpretation. His piano pieces are in the same miniature vein as Chopin's, but they are somewhat less idealistic and virtuosic and of a more personal introspective style. His attempts in the symphonic and sonata forms, undertaken later in his life, were less successful, and, again like Schubert, it is the youthful Schumann who speaks more directly, poignantly, and pleasingly to the modern listener.

THE PROGRAMMATIC IDEAL:

BERLIOZ

Introduction: The Increasing Role of Literary Ideas

All in all, the Romantic period was a time of considerable literary influence upon musical style. Following Schubert's and Schumann's fusion of poetry and music in the art song, composers, beginning about midway in the century, increasingly sought literary connections in music. These ranged from rather brief titles applied to movements or sections of orchestral pieces (as in Liszt's *Faust Symphony,* in which the titles of its three movements are drawn from the three main characters in Goethe's *Faust),* to more elaborate texts set to music, as in Berlioz's *Symphonie fantastique* (1830) and Liszt's *Les Preludes* (1848). Wagner's use of mammoth plots in his operas (music dramas), and Mahler's extended texts in his gigantic song cycles and symphonies, represent the epitome of the literary influence in late nineteenth-century music.

Of course, the practice of combining music and words is as old as music itself. But what is so significant in the nineteenth century is the tremendous emphasis placed upon literature (poetry and prose) as a source of ideas and inspiration. Moreover, what makes this aspect of romanticism so pronounced is the fact that the literary influence was considerably less in the preceding period. For we noted that the characteristic expression of the classical era was predominantly "pure music," that is, abstract instrumental music in the form of the symphony, sonata, or concerto.

The basing of orchestral music upon some literary or extramusical idea is, of course, referred to as "program music," and is mainly the achievement of the romantics in the last half of the century. The practice was applied to the symphony, symphonic poem, and the symphonic song cycle. Beethoven, it may be recalled, is generally cited as the first romantic composer to employ this technique principle in the orchestral field, specifically in his Sixth, or "Pastoral," Symphony. Berlioz, however, was the first leading romantic to treat the programmatic idea in a more elaborate and realistic fashion.

Berlioz: Precursor of Late Romanticism

Hector Berlioz, the composer who laid the foundations for the final burst of romanticism in the orchestral field, was a Frenchman, born in 1803. His first major work, the *Symphonie fantastique,* composed in 1830, stands as a milestone in the romantic movement. As with many significant works frequently appearing in advance of their rightful period, this powerful symphony seems out of place among the predominantly aphoristic expressions of Schubert, Chopin, and Schumann. But when we observe that the *Symphonie* followed Beethoven's Ninth by only six years, we come to the full realization that the Beethovenian spirit of dynamic, sweeping romanticism never expired, even in a time of feverish interest in the poetic vein of composing. Thus, Berlioz stands as a connecting link between Beethoven and late romanticism.

The presence of these contradictory streams of romanticism in the 1830s— that of the poetic and the powerful or profound—can be partially explained by their geographical origins and the shifting of the nerve center of romanticism. The poetic musicians Schubert and Schumann were German romantics, living and breathing the "poetic" atmosphere of Heine, Jean Paul, and Eichendorff. The composer of the *Symphonie fantastique,* on the other hand, created in a different atmosphere and locale. Berlioz's work stemmed from the age of revolution in French art—when French theater dramatically turned away from the classical "unities" to an intense, individualistic expression heralded by Victor Hugo's *Hernani.* This unusual drama was first presented in 1830, the same year as Berlioz's famous *Symphonie.* Thus the center of romanticism shifted to France, as attested to by the abundance of extraordinary achievements in the fine arts, including the writings of Hugo, the paintings of Delacroix, and the music of Berlioz and Liszt. The French dominance in music was only momentary, however; the German musicians soon again resumed their leadership, which they held to the end of the era.

It would be incredulous, of course, to call Berlioz the founder of the late romantic style, since the traits of late romanticism were present in a dormant state in much early romantic music. There is, however, considerable justification for referring to Berlioz as the first composer to consistently employ the underlying artistic creed that is woven through most late romantic music, namely, the extreme amplification of *imagination, mysticism,* and *human feeling.*

Berlioz was, indeed, the pacesetter for the movement. For shortly after the appearance of his monumental works (such as the *Symphonie fantastique* of 1830, *Harold in Italy* of 1834, and the *Damnation of faust* of 1846, among others) there appeared in quick succession a series of similarly styled compositions: twelve of Liszt's symphonic poems (1848-1858) and his *Dante* and *Faust Symphonies,* and Wagner's elaborate music dramas, which began to emerge after 1850. These highly romantic works, although of differing form, are bound together, not only by their exaggeration and amplification of human feeling, but also by the more serious and intellectual tone of romanticism that they employ. In short, Berlioz and his immediate successors signalized the radical shift in aesthetic ideals that had taken place by mid-century: from the small scale to the large, from light to heavy, from the intimate poetic expressions of the art songs and piano pieces to the epic symphonic and operatic structures.

Berlioz: His Life

Born in 1803, near Grenoble, France, Hector Berlioz grew up in a strong cultural environment in which an interest in the classics and music was cultivated as a natural way of life. His father, a successful physician, fostered the youth's artistic bent by teaching him what little he knew of music. At the same time, he hoped that young Berlioz would follow a medical career. However, these efforts, which remind one of Schumann's similar creative path, were in vain for the youth's interest in medicine was clearly subordinated to music.

After a short period of college medical studies, the high-strung Berlioz was finally permitted to carry out his ambition, that of studying music at the famed Paris Conservatoire. During this period of study he competed several times for the Prix de Rome, finally winning it in 1830 with the composition *The Death of Sardanapalus,* inspired, apparently, by Byron's poem or perhaps by Delacroix's painting of 1829. The Prix de Rome carried with it three years of study, but Berlioz spent only part of the time in Rome, where he made some revisions in his first symphony and composed his second, *Harold in Italy* (1834).

Unfortunately, much of Berlioz's music was not warmly received in Paris. Hence, under economic pressure, he turned to journalism in 1835 and became a music critic for the *Journal des Debats,* remaining in this post for nearly thirty years. His work in this field, like Schumann's, constitutes an important body of writings in the history of musical criticism. However, his creative energy in music did not subside, for we note the following works from the years 1835-1855: the third and fourth symphonies (the *Symphonie funebre et triomphale* of 1840 and *Romeo and Juliet* of 1839), his first opera, *Benvenuto Cellini* (1838), the mighty *Requiem Mass* (1837), and the *Damnation of Faust* (1846), based on Goethe's famous drama.

It is lamentable that Berlioz's works fared so poorly in Paris—beginning with his early unsuccessful attempts to acquire the coveted Prix de Rome, the failure of *Benvenuto Cellini* to win the opera public, and the production of the *Damnation of Faust,* which put the composer seriously in debt. In contrast, his foreign travels to Germany and England as a conductor, beginning in the 1840s, brought him fame. Ironically, acceptance in his own country was not achieved until late in his life, when, in 1856, he was elected a member of the famed French Académie.

The Berlioz musical profile is much the same as his personality: high-strung, compulsive, imaginative, grotesque, melancholy, eccentric, and intense. Berlioz, like Schumann, put his whole self into his music and thrived on the extramusical idea, which served as a kind of catalyst for his creative imagination. Schumann, we found, reflected his sensitive, introspective nature in his piano music and songs. Berlioz seems to have projected his compulsive and bombastic nature into his highly dramatic orchestral works. Historically, his significant contributions and characteristic romantic disposition place him in the same circle with his leading contemporary Frenchmen in the arts: Hugo, the master of the new French romantic drama, and Delacroix, the most outstanding French painter of the nineteenth century. This trio of artists is, moreover, bound by the same artistic philosophy: an interest in the strange and the macabre, depicted in the most vivid and realistic manner. Witness for example, Hugo's literary masterpieces *Les Miserables* and *Hernani,* and Delacroix's *Dante and Vergil in Hell, The Lion Hunt,* and the *Massacre at Scio.*

Berlioz, Paganini and Virtuosity

Before we close this discussion on the musical scene in France, we should bring the name of Paganini into the picture. His name is synonomous with virtuosity which now comes into prominence in romantic music. Although present in practically all musical endeavors of this era, the virtuoso image (the "superstar" performer, possessing amazing skill) is associated with the pianists Thalberg, Liszt,and especially with the greatest violin virtuoso of the era, Nicolò Paganini. Paganini's influence was especially pronounced in the endeavors of Liszt and Berlioz. In the former it was reflected in transcendental performance skills in piano (which Liszt also transferred to the orchestra in his symphonic poems); in the latter, the influence reveals itself in expanded musical expression rather than in pure virtuosity.

Paganini was both a showman and an artist. The first side of the musician is shown in numerous feats which won him a huge throng of admirers. Paganini's unusual appearance—a highly publized mystique—is best depicted in Delacroix's famous painting. The other side of this phenomenal figure—the true musician—is known to every violinist through his many compositions for the instrument, many of which fully exploit the technical capabilities of the instrument.

The *Symphonie fantastique* was inspired by Harriet Smithson, a British actress whom Berlioz later married. Upon seeing her in Shakespeare's *Hamlet*, he immediately fell in love with her. Deluging her with letters, she refused to become interested in the young artist. In a state of dejection, according to the Berlioz legend, he composed the mammoth *Symphonie*, identifying himself as the musician in the accompanying program and Harriet as the object of the young musician's dreams.

The *Symphonie fantastique*, referred to as an "instrumental drama" by its composer, was probably influenced in part by De Quincey's *Confessions of An English Opium-Eater,* which appeared in France about this time. The "program" devised by Berlioz centers around a young artist who, under an overdose of opium, has a series of dreams, most of which are bizarre and grotesque. The dreams evolve about the artist's beloved, who is represented throughout the symphony by a recurring theme or *idée fixe* (fixed idea). The program or story or the five-movement symphony unfolds in the following manner:

The first movement, entitled "Reveries and Passions," depicts, through compulsive shifting rhythms and sensuous harmony, the artist's longing for the beloved. It begins in a serious, melancholy mood, apparently representing the artist's state of mind prior to his meeting of his beloved, then suddenly the tempo changes into allegro and we hear for the first time the idee fixe in the violins and flutes. The movement closes with organlike chords, suggesting perhaps a state of religious consolation, as mentioned by Berlioz in his accompanying program (see thematic chart).

The second movement has this caption: "A Ball: At a ball, in the midst of a noisy, brilliant fête, he finds the loved one again." Here, the young artist sees only glimpses of her as the party dances a rather fast and graceful waltz. The third movement, which has a pastoral setting, is entitled "In the Country." He hears two herders, who serenade each other with shepherd melodies, one played by the English horn and the other by the oboe. In the fourth movement, "March to the Gallows," he dreams that he has murdered his beloved and thus suffers the consequences under the guillotine.

The fifth and last movement, "Dream of a Witches' Sabbath," depicts a grotesque orgy in which sorcerers and monsters gather together for the artist's funeral. Orchestral shrieks and groans and high-pitched clarinet squawks nearly blot out the melody of the beloved, which is now, however, sounded as a bizarre dance tune mingled with the weird sounds of the *Dies Irae* (toll for the dead), played by the bells. (Principal themes are given below.)

Summary

Berlioz occupies a very important position in the romantic movement. In fact, it might be said that much of the music of the late nineteenth century rests upon his many innovations. Uppermost of these is the programmatic principle and his numerous contributions to orchestral technique. These are so numerous that all we can do here is mention a few, such as his use of orchestral sonority for its own sake, that is, for sheer coloristic effect; the introduction of many new instruments in the orchestra, such as the English horn, bass clarinet, contrabassoon, harp, and exotic percussion; and use of the new valved brass instruments. Berlioz, also greatly expanded the number of instruments in the orchestra and deployed them in a virtuosic manner, as if the total orchestra were a solo instrument capable of executing great feats of technique.

His most important contribution to musical form is the recurring theme idea (idée fixe), which permitted his successors to unify greatly extended compositions. As romantic composers increasingly turned away from the classical symphony form to a lyrical conception of composing, this structural device enabled them to coordinate and to tie together long strands of musical ideas. Notable examples are round in the works of Liszt and Wagner—Berlioz's leading romantic successors.

FRANZ LISZT

The Symphonic Poem

If we may judge music reviews and reports correctly, Franz Liszt was undoubtedly the leading pianist of the romantic era. As a performer he was a virtuoso and showman par excellence. As a true artist—a role he assumed when excessive virtuosity and theatricality did not dominate—he was the foremost champion of the piano music of the great masters. Unfortunately, the taste of the French salons (Liszt's habitat as an aspiring musician) leaned heavily toward philistinism, including the showy, bravura style of performance staged by such keyboard acrobats as Kalkbrenner and Thalberg. In this atmosphere Chopin, too, had found that "solid musical fare had to be served with decorative garnishes." Further indication of an empty, frivolous society, strongly reminiscent of the rococo, was the need to demonstrate pianistic supremacy via a public contest, such as was held between Liszt and Thalberg. It is little wonder then, that our present-day image of Liszt should be so strongly associated with "technique" rather than with creation. But beneath the facade is the lesser-known side of the musician, which came to the surface in his expressive performance of the masters and in his later life, when he supplanted the career of a virtuoso with that of a composer, conductor, and teacher. In this vein, he made three main contributions to the romantic movement: (1) the development of a new musical form called the *symphonic poem,* or *tone poem,* which was used extensively by his successors up to the early twentieth century; (2) the principle of *thematic transformation* (similar to Berlioz's idée fixe except that the recurring theme is presented in different guises); and (3) the expansion of piano technique.

Understandably, Liszt's stature as a composer is not that of a major figure. In fact, his total output, though highly diffuse, is negligible in the area of the larger forms, consisting of two symphonies, the *Faust* and the *Dante,* a dozen symphonic poems and two piano concertos. The remainder of his catalogue is chiefly that of miscellaneous vocal works and arrangements and a large body of didactic piano literature.

Uppermost among the major works of Liszt performed today are the *Faust Symphony* (three character studies of Faust, Gretchen and Mephistopheles), the Piano Sonata in B minor, and the symphonic poem *Les Préludes.*This highly melodramatic work, composed in 1848, is perhaps the most popular of Liszt's orchestral works. It exemplifies a particular kind of program music that was widely emulated by subsequent romantic composers. Instead of basing his symphonies and symphonic poems on an elaborate story, Liszt merely gives us a musical characterization, as suggested by the themes or titles of the works. Thus, he is chiefly concerned with abstract sounds rather than with objective depiction of human action and events (as in Berlioz's *Symphonie fantastique),* or, as one writer commented, he gives us "tone paintings" rather than realistic tonal "pictures" or stories.

Liszt composed *Les Préludes* in 1848. Two years later he revised it with an appended program note derived from Lamartine's *Méditations poétiques.* In the original edition, the title of Liszt's symphonic poem is provided in quotation marks: "What is life but a series of preludes to that unknown song whose first solemn note is tolled by death?" The complete text of the poem is as follows:

> Is not our life but a series of preludes to that unknown song whose solemn tone is tolled by death? Love is the enchanted dawn of every life, but are not the first joys of happiness disturbed by some tempest whose force destroys its glorious illusions? And where is the deeply wounded soul which upon experiencing such a tempest does not attempt to find peace and solace in the calm of pastoral life? Yet, man cannot linger long in the existence of nature and seeks out the dangerous post whenever the trumpet calls him to its ranks in order to regain knowledge of himself and full control of his energy.

Liszt's program deals with a theme favored by the late romantics: man against fate. This type of weighty, philosophical probing of man's nature—as opposed to the psychological revelations of Schumann and other poetic romanticists—is characteristic of late nineteenth-century music. This aesthetic ideal is so prominent that we may call this phase of the movement "profound romanticism." Vast tonal dialogues inspired by cosmic themes, such as the destiny of man, death and transfiguration, pervade much of the music of the late nineteenth century, especially the works of Wagner, Mahler, and Richard Strauss.

Les Préludes, as we have mentioned, is in the *symphonic poem* form, Liszt's chief contribution to the romantic movement. The essential features of the form are as follows: it is in the orchestral medium, of one continuous movement and has an underlying program, related to or suggestive of a story, poem, philosophy, scene, and so on. *Les Préludes* is divided into four sections, which correspond to the four basic ideas in the Lamartine poem. It opens with a rather lengthy introduction, in which the all-important, unifying, three-note germinal theme is announced softly in the strings and forcefully in the brass:

(a) Germinal motive, beginning of *Les Préludes*

(b) Motive (bracketed), opening brass passage

Four preludes follow, each of which conform to the four varying moods of the poem: (1) love, the greatest fulfillment of life, (2) the struggle for an ideal, (3) the solitude of nature, and (4) the return to conflict.

Liszt employs his technique of thematic transformation throughout all of *Les Preludes;* in other words, the three-note germinal theme identified by its upward inflection (skip of a fourth) is to be heard in varying guises in all of the four sections. Sometimes it is in a different key or in a different rhythmic setting, or is set in a different timbre or instrumental color, but it is always recognizable as a constantly recurring idea in the vast tonal structure. It should be pointed out in this connection that Wagner adopted the same formal principle for his gigantic music dramas, calling it a *leitmotif,* or *leading motive.*

Following Berlioz's general esthetic, Liszt scored *Les Préludes* and his other orchestral works for a large orchestra of strings, woodwinds, brass, and percussion, including the "new additions" made by Berlioz, such as the harp, English horn, bass clarinet, and contrabassoon. Outside of Liszt's virtuosic deployment of instruments (an idea carried over from his piano idiom), his striking romantic sound can be attributed chiefly to a lush, colorful harmony. Chromatic harmony (dissonant-sounding chords containing notes "outside" the prevailing key), largely the innovation of Chopin, was further developed by Liszt for conveying various romantic states of mind such as suspended, transitory moods, tension, longings, and unequalled dramatic climax. Wagner, whose work represents the final stage of this harmonic style, carried the idea of chromatic harmony to its complete exploitation at the end of the century. However before turning to Wagner, let us briefly examine the musical style of Brahms, the "conservative" romanticist.

JOHANNES BRAHMS

Classical Point of View

The leading conservative of the romantic movement, Johannes Brahms, was born in Hamburg in 1833. His life span (1833-1897) places him in the same era as Liszt and Wagner. The relationship ends there, however, since Brahms' aesthetic principles were quite different from his two contemporaries. Whereas his fellow romantics were representative of the avant-garde, Brahms continued the classic tradition of the symphony and sonata as inherited from Haydn, Mozart, and Beethoven.

In 1853, during a concert tour as an accompanist to the noted Hungarian violinist, Remenyi, Brahms met the dashing celebrity, Liszt, who showed considerable interest in his compositions; the musical interest, however, was not reciprocated. Also on this same tour Brahms met Schumann, who praised the young musician in an article in his *Neue Zeitschrift für Musik.* Subsequently, a strong friendship developed between Brahms and the Schumanns, resulting in a further strengthening of Brahms' high artistic ideals. When Schumann died in 1856, Brahms comforted Clara in her time of sorrow. Ironically, the strong devotion he showed Clara for many years after the death of her husband never developed beyond the level of friendship. Brahms' first phase of creativity, which began in the 1850s, was primarily in the chamber idiom, completing some twenty-four works over a forty-year period from 1854 to 1894. These include sonatas for violin, cello, and clarinet piano trios, and various kinds of quartets and quintets, for strings alone and strings and piano in combination. In the period 1860-1870, his choral decade, Brahms turned out some of his finest choral music, notably the famous *Deutsches Requiem* (1868), *Alto Rhapsody,* and the scintillating *Liebeslieder Waltzes* for mixed voices and piano duet. The more than two hundred songs cover a span of some forty years. These are generally modeled after Schubert; however, the piano part plays a secondary role, which sets these songs apart from those of Schubert and Schumann. It is in the texts of the songs, which abound with amorous subject matter and sentimental moods, that we note the true romantic nature of the composer.

The orchestral idiom occupied much of Brahms' creative energy in the latter part of his life. Outstanding instrumental examples include the *Variations on a Theme by Haydn,* a violin concerto, two overtures, the *Tragic* and the *Academic Festival,* which was composed to commemorate his honorary doctorate from Breslau University in 1879. Brahms also wrote a virtuosic double concerto for violin and cello, and four magnificent symphonies. The first of which, the Symphony in C minor, dates from 1876 (when Brahms was forty-three) and the last in E minor, from 1885.

Symphony No. 2 in D major (1877)
Symphony No. 3 in F major (1883)
Symphony No. 4 in E minor (1885)

The Classic vs the Romantic Nature of Brahms

Indications of Brahms' deep concern for the restoration of classic principles of balance and restraint are to be noted in both his creative work and in his protestations against the futuristic trends represented by Wagner and Liszt. The programmatic principle of Liszt and the elaborate music drama of Wagner were not akin to Brahms' creative outlook and temperament. Although Brahms held to the classic principles of Haydn, Mozart, and Beethoven, a definite romantic tone pervades most of his music. Let us examine this dualism in greater detail.

Romantics, we have found, favor color either in harmony, melody, or orchestration, or in all of these elements. For example, Schumann and especially Chopin stressed a colorful harmony, as shown by their use of chromatic chords (diminished sevenths, augmented chords, and the like). Berlioz contributed a colorful spectrum of instrumental sounds through a skillful orchestration technique and new instrumental additions to the orchestra. Brahms' romantic side is revealed chiefly in the underlying harmony, a love of dark-toned sonority of cellos and horns, and secondly in the melancholy, brooding mood that prevails in many works.

In Brahms' style there is a very strong relationship to Beethoven's. In his instrumental works, Brahms, like Beethoven, prefers to express general states of mood or emotion spread over large, spacious tonal areas. Also, the Beethoven principle of dynamic development, leading to a definite climax and resolution of tension is also common to Brahms, especially in the large forms. The romantic temperament is seen, too, in his use of minor keys, large-striding melodies spanning over an octave as in the opening of the Third Symphony, and an all-pervading, dark tone quality resulting from heavy emphasis on low-pitched instruments in the orchestral scoring.

As a classicist Brahms was deeply concerned with matters of form, balance, and restraint. Notably absent is the nervous, compulsive shifting of mood and the grotesque and eccentric expressions so common to Berlioz's *Symphonie* and Liszt's *Faust Symphony*. Instead, restraint of movement and power, and an over-all calm seems to prevail. Other classic traits can be readily observed in his use of the sonata form (generally in the opening movements of his larger forms), where classical balance is represented in the exposition-development-recapitulation scheme. And, like Haydn and Beethoven, Brahms employs the conventional or classical instrumentation in his symphonies: woodwinds in pairs, the standard brasses, timpani, and the usual string group.

The progressive orchestral methods of Berlioz, Liszt, and Wagner, which were chiefly coloristic and virtuosic, did not interest Brahms, who observed traditional procedures of scoring. In the following example (fourth symphony) note several Brahmsian trademarks: (1) his technique of dividing themes up among various instruments, thus producing a "broken-work" type of orchestration (as opposed to assigning large segments of thematic material to single instruments or a group of instruments); (2) the absence of any programmatic content—the music is totally abstract; (3) the ever present idea that melody must be ingratiating, memorable.   Without question Brahms possessed a gift of melody which is at the center of his particular brand of romanticism. It usually has a warmth about it resulting from the simplicity of tonal movement and also from his distinctive scoring of instruments favoring darker-toned instruments in the middle-lower register such as the cellos and French horns. Finally, a melancholy, reserved, almost austere personality is stamped into practically everything he composed, be it art song, piano sonata, or symphony. In this example, opening of the fourth symphony, the principal melody is sounded in the upper part (violins), while the basses and cellos provide an accompaniment in broken chords.

J. Brahms, opening of fourth symphony

THE CULMINATION OF ITALIAN ROMANTIC OPERA

Forerunners of Verdi: Rossini

In the year 1813, one year before Napoleon's eclipse, two figures were born who were later to command one of the richest epochs in the history of opera: Wagner and Verdi who were influenced in different ways by the phenomenon of romanticism. Wagner, who was attracted by the literary aspects and medieval imagery, remained close to the heart of the movement which he enunciated in a progressive language and form. Verdi, of an entirely different musical personality, was intrigued by the expressive potential of the human voice set within a traditional form and language. These and other fascinating comparisons will be the principal emphasis in these pages. For a better understanding of the reasons for Verdi's creative position we should first look at the state of opera and its form when Italian taste for things romantic was beginning to flower, specifically to the time of Rossini, Bellini and Donizetti, roughly 1820-1840.

Structurally, the operatic form used by Verdi's forerunners is much the same as that of the eighteenth century. The whole is divided into two or three acts (later four) and each act is further divided into two "numbers" consisting of arias, recitatives, duets and choruses. The musical centerpiece of earlier opera, the aria, is generally substituted by a *cavatina* which has a distinct popular flavor as opposed to the more reserved manner of the earlier aria. Also, instead of the classic symmetry and suavity of the da capo aria (in A B A form) the cavatina had a slow expressive opening followed by a lively closing called a *cabaletta.*

The two branches of opera, *opera seria* and *opera buffa,* which were established in the eighteenth century, continue in the early nineteenth. However, after Rossini, the comic idiom is almost completely obliterated by the popularity of opera seria. The plots of serious opera were altered considerably: from legends of classic antiquity and stories of courtly, sophisticated intrigue to historical themes and sentimental love. Interestingly, the strict code for happy endings of the eighteenth century opera is also changed very frequently to reflect the unpredictable (romantic) pattern of life.

One of the most successful composers (and businessmen) to emerge from this early transitory phase of Italian opera is Gioacchino Rossini (1792-1868). A highly prolific composer, he turned out approximately forty operas by the time he was thirty-seven. Of these, the following are most widely known: *Tancredi* (1813), *L'Italiana in Algiers* (1813), *Il bariere di Siviglia* (1816), *Semiramide* (1823) and *Guillaume Tell* 1829).The contrast between old and new is most striking in the music of Rossini. The new spirit, marked by its definite popular appear, is identified in two ways: by its simple melody and clear-cut rhythms. These undoubtedly originated from Rossini's innate flair for theatricality that was fired by the Napoleonic era.

The orchestral aspects of Rossini's operas, especially the brilliant overtures, are some of the most valued features which continue to please audiences everywhere. Clearly, Rossini was the principal Italian orchestral representative of the first half of the century; Verdi of the second half. In contrast to the German school of Wagner which favored the "total" sound, Rossini's thrust was through the strings in which the winds are in a subordinate role. The overriding quality in the Rossini-sound is brilliance, achieved by using primary instrumental colors rather than the mixed palette of his northern contemporaries.

Donizetti and Bellini

As romanticism captured the imagination of Italian composers and audiences, the bright showpieces of Rossini were supplanted by a style heavily tinted with melancholy. This trend coincides with the adoption of "romantic" literary sources used for the libretto. It is shown most vividly in Donizetti's operas which constitute a "gallery" of famous women: Lucia de Lammermoor, Anne Boleyn, and Lucrezia Borgia. This phase of the movement is thus identified by a concentration on what might be called the "love-theme" genre, ranging in expression from the gallant, *L 'elisir d'amore* (The Elixir of Love) to the violent and tragic *(Lucia di Lammermoor)*. The latter work, composed in 1835, is Donizetti's most important contribution to the romantic movement.

Vincenzo Bellini (1801-1835) is also a part of this trend. However, his style, very appropriately referred to as "elegiac melancholy," is more refined than Donizetti's, and far distant from Rossini's theatricality. *Norma*, composed in 1831, is without a doubt Bellini's masterpiece and perhaps the finest example of Italian tragic opera. As with its predecessor the plot centers around amorous intrigue. However, *Norma* is much more complex in scope and depth of feeling that is climaxed by a powerful ending reminiscent of later Verdi. Even Wagner, that vehement critic of Italian opera, was greatly impressed: "The action, bare of all theatrical coups and dazzling effects, reminds one of the dignity of Greek tragedy...Those who can hear in *Norma* only the usual Italian tinkle are not worthy of serious consideration. This music is noble and great, simple and grandiose in style."

The setting for this seventh opera by Bellini is in ancient Gaul during the occupation of the Romans. The story is as follows:

> Norma, high priestess of the Temple of Esus, has had an affair with a Roman officer named Pollione; this illicit episode has resulted in the birth of two sons. Norma reveals her feelings of guilt to her close friend, Adalgisa who, unbeknown to Norma, is also in love with Pollione. Despair turns to rage as Norma discovers that she and Adalgisa are in rivalry over the same man. Likewise, plans of annihilation—of herself, her children and of Pollione (who remains steadfast in his love for Adalgisa)—change to self-sacrifice. In the final scene she plunges to her destruction in a flaming pyre, followed by Pollione who she prophesied would be united with her in death.

Unfortunately, Bellini's short life (he died in his early thirties) did not give him sufficient opportunity to develop his unique style. Even though short-lived, his style appeared as a kind of Italian renascence, for once again the innate power of this great heritage was placed in the foreground. To summarize, the Bellinian aesthetic places total emphasis on the vocal line which in effect becomes a drama in concentrated, intimate form. In *Norma*, for example, moments of extensive coloratura are balanced by interludes of the classic *bel canto*, a melodic style characterized by its unusual purity and simplicity. Harmony never exerts itself, and orchestral effect is held carefully in check. The accompaniment is basically one of poetic enhancement, "simply a frame," as one writer commented, "for a lyrical etching in silver point." A continual favorite among opera lovers is the "Casta Diva" section from Bellini's *Norma*. This begins with a short introduction of arpeggiated figures in the strings followed by a solo flute passage.

"Casta Diva" from Bellini's *Norma*

GIUSEPPE VERDI

The "Theatre of Character"

Verdi brought the romantic movement in Italian opera to an illustrious climax. Although working within the traditional operatic framework and harmonic principles, he achieved considerable diversity of effect through wide-ranging subject matter and especially an abundant melodic technique. Disinterested in "progressive" northern harmonic practices and enriched orchestration, Verdi struck off on the primary route of all Italian musical art. He proved that a singular emphasis—simple, tuneful melody—could carry most of the weight of an operatic score. We should hasten to add, however, that with increasing maturity of style, especially in the final period, two other ingredients were given prominence: dramatic unity and strong orchestral support.

Italy, unlike Germany and France, did not have a strong heritage of drama upon which to build the new romantic form of opera. Verdi, however, filled the gap with "imported" literary works by Schiller, Dumas, Hugo and Shakespeare, thereby ushering in the Italian form of music drama, quite distinct, of course, from the German. From the wealth of literature offered by Schiller, Hugo and others, Verdi drew his inspiration and fashioned his essential claim to fame: the "theatre of character." Rarely had there been such a skillful drawing out of characters from the story and their development through musical means. With such works as *La Traviata* and *Rigoletto* the emphasis shifts notably in two ways: from themes of sentimental love (Donizetti) to action and character dramatization; and from virtuosity and stage effect to intrinsic musical development of the character's feelings, tensions and passions. In a moment we will see how *La Traviata* mirrors these aesthetic changes.

A few comments on the differences between Verdi and Wagner must be made. Though Wagner and Verdi sought the same general goals in musical and dramatic achievement, their respective paths differed considerably. Building on Donizetti and Bellini, Verdi continued his predecessor's conception of opera as basically "lyrical drama." This type places melody in the dominant position, as the ruling agent over harmony and orchestration. Wagner's type of opera, "declamatory drama," differed with its speech-like melody, harmonic richness and especially the dominance of the orchestra, which as we shall see, becomes the soul or conscience of the opera. The "rule of melody" in Verdi's lyrical drama had a profound effect. The popular appeal of repeated melodic sections and vocal solos required sections and divisions between arias, duets and choruses. In contrast, Wagner's structures (*The Ring*) are continuous with focus on dramatic continuity as opposed to solo melody.

La Traviata (The Fallen Woman) is based upon Dumas' play's *La Dame aux Camelias.* In 1852 Verdi saw the new play in Paris during the time he was working on *Il Trovatore.* He subsequently constructed a plan for an opera on Dumas' story and sent it to his librettist, Piave, who had collaborated with Verdi on previous works. Verdi worked with incredible speed. Just seven weeks after *Trovatore* was premiered in Rome on March 6, 1853, *Traviata* was presented in Vienna. Amazingly, Verdi had composed the musical portion of *Traviata* in four weeks. The following is a brief synopsis of this opera:

> In a heartfelt moment in which Violetta sings a short soliloquy (given below), she ponders the overture of Alfredo Germont, a wealthy bachelor from Provencal. Eventually she decides to abandon her dissolute existence which is slowly killing her, and live with him in a country villa near Paris. However, in the second act, after Alfredo's father tries to persuade her to leave Alfredo, Violetta agrees to sacrifice herself and returns to her life of pleasure. In the last act Alfredo, having

learned of her sacrifice for his family and her terrible state of health, rushes to her side. Violetta, ravaged by consumption dies in the arms of her lover.

Violetta's soliloquy, a portion printed below, is preceded by a short wood-wind introduction of three measures.

Violetta's Soliloquy from first act of *La Traviata*

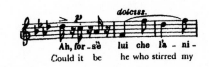

CHAPTER SEVEN

CLIMAX OF ROMANTICISM
1850-1900

STRIVING FOR THE SUMMIT

German Hegemony

The period extending from the middle of the nineteenth century to the early years of the twentieth marks the culmination of a remarkable epoch in musical art. From the rich background of Germanic culture emerged Wagner, Bruckner, and Mahler—Wagner, who drew his creative inspiration from German mythology; Bruckner, from the Austro-German vein of melody and Baroque mysticism; and Mahler, from German folk melody and poetry. As with the earlier romantics, there is no clear-cut style system evident among these highly diversified composers. However, there is a particular aesthetic concept, generally shared by all: an extraordinary inclination to expand the boundaries of expression in every aspect of composition. For example, an intense desire to amplify feelings and emotions, to seek an understanding of the profound mysteries of life, and to extend the limits of musical art, including its time scale (performing time), its subject matter, its harmonic foundations, and its performance medium, which now reaches gargantuan proportions. The late nineteenth century was, to be sure, an era of grandeur, immensity, and superlative expression unequalled in previous periods of music. These traits are most completely personified in the music of Wagner, Bruckner and Mahler.

The musical heritage of Wagner, Bruckner and Mahler stems from the very heart of the romantic movement in music—Germany and Austria. Although they are markedly different in style, they possess the intense drive to ascend to the highest mystical regions and pronounce to the world their ultimate statement of romanticism. Thus, the late romantic composer frequently looks to the world beyond, to the mystic regions of legend, mythology, and the supernatural for inspiration. The early romantic, in contrast, turned to his own immediate world and expressed his feelings and thoughts regarding less complicated subjects,such as sentimental love, childhood reveries, and pastoral scenes. To be sure, the early romantic delved into nocturnal shadows, but for the late romantic these shadows were darker and more mysterious.

Time-Line: Late Romanticism

1851	Wagner: *Oper und Drama*
1859	Wagner: *Tristan und Isolde*
1869	Brahms: *Liebeslieder Waltzes*
1874	Bruckner: Symphony No. 4 "Romantic"
1876	Brahms: Symphony No. 1
1882	Wagner: *Parsifal*
1883	Death of Wagner
1896	Bruckner: Symphony No. 9
1897	Death of Brahms
1907	Mahler: *Symphony of 1000*
1909	Mahler: *Das Lied von der Erde*
1911	Death of Mahler

The striving for the summit that we feel so strongly in the works of these late romantics seems to be analogous to pursuing the summit of some gigantic peak. This idea is not perhaps as naïve as it may appear when we examine the great struggle for an ideal in the life of Wagner, and particularly the nature of his musical style. Wagner's melodies, and many of those of his two leading contemporaries Bruckner and Mahler, are generally long, sweeping, and seemingly endless, stopping only briefly on tonal plateaus, which are momentary resting points in what seems to be a great ascent. With the long-awaited climax there is an overwhelming release of tension, as the constant stream of dissonant harmony becomes resolved in tonic harmony, and concerted sounds of cosmic magnitude and force bring the work to a triumphant close. Although Beethoven emphasized this aesthetic aim, never before in the history of music has so much attention given to the *climax*. A series of dramatic situations or episodes, skillfully designed in the manner of a Dostoevski novel and containing powerful germinal motives, are woven together into a vast tonal drama that gradually gains in momentum and tension.

The ultimate in musical forces is required. Orchestral bodies had to be expanded to more than twice the size of the late classical orchestra, and new instruments created (such as the haunting Wagner tubas). New instrumental combinations for a richer, thicker sonority were devised, and the emphasis on a dramatic gradual buildup of tension, led to greatly extended musical forms. The effect of all of these newly devised musical techniques is perhaps what Wagner was aiming for: a suprapowerful musical force that would transport and engulf the listener in vast tonal waves of volume, orchestral color, and lush harmony.

The Role of Folklore and Nationalism

The presence of folk, religious and mythological subjects in the late romantic period is easily understood, for the nineteenth century, in general, was a time of unprecedented interest in German culture—an interest that extended to all of the arts, painting, literature, poetry, drama, and music. From the very beginning of the romantic movement, writers, artists, and musicians maintained a close connection with German folk poetry, legend, and medieval heritage.

In music, the first signs of approaching German nationalism were announced in the opera form by E. T. A. Hoffmann, a celebrated literary figure and painter; his best known opera, *Undine* (1816), discloses characteristic romantic traits in its folklike melody and supernatural scenes. But the real founder of German romantic opera was Carl Maria von Weber whose famous operas, *Der freischütz.* (1821) and *Oberon* (1826), established the framework of German romantic opera, later culminated by Wagner. Abounding in Weber's works are forested German landscapes, the supernatural and ancient folk tales.

One of the most important cultural developments to have a great impact on practically all of German music in the romantic era was the popular folk music movement which began in Germany about 1770. Included among the earliest collections of folk music were J. A. P. Schulz' *Lieder im Volkston* (1782), J. A. Hiller's *Lieder für Kinder* (1769), and Herder's *Ossian und die Lieder alter Volker* (1773). In turn, the poetry of Goethe and Heine, whose work was often inspired by these folk collections, served as the basis for the art songs of Schubert and Schumann, and were used as late as Brahms and Mahler. In particular, the stylistic roots of the last leading German romantic, Gustav Mahler, are to be found in the gigantic collection of German poems, folk songs, and carols (dated as early as the sixteenth century) collected under the title *Des Knaben Wunderhorn (*The Youth's Magic Horn*),* by the poets von Arnim and Brentano and published 1806-1808.

Painters also rediscovered the Rhine, German village scenes, mountains, and Gothic castles captured in a dark-toned, nostalgic mood. Also, Carus (d. 1869) provided a metaphysical approach to painting nature. In his *Nine Letters on Landscape Painting,* he writes:

> A man contemplating the magnificent unity of a natural landscape becomes aware of his own smallness and, feeling that everything is a part of God, he loses himself in that infinity, giving up, in a sense, his individual existence. To be engulfed in this way is not to be destroyed; it is a gain; what normally one could only perceive with the spirit almost becomes plain to the physical eye.

The movement in German art attained its highest point in the paintings of Caspar David Friedrich (d. 1840), the most important of all German romantic painters. In many of his works, such as *The Chalk Cliffs of Rugen* (1818), *The Couple Looking at the Moon* (1819), and *The Cross and Cathedral in the Mountains* (1811), we can sense many of the same qualities that are suggested in Wagner, Bruckner, and Mahler. These include a vastness of form, strength and massiveness, a reaching for infinity, and the subordination of man to the mysteries and power of nature and the supernatural.

RICHARD WAGNER

Of all the late nineteenth-century composers Wagner (1813-1883) must be placed at the pinnacle of the romantic epoch. He greatly extended and enriched the romantic concepts of harmony, melody, orchestration, and form, and brought to complete fruition the romantic ideal of unification of the arts.

We have observed that the romantic styles throughout this period have been as numerous and highly divergent as the composers who created them. These musicians were, however, bound by their common interest in originating a new language, one that was governed less by rules or social custom and more by individual temperament and personality. Actually the language was not new. It was basically the traditional system of harmony and melody greatly enriched by extensive chromaticism and placed into new molds. It was "new" in the sense that tonal combinations were employed *freely* for their *psychological* rather than *rational* meaning, that is, for their power to express emotional connotations. Whereas the earlier romantics used the new musical language to suggest various emotional states and to enhance the dramatic content of a text or story, Wagner carried the idea one step further. His objective was to completely transport the audience into the world of feelings, moods, and emotions via the medium of total theater, in which drama and music are one.

A Brief Look at His Life and Work

It is hard to believe that Wagner, born in Leipzig in 1813, entered the world at the same time as the poetic romanticists Schumann and Chopin, who developed an entirely different musical aesthetic. Perhaps our perspective of Wagner's life will become clearer when we note that he began to reach his stride after 1850, at a later age than his predecessors, who attained their creative peak earlier in life. Also, Wagner, who died in 1883, lived a much longer life than most romantics, completing most of his major works in his later years, in contrast to the youthful contributions of Schumann, Schubert, and Chopin.

Wagner's educational background and early music experiences do not disclose signs of extraordinary latent talent in musical and literary creativity. At the Kreuzschule in Dresden, young Wagner showed much interest in Greek and German poetry and tragedy but little enthusiasm for music. It is quite remarkable that the operatic giant of the romantic movement did not show a real interest in music until his late teens, when he finally plunged into an intense study of Beethoven's works. Several minor compositions, including a symphony and a piano sonata, were composed at this time. However, at the outset of his career his chief interest lay in conducting.

From 1833 to 1849 Wagner held numerous operatic conducting posts in Germany, the most important of which was at Dresden from 1843 to 1849. Also, his earliest operas were composed during this period: *Rienzi* (1842), *Der fliegende Holländer (*The Flying Dutchman*)* (1843), and *Tannhäuser* (1845). The last of this series of traditional-styled operas, *Lohengrin,* was completed in

1850. This opera foreshadowed his future music dramas in its more continuous flow of music (as opposed to the sectional style of traditional opera, with its recitative-aria sequence), its use of symbolism, and recurring theme idea, or *leitmotif.*

The turning point in Wagner's life came in 1849, when, as a result of his participation in the May Revolution of that year, he was forced to migrate to Switzerland, where he remained in exile for about ten years. Here, he wrote his theories on art, including the famous *Oper und Drama* (1851), an exhaustive study on aesthetics that forms the philosophical groundwork for his invention, the *music drama.* This new form of opera became the framework for his gigantic tetralogy, *Der Ring des Nibelungen (*The Ring of the Nibelungs*).* This collosal work, which was partially completed during his exile, consisted of *Das Rheingold (*The Rhine Gold*), Die Walküre (*The Valkyrie*), Siegfried,* and *Götterdämmerung (*Twilight of the Gods*).* The entire work, which was finally completed in 1874, represents the sum expression of Wagner's theories and the capstone of his creative work. Three other music dramas were completed in the latter part of his career: *Tristan und Isolde* (1859), *Die Meistersinger von Nürnberg* (1867), and *Parsifal* (1882).

Among the many features of the Wagner mystique, we must mention the Gothic influence which also touched Bruckner and Mahler. For example, the castle motif and settings in Wagner's *Lohengrin* and the *Ring,* the use of medieval chant and deep, dark sounding horns in the Ring and in Bruckner's symphonies. As a side note, Wagner was also associated with the magnificent Neuschwanstein castle located high in the Bavarian alps. King Ludwig II, who constructed the ediface, became a personal admirer and financial backer of Wagner. The young king intended the castle to be a "temple" in Wagner's honor and thus had the structure decorated with numerous murals depicting scenes from the Wagnerian operas. Ludwig also the assisted Wagner financially in the building of the composer's famous opera house at Bayreuth, completed 1876.

As to some of the main ideas presented in his comprehensive treatise *Oper und Drama,* those pertaining to the rationale for breaking with traditional opera and his phenomenal plan for assigning equal rights to "tone" and "word" are most pertinent here. Deploring the terrible state that opera had fallen into, Wagner cited two basic causes of the dilemma: first, the superficial librettos, which were addressed not to humanity but to "the cultured sensibilities of a select social group," and, secondly, the traditional structure of opera with its emphasis on the aria, which had been designed to show off the singer's technique rather than "display any truth of feeling." In essence, music which should be the *means,* had been made the *end,* and drama had become the means.

A guiding factor in Wagner's creation of a new operatic ideal was provided by Beethoven. In his study of the Beethoven symphonies, a new logic founded not on reason but on inner feeling was revealed to Wagner. He believed that the great orchestral genius had cultivated the expression of human feeling to a high degree, but the limits had been reached in the instrumental idiom. However, in his Ninth Symphony, Beethoven had demonstrated that it was possible to extend the boundaries by the addition of *voices.* Thus, where instrumental music previously provided only an incomplete representation of emotion, music could now become complete with the addition of the *word*. Hence, in the Wagnerian music drama the outer action is carried by the sung words, while the inner action (that which is beyond words, such as feelings and desires) is carried by the orchestra. Actually, the focal point of Wagner's music drama is not the melody but the orchestra, which functions at the subjective and even subliminal level of the listener, calling forth images of persons, places, feelings, and desires, each of which is associated with its own particular recurring theme or leitmotif.

Since the essence of drama is conveyed through feeling and not understanding, the new art form must be centered around the senses rather than the intellect. Consequently, the drama's action must transcend the world of reality. The customary historical subject matter of traditional opera, with its emphasis on everyday physical things, is therefore to be replaced by mythological subject matter. Moreover, to enhance the aesthetic impact of the drama, all of the arts—painting, music, poetry, sculpture, and dance—were to be brought together on the stage. The aim: to transport the individual member of the audience "out of himself," and to make him completely responsive to the artistic expression of the various media presented on the stage. Emotion, then, becomes "the supreme and unique legislator." Thus romantic ideals attained their zenith with Wagner.

Wagner's Orchestral Contributions

Wagner's distinctive treatment of the orchestra and its instruments is one of the most significant contributions of the entire romantic movement, influencing practically every musician of his era. And when his music dramas are not readily accessible, concert audiences experience the Wagnerian "mystique" through his overtures, which are widely performed by symphony orchestras throughout the world. These overtures owe their lasting quality to their musical invention, richness of orchestral effect, and completeness of expression, for they are, as it were, miniature orchestral music dramas. Also regularly performed are the orchestral pieces extracted from the Wagner operas, including: "The Magic Fire Music," and the "Ride of the Valkyries" from *Die Walküre*, "Siegfried Idyll" from *Siegfried;* "Good Friday Spell" from *Parsifal,* and the powerful and dramatic "Siegfried's Funeral March" from *Götterdämmerung*, which we will discuss next.

It is obviously difficult to measure the impact that Wagner's orchestral techniques had upon his fellow romantic composers, Bruckner and Mahler, and upon the leading post-romantic composers of the twentieth century, such as Strauss and Sibelius. The influence is perhaps best described as a general philosophy of orchestral writing that permeated the musical atmosphere of the late nineteenth century and early twentieth. Its essential features include virtuoso treatment of the total complex of players (individually and as a group); unusual weight, strength, and breadth of orchestral sound; a rich sonority rooted in full brass; and extension of the orchestral range, both high and low, to its limits.

(a)	(b)	(c)
(Essentially strings, couple of woodwinds, horns & harpsichord)	(Strings dominant, wind section established, brass, tympani.)	(Four complete and independent sections of the orchestra; orchestra doubled in size of Classic Period)
(a) Early Haydn 1760s	(b) Beethoven	(c) Wagner

Comparative orchestral makeup

Aside from its emphasis on massiveness of sound produced by a large orchestra, the Wagnerian style calls for individuality of all instrumental sections. For example, no longer do the strings hold the continual focus of musical ideas, for now not only does every section possess executant powers—that is, is capable of extended solos as a group—but each has a complete instrumentation and is assigned full chords, which provide a richness of sonority never heard before.

The English horn, bass clarinet and contrabassoon, which were of course used before by Berlioz, now are regular members of the woodwind section. For Wagner and all late German romantics, the brasses serve as the organic foundations of the grand orchestra, establishing the deep, resonant sonority so characteristic of their work. In *Die Götterdämmerung* Wagner employed a huge brass section, including four French horn-like instruments of his own invention called the "Wagner tubas," eight regular French horns, three trumpets, bass trumpet, three trombones, bass trombone, and tuba. The technical capabilities of the horn, trumpet, and tuba were greatly expanded at about this time, with the wide acceptance of the new modern valve system invented by Blühmel earlier (1818) in the century.

What better example for showing off the Wagnerian techniques than that of "Siegfried's Funeral March" from the final portion of *Die Götterdämmerung*. Frequently played as a separate work on symphony orchestra programs, it fully displays Wagner's strengths as an orchestrator and dramatist. In this scene, the hero, Siegfried, has just met his end in a violent sword fight with Hagen. The funeral music that follows this tragedy is presented in a setting favored by the romantics of this era. It is night, mists rise up from the Rhine as Siegfried's body is carried off by his mourners into the forest shadows. We hear the powerful brass entone the death motive: two explosive chords and swirling triplet figures:

Summary

Wagner's unusual sonority—a "cosmic sonority," as one writer described it—is attributed to the complete instrumentation and harmony in each section of the orchestra, expanded orchestral range (deeper range through the addition of lower-pitched brass instruments and higher string range) and, above all, to the subdivision of the string section. That is, the violins, violas, cellos, and even basses are divided into several sections, each playing a separate part, as opposed to the classic method of giving each string section, violins, violas, etc., one or two parts played by all instruments in that section. Thus, the "splitting up" of each string section into several parts provides an ethereal quality especially effective with muted instruments, as in the opening of *Parsifal*.

Beneath the huge orchestral facade is the unique Wagnerian harmony (actually an extension of the Chopin-Liszt style), characterized by its constant movement of voice parts, thick, quasi-contrapuntal texture, and extensive chromaticism. In conclusion, in addition to creating a new form of opera, Wagner expanded the orchestra to its maximum and created new techniques of orchestration that greatly influenced his post-romantic successors. Also, he extended the traditional tonal system of major and minor keys and chords to its maximum limits, eventually giving rise to new harmonic systems under the impressionists (Debussy) and the expressionists (Schoenberg)

ANTON BRUCKNER

Late Nineteenth-century Trends

In the wake of Wagner's spectacular achievements in music drama, musical style reached a crossroads in the last two decades of the century. Two stylistic trends became apparent: one, the continuation and expansion of German romanticism by Bruckner and Mahler and, the other, the beginning of the impressionistic movement by Debussy in France.

Firmly steeped in the Viennese tradition, Anton Bruckner (1824-1896) and Gustav Mahler (1860-1911) provided a superlative finale to the century of romanticism. Committed to the romantic belief that instrumental music could express something deeper than words, a belief especially true of Bruckner, these Viennese romantics chose as their chief musical medium the symphony form of Beethoven. Thus, the creative focus of this final stage of romanticism shifted from the theater to the concert hall, and specifically to the symphony, which became increasingly mystical in character and titanic in proportion.

The Wagnerian influence is particularly striking in these late symphonies, especially in the strength and breadth of the orchestra, whose gigantic sounds seem to echo some primeval or cosmic origin. The Wagnerian spirit is also noted in the greatly increased time span of the symphony; a single Bruckner movement is sometimes as long as a complete classical symphony. Moreover, the orchestration of these late romantic composers, especially Bruckner, is truly

Wagnerian—thick, richly colored, and founded upon heavy, dark, brass sonorities. However, the intrinsic features of the Bruckner and Mahler compositions are, as we shall observe, highly individual and original, bearing little relationship to Wagner.

Unquestionably, Anton Bruckner is one of the most fascinating (and enigmatic) symphonic composers of the romantic era. Often criticized for their great length and enormity of conception, Bruckner's works possess a particular haunting, pastoral quality quite different from any other romantic symphonist. Unfortunately, the Brucknerian character has only recently been revealed to concert audiences in this country. Naturally, Bruckner's art has encountered much difficulty in our fast-moving, materialistic age. The modern listener, in making his initial acquaintance with one of the most mystical of romantics will need a different "preparatory set," than that which he would bring to a more abstract, late twentieth-century composition. With Bruckner there is no compromise, no reliance on programmatic elements, no substitution for complete involvement on the part of the listener. For true appreciation one must succumb to his quaint world of murmuring forests, pastoral valleys, and peaks that resound with medieval hymns of praise.

Life Sketch

Hans Redlich's distinctive study of Bruckner's life and music discloses a picture of a quiet, unpretentious, introverted, rustic, village musician intensely dedicated to the Catholic Church. However, these characteristics mask a composer whose creative expressions plumb the depths and soar to great heights of religious joy, calling to mind the sacred music of the Gothic and the Baroque. Some writers suggest that perhaps Bruckner was actually a "mystic" or a kind of rustic genius who, unlike Wagner, did not champion his own cause but rather worked in anonymity. Bruckner's religious devotion and inspiration is sensed in practically every page of his scores. His musical moods, ranging from pastoral-like simplicity and a strange celestial calm to mighty exhortations of joy and jubilation, afford a refreshing change in the romantic style at the peak of its movement.

The essence of this peculiar brand of romanticism seems to be an all-pervading tone of religiosity, which undoubtedly stemmed from Bruckner's long affiliation with the Catholic Church. Born in 1824, the composer spent his boyhood in a remote Austrian village where life had changed little in a century, and where the Church had remained strong as a dominant cultural influence. Representative of this religious heritage is the famous monastery of St. Florian's, renowned for its great library, choral music traditions, and beauty of its Baroque-styled architecture. Its dramatic atmosphere, with its ornate designs, complexity, and grandeur, bear more than a casual relation to Bruckner's Baroquelike masses and symphonies.

Desirous of following a schoolmaster's profession like his father, young Bruckner became a student and chorister in the St. Florian monastery. It was here that he began his lifelong association with the Catholic Church and its musical heritage, and it was also here that he assimilated the germinating elements of his grand masses and symphonies. After St. Florian's, he held several schoolteaching posts and organ positions in various Austrian villages. In 1856, competing against many rivals, Bruckner won the organ position at the Cathedral of Linz, where he remained for twelve years. In the interim he traveled frequently to Vienna, where he studied counterpoint with the renowned Simon Sechter, teacher of theory and organ at the Vienna Conservatory.

It was during his Linz tenure that Bruckner wrote the bulk of his choral music, including three great masses: the Mass in D minor (1864), the Mass in E minor (1866), and the Mass in F minor (1868). The shifting of his creative outlook, from the choral to the symphonic idiom, was undoubtedly influenced by his hearing of Wagner's music, particularly a performance of *Tristan und Isolde* in Munich in 1865. It was then, as one writer jokingly stated, that Bruckner met his second deity, Richard Wagner, to whom the quiet admirer later dedicated his Third Symphony (1873).

As Bruckner grew in musical stature, he eventually settled in Vienna (1868), where he succeeded the deceased Simon Sechter as professor of theory and organ at the Vienna Conservatory. During his Vienna period Bruckner concentrated chiefly on the symphonic idiom, completing nine monumental works in this form. Two other symphonies, in F minor and D minor, were regarded by the composer as student works and outside of his canon of nine. All but the First Symphony were composed in the Vienna period, and all underwent considerable revision and modification.

> Symphony No. 1 in C minor (1866)
>
> Symphony No. 2 in C minor (1872)
>
> Symphony No. 3 in D minor
> "Wagner" (1873)
>
> Symphony No. 4 in E flat major
> "Romantic"   (1874)
> Symphony No. 5 in B flat major (1877)
>
> Symphony No. 6 in A major (1881)
>
> Symphony No. 7 in E major (1883)
>
> Symphony No. 8 in C minor (1885)
>
> Symphony No. 9 in D minor (1896)

Bruckner Musical Profile

The problem of summarizing the characteristics of Bruckner's style is somewhat less than with many romantic composers. The reason is that Bruckner's music did not undergo a stylistic evolution, as with Beethoven nor a periodic fluctuation in choice of forms, as with Schumann. Although there is a noticeable difference between early and late symphonies, the Brucknerian "fingerprints," which are clearly engraved in the First Symphony, are imbued in all his other works.

His creativity, falling neatly into the choral idiom in his early period (prior to Vienna) and in the orchestral in the late, sprung from profound religious experiences. During his long association with the Catholic Church, Bruckner developed a predilection for certain liturgical elements that served as cornerstones for his masses and then later for his symphonies. These elements include a polyphonic texture (at times heavily homophonic in the symphonies), use of ecclesiastical modes, chorale themes (especially in finales of symphonies), the continuous melodic movement so characteristic of sacred medieval and Renaissance polyphony, and an all-pervading "religious" mood. The characteristic romantic obsession with pure sound as a mystical power of communication is perhaps most amply demonstrated in the music of Bruckner. Schumann and Chopin applied the concept to smaller piano forms, and Berlioz and Liszt, using it in conjunction with an accompanying program, applied it to the orchestral idiom. But Bruckner, perhaps, is more successful since he does not rely on a program that frequently detracts from the mystery of sheer sound. Having no definite connection or relation to verbal or literary meaning, the mysticism is that much more enhanced.

Bruckner's symphonies, with their solemnity of procession, vast sonority, and enormous power, seem to be giant paeans of religious faith and ecstasy, spiritual transformations from some great religious epoch of the past. They are, like his earlier masses, thick textured and imbued with various liturgical elements, such as plainsong, triads in root position giving an austere harmonic sound reminiscent of Palestrina, slow majestic chorale melodies and rhythms, and an organlike sound in the orchestration.

The symphonies are modeled after the four-movement plan of Beethoven: Allegro, Adagio, Scherzo, Allegro. However, in place of the tightly knit, logical Beethovenian structures, Bruckner emphasizes mood rather than themes, creating long, rambling movements that stretch the symphonic mold to its breaking point. For example, the length of the Seventh Symphony is about eighty minutes. Rooted in the Ninth Symphony of Beethoven, which begins with a vague, primordial stirring, Bruckner's creative esthetic stresses the subconscious level rather than objective classic procedures. To illustrate, instead of clear-cut thematic details, tonal complexes or masses, chiefly in harmonic form, seem to hover on the threshold of comprehension, as vague-sounding unities, emerging from time to time as themes in complete, concrete form. Such an aesthetic tends, of course, to negate symphonic form and to stretch it to unusual proportions. Rather than following a logical plan of stating and developing themes in a nice, taut, compact form, Bruckner prefers to meander over immense areas, progressing in a terraced fashion from one plateau to another, each generally differentiated by a huge climax. The development technique is used, but it lies unobtrusively beneath the powerful waves of sound.

The allegro tempos are not "fast" allegros, since their ponderous orchestration and processional majestic rhythms tend to restrain their forward propulsion. In this regard, Capell has pointed out the similarity of Bruckner to Wagner. Both, he states, command a majestically deliberate pace unknown to other composers. Bruckner's scherzos (more so than any other movement) usually have the closest connection to our earth existence. Based on the Austrian dance called the *Ländler,* the scherzos have a boisterous, rustic effect resulting from a strong rhythmic figure. Generally, Bruckner adheres to rhythmic and metrical simplicity, preferring four-square meters and phrases and majestic rhythmic figures reminiscent of liturgical practice, particularly the quintuple figure which is a distinctive Bruckner trademark:

Bruckner's themes, possessing strong masculine and heroic qualities, are quite unlike those of many earlier romantics, such as Schumann and Chopin. At times, however, there is a very sweet lyrical quality similar to Schubert. Most of the principal themes have a wide-leaping melodic movement, encompassing intervals of a fifth, seventh, or octave, and when sounded are like chiseled or sculptured blocks of tone.

Bruckner, Symphony No. 3, first movement

Bruckner's statement of these themes generally follows a particular pattern in the opening movements. After a vague or perhaps mysterious tremolo of the strings or woodwinds, the main theme, sounded by a horn seemingly from afar, dramatically "announces" the symphony, that is, provides the setting, atmosphere, or mood of the work. And then gradually there is a general stirring of the vast orchestra, indicating the presence of some mighty dormant force.

The Fourth Symphony

Subtitled the "Romantic," the fourth, which ranks with the seventh in popularity, departs from the serious tone of the first three symphonies and radiates a joyful, pastoral quality. The Fourth as well as the Fifth and Sixth Symphonies are more optimistic, and generally suggestive of pastoral scenes similar to Beethoven's Sixth. In addition to evoking visions of spacious landscapes, the listener will hear stirring horn calls, (which some writers suggest huntsmen in the far distance) and peasant dances in the scherzos. In true late romantic fashion, Bruckner's vast majestic peaks and deep valleys seem to completely engulf the human element, in much the same manner as Caspar David Friedrich.

The fourth symphony offers an ideal introduction into the world of Bruckner. It begins in typical Brucknerian fashion: a soft tremolo pedal (sustained tone) is heard in the strings. With gradual increasing intensity the symphony begins to stir, to come to life from out of its primordial state. As the musical content begins to take shape the listener becomes aware of immense power, depth and grandeur of procession—qualities which portent the vast time-scale the symphony is to follow. Above the string tremolo we hear immediately the distinctive first theme (sounded by the French horns) which like many of the composer's opening themes is characterized by its austerity and slow majestic rhythm.

The final set of symphonies (Nos. 7, 8, and 9) return again to the solemn procession and gravity of the earlier works. Thematic quotations from various earlier Bruckner sacred works abound in these, and in general the tone, is very mystical and intense. This is especially true of the Ninth Symphony, which in its piercing, searing dissonance, angular themes, and deep sense of tragedy, points to Mahler and beyond.

GUSTAV MAHLER

The most important aspect of composition is that every voice
be a song…the bassoon, the bass tuba, and even the tympani
must be songlike. Gustav Mahler

With the music of Gustav Mahler (1860-1911) we reach the end of the great movement that had inspired a century of unprecedented creativity in the arts. With monumental designs and unequaled profundity of subject matter, Mahler carried the late romantic idea of seeking the infinite to its ultimate conclusion. Using the forms of song cycle and symphony, Mahler attempted to make music a vehicle for projecting his thoughts about the nature of existence, life and death, and immortality. In a sense then, his compositions are a mirror of his soul, are spiritual autobiographies.

Although he is sometimes referred to as a post-romantic, it would perhaps be more appropriate to regard Mahler as the last important member of the late romantic group. Aside from exhibiting a high degree of originality, his intense sincerity toward his art and complete exemplification of romanticism in his music and life justifies a searching examination of Mahler's work and contributions to the movement. His designation as "last of the great romantics" is readily defensible when we look at succeeding romantic composers. Much of the romantic-styled music of Bruckner's and Mahler's successors (such as Strauss and Franck) seems, in contrast, artificial and highly melodramatic—indeed, as ineffectual strivings to recapture the spirit of romanticism.

In our haste to group everything under the heading of "German romanticism," the dominant trend in nineteenth-century arts, we should not underemphasize the fact that the movement in music was from beginning to end centered in Vienna. Such names as Beethoven, Schubert, Brahms, Bruckner and Mahler—practically all of the major figures of the romantic era—were closely affiliated with the musical life of this famous city. Here the representative forms of the romantic movement, the symphony, piano piece, and lied, first acquired their romantic cast. Of these, the romantic symphony was the most important contribution of the Viennese. Beethoven, especially in his Ninth, set the general pattern and character of the romantic symphony, Schubert contributed the characteristic lyricism, Brahms restored the classical principles, and then Bruckner gave the four-movement plan unequaled power and mysticism in the Baroque manner. And now the long history of the Viennese symphony comes to an end with Gustav Mahler, who sought to reconcile the essential romantic forms of symphony and song.

Outline of His Career

Gustav Mahler was born into a family of poor Moravian Jews in 1860, one year after Wagner composed *Tristan und Isolde*. Mahler's musical education, pursued simultaneously with his private gymnasium studies, began at fifteen when he entered the Vienna Conservatory. Here he studied harmony, piano, and composition for three years, graduating with the diploma in 1878. After graduation he embarked on a conducting career. Beginning with small German opera houses, his appointments eventually included the Prague Opera, Budapest Opera, and the esteemed Vienna Royal Opera, where in his ten-year period (1897-1907) he became world renowned as a conductor and champion of the great works in the operatic repertoire, including the operas of Mozart, Cluck, and Wagner. In 1907 he accepted the conductorship of the Metropolitan Opera in New York, and in the fall of 1909 he took over the directorship of the New York Philharmonic Orchestra, a post he held until 1911, when he was forced to resign due to ill health.

Conducting was Mahler's chief occupation, but, as time went on, his great interest in composing gradually usurped more and more of his hours. His creative inspiration, which sprung from the lied, followed two basic directions, one being the *song-cycle* form (a song cycle is a group of songs based on poems usually by one poet and connected by a general idea) and the other the symphony. At first Mahler was occupied with large-scale song cycles, beginning in 1880 with *"Das klagende Leid"* (The Plaintive Song), for solo voices, chorus, and orchestra and based on the composer's adaptation of a text by the Grimm brothers. More song cycles followed, including *Lieder eines fahrenden Gesellen* (Songs of a Wayfarer), completed in 1885 and consisting of four song settings of a text by Mahler. His next cycle, *Des Knaben Wunderhorn* (The Youth's Magic Horn, 1889), was inspired by a gigantic collection of German folk poetry dating back to the sixteenth century. This collection, also entitled *Des Knaben Wunderhorn,* was compiled by the poets von Arnim and Brentano during the years 1806-1808. The pathetic-toned *Kindertoten Lieder* (Songs on the Death of Children, 1904), is a cycle for solo voice and orchestra, set to the poems of Rückert. The high point in this phase of Mahler's creative work came with *Das Lied von der Erde* (The Song of the Earth, 1908), a song cycle based on ancient Chinese poems for tenor, contralto, and orchestra. This is generally regarded as Mahler's finest contribution.

Musical Personality

During the short span of time, 1888-1910 (a period of intensive conducting duties), Mahler turned out ten symphonies, the last of which was left uncompleted. As the final composer of the long line of illustrious Viennese symphonists, Mahler continued the essential outlines of the great classical form. However, his conception of the symphony, markedly different from his predecessors, was heavily influenced by three factors: (1) the far-reaching shadow of Wagner, (2) his own deep romantic roots in German folklore, and (3) his true romantic obsession for reflecting states of the soul. And particularly his penchant for a large performing body (reaching colossal proportions in the Eighth Symphony), along with his attempt to express through music the intangible, the infinite, the philosophical, and the metaphysical, indicates Mahler's roots in the Wagnerian world.

The fundamental characteristics of Mahler's art include an unusual mastery of orchestration: a unique "chamber style" in his symphonies, that is, his unusual deployment of a small number of instruments within the framework of the full orchestra; and the conscientious use of the German lied and folk elements. The spirit of Schubert is felt in Mahler's ingenious melodic lines, while the folk elements (folk poetry, march and dance tunes, and pastoral bird calls) stem from Mahler's extraordinary interest in German folklore, a major source of which was *Des Knaben Wunderhorn.*

The programmatic element is either expressly intended in his symphonies or strongly alluded to. For example, the musicologist Hans Redlich mentions that the Symphonies No. 2, 3, and 4 "represent a symphonic trilogy reflecting the composer's struggle for a lasting religious belief and ultimate finding of it in the victory of love and forgiveness over doubt and fear." At the heart of each symphony emanates a religious message from *Des Knaben Wunderhorn,* which expresses Mahler's faith in resurrection and eternal life through love. As much as Mahler frequently spoke out against program music, he apparently relied heavily upon the technique for creative inspiration, for in a letter written in 1897, he makes the following statement in regard to his second symphony:

> When I conceive a great musical organism I invariably arrive at a point where I feel compelled to call in the art of words as a carrier of my musical idea...In the case of the last movement of my second symphony this went so far that I had to search through the whole world of literature, down to the Holy Bible in order to find the appropriate words.

Of the ten symphonies by Mahler, the Second, the "Resurrection" (1894), the Fourth (1900), and the Eighth, "Symphony of a Thousand" (1907), are best known. The Second is so called because of the poem, "The Resurrection" (by Klopstock), which serves as the program for the finale of the five-movement symphony. This work fully exemplifies the lofty, profound mysticism that prevails throughout most of Mahler's music. It is, according to Redlich, a deep-probing, soulful mysticism that generally reflects Mahler's thoughts on the Resurrection, the mystery of life, the tragedy of death, and evidently his own spiritual loneliness and longing for inner peace.

The fourth symphony opens with the sound of a sleigh-bell motif which keeps recurring throughout the movement. It is immediately clear that this is a happy, uncomplicated work. As the movement unfolds we notice that the bouyant mood has a characteristic Mahler dualism: a combination of both innocent youthful joy and sophisticated humor or *parody*—shown in garish changes in dynamics, orchestral timbre and sudden abrupt endings and starts. In the finale (see below) Mahler turns to his favorite medium of expression: the leid.

Here, a soprano soloist joins the orchestra in a truly remarkable setting of a text ("Life in Heaven") from the German folk collection, *Des Knaben Wunderhorn.*

Translation of Text "Life in Heaven" (opening lines)

> We enjoy the pleasure of heaven
> And therefore avoid the earthly.
> No worldly strife
> Does one hear in heaven;
> Everything lives in sweetest peace!
> We lead an angelic life,
> Yet are as merry as can be.
> We dance and jump.
> We skip and sing,
> While St. Peter in heaven looks on.

The Eighth Symphony or "Symphony of a Thousand," so named because of its huge body of performers, is a colossus of romanticism. It is scored for an immense orchestra, with auxiliary brass choir, two choruses, boys' choir, and seven vocal soloists. The program for the symphony, which is in two parts, is drawn from the hymn *Veni creator spiritus* and from portions of the second part of Goethe's *Faust.*

Summary

Romanticism has run its full course, beginning early in the movement with a renascence in the artistic representation or personal feelings, moods, and nature, and concluding with the contemplation of deep philosophical and religious thoughts. At times, in Mahler's later works, strong dissonant passages seem to be a harbinger of *expressionism,* an important style period to be discussed in the next chapter, the "twentieth-century."

CHAPTER 8

20TH CENTURY and BEYOND

IMPRESSIONISM AND EXPRESSIONISM

Impressionism and expressionism held the center of interest in the music world during the early years of the twentieth century. Impressionism is represented chiefly by the work of Claude Debussy (1862-1918) and expressionism by Arnold Schoenberg (1874-1951) and his followers. Our opening discussion will center on Debussy, and then later, upon Schoenberg and the various succeeding experimental trends that closed out the twentieth century.

Paris: The setting of the New Style

In the last decades of the nineteenth century, the cultural center of Europe shifted from Germany to France, and specifically to Paris, the mecca for artistic innovation since medieval times. Given impetus by a wave of prosperity following the French financial crash and depression of the 1870s, a social climate of opulence and luxury arose in Paris. Parisian artistic taste became permeated by a kind of sophisticated sensuality mixed with a cool, reserved intellectualism—important traits

Time-Line Impressionism	
1894	Debussy: Prelude, *After-noon of a Faun*
1899	Debussy: Nocturnes for Orchestra.
	Ravel: *Pavane for a Dead Infanta*
1903	Ravel: String Quartet
1905	Debussy: *La Mer*
1908	Debussy: Children's Corner (piano)
1910	Debussy: Preludes Book I
1912	Ravel: *Daphnis and Chloé*
1928	Ravel: *Boléro*

common to all of the French fine arts of the era. This period of affluence, which continued until the outbreak of World War I in 1914, marked the end of not only the old world but a way of political and social life. Artistically the era was headed by such important painters, musicians, poets as Monet, Renoir, Debussy, and Mallarmé, whose work clearly signalized the formation of the impressionistic style.

The period to be discussed, the impressionistic, covering the last decades of the nineteenth and opening of the twentieth centuries, is generally referred to as the *fin de siècle;* it could also be appropriately labeled the *sensate age* in French culture. It is in some respects a continuation of the romantic movement, especially in its pursuit of rich, luxuriant color effects in all of the arts. However, what immediately separates the two movements is the impressionists' interest in the small instead of the large and, especially, their substitution of sensualism for the romantics' love of conflict, drama, mystery, and passion.

A partial explanation for these characteristics of impressionism is to be found, as was intimated earlier, in the French life of the times. For example, the *fin de siècle* represents the epitome of an age, the climax in luxurious living and personal pleasure. In this hedonistic society people regarded the arts as a form of escape from reality, that is, from the practical and routine way of bourgeois life. The tendency was, in the words of Hauser (*The Social History of Art*), "to seek a higher, more sublimated and more artificial world than the previous romantics."

CHARACTERISTICS OF MUSIC AND ART

Origins in Painting

Impressionism, as a fairly definite movement, came into focus in 1874, when the first impressionist exhibition was held in Paris. It was the critics of the first impressionists who called their works "impressionistic," using the term, of course, in a derogatory sense like so many style names we have noted in earlier periods. The word itself was derived from the picture *Impression: Sunrise*, exhibited by Claude Monet in the same showing of 1874, and which he referred to as "an impression of the sun rising through mist over the Thames."

The movement was at its height from 1874 to 1886 the date of the last exhibition in Paris. Gradually, the style became more formalistic and mathematical and less casual and spontaneous, particularly in the work of Georges Seurat. His famous painting of 1886, *A Sunday Afternoon on the Grande Jatte,* marked the trend away from the naturalistic, representational mode toward the modern concept of nonrepresentational art (abstract paintings bearing no lifelike imagery).

The impressionists' interest centered upon familiar, daily events and scenes, garden settings, still life, and seascapes. A spontaneous, almost accidental approach to the subject matter generally prevailed, the aim being to capture a feeling, emotion, mood, or atmospheric condition at a given moment.

In quite the opposite vein to the romantics, these artists generally depicted the lighthearted qualities of humans at play or work rather than the profound, tragic, and passionate experiences of life. The principal elements or qualities stressed in their paintings include much emphasis on the full spectrum of color, preferably the quiet tints rather than the brilliant, forceful colors of the romantics; a vagueness of form and outline; a tendency toward emotional neutrality (avoidance of extremes such as violence, despair, anger, and the like) and understatement, that is, never quite filling in the details to make a concrete form.These characteristicse are qually applicable to the music and poetry of the age.

Unity of Ideals

What connects Debussy's *La Mer*, Monet's *Rouen Cathedral*, and Baudelaire's poem, "*Correspondences*"? All of the impressionists—the painters, musicians, and the symbolist poets—seemed to have shared one ideal: to suggest rather than describe or depict. They were essentially interested in presenting their impression of some object, scene, or event. Somewhat different in their approach, the symbolist-poets likewise refrained from stating the object in concrete fashion and instead, employed symbols that would evoke sensual feelings and other associations. The painters', poets', and musicians' creative path was the same—through the use of sensual elements, either in beautiful, shimmering hues, words carefully chosen for their "musical," poetic qualities, or lush-sounding melodies and harmonies.

The manner in which Debussy carries this idea out in music is actually a continuation of the programmatic principle. However, instead of telling a story (as in Wagner), using concrete themes and printed program (as in Berlioz), or depicting psychological depths of feeling (Mahler), Debussy prefers to evoke the simple, untroubled mood or atmosphere of an object or scene as designated by such titles as *Footsteps in the Snow*, and *Reflections in the Water*.

Fusion and Intensification of Sense Impressions

The poet and the musician were intrigued by the relationships that existed among the stimuli of the various senses. Words suggestive of various sensations—tactile, visual, aural, and so on—were frequently fused together in a highly sophisticated and abstract manner. This is borne out in a few lines from from *Correspondences* by the symbolist poet, Baudelaire:

> Perfumes there are as sweet as the oboe's sound,
> Green as the prairies, fresh as a child's caress,
> And there are others, rich, corrupt, profound
>
> And of an infinite pervasiveness,
> Like myrrh, or musk, or amber, that excite
> The ecstasies of sense, the soul's delight.

The musician also wished to translate into musical tones a wide variety of sensual or physical impressions, as indicated by the very titles of Debussy's works: *Les parfums de la nuit* (Perfumes of the Night), *Le vent dans la plaine* (The Wind in the Plain), *Des pas sur la neige* (Footsteps in the Snow), *La fille aux cheveux de lin* (The Girl with the

Flaxen Hair), *Reflets dans l'eau* (Reflections in the Water), and *Dialogue du vent et de la mer* (The Play of the Wind and Sea). Although it is impossible to represent these fundamentally tactile, aural and visual sensations in tone, Debussy clearly wished to translate the essence of the experience into tonal patterns.

The painter followed the same artistic path. He reached beyond the romantics in his attempt to intensify the sensual approach to his art—almost to the point where the viewer may vicariously reach out to feel the vibrant warmth of the sunlight and to touch the richly colored foliage of a Renoir garden scene (for example, *Monet Painting in His Garden in Argenteuil* by Renoir, 1873), or perhaps feel the empathy of a moving crowd on a bustling French boulevard (Pissarro, *The Pont Neuf,* 1901), or sense the damp, heavy fog that enshrouds many of Monet's scenes (*Westminister Bridge,* (1871).

The Coloristic Interest

We might think of Debussy as a highly refined and skilled painter of tone colors, rather than as a sculptor or architect of giant structures in the manner of Beethoven or Wagner. Just as the impressionists Monet and Renoir sought a fuller spectrum of colors and explored the broken-color technique, that is, the use of patches and dabs of color, so, too, did Debussy look beyond the romantic musicians' palette to a realm of kaleidoscopic tones and shadings. Debussy, like his painter counterparts, used what might be described as the *broken-color principle* in scoring, whereby instrumental tones are deployed on his "musical canvas" in small dabs and splotches for pure coloristic affect.

Generally speaking we can designate three ways in which the leading tone-painter created color in his works: (1) shading or "coloring" of the fundamental scale tones through either chromatic alterations or adoption of exotic pentatonic and whole-tone scale patterns (melodic color); (2) combining of unusual dissonant tone combinations into complex chord structures (harmonic color); and (3) unusual methods of scoring for instruments (orchestral color).

Impressionists' Use of Color—"Exotic Scales"

(a) Whole-tone scale (b) Pentatonic Scale (c) Ancient Mode (Dorian)

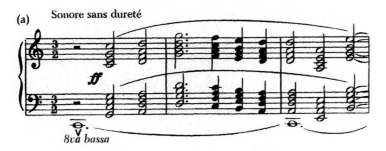

Impressionists' Use of Color—Harmony

(a) Debussy: "The Engulfed Cathedral" (b) Debussy: "Footsteps in the Snow"

Other Points of Similarity: Dissolution of Form

Another fundamental characteristic of impressionism is the tendency to dissolve form. With emphasis on the mood of the scene rather than the scene itself, the artists' canvases became bathed in shimmering light. Primary colors are frequently reduced to subtle gradations and solid outlines are dissolved into spots and dabs of colors.

In a similar vein, the symbolist poets glorified the fleeting rather than the permanent. Feeling replaced fact, with more being communicated "between the lines" than through the lines themselves. A corresponding dissolution of form resulted that at times is practically complete; witness the difficulty of comprehending (let alone translating) the complex poetry of this school. The symbolists, like their counterparts in art and music, strove for a multisensory approach, using words symbolical of strange and exotic sounds, rhythms, odors, and colors, which were woven together in dreamy, ethereal forms.

Understandably, the romantics' heavy equipment of heros, epic themes, passion, pathos, power, sweeping forms, and gigantic frescos did not interest the symbolists, nor the painters and musicians. Mirroring their own age of opulence they preferred the enchantment of sensual colors and sounds and to escape from the dynamic problems of the world. The same trend is also found in late nineteenth-century drama, in the works of Chekhov, whose plays exemplify the creed of impressionism: a renunciation of all formal organization for fleeting, passing moods, passiveness of character portrayal, understatement of ideas, and negation of dramatic conflict. Debussy, too, dissolved the large tonal structures, heavy melodic lines and forms of the romantics into irridescent, shimmering, and vague splotches of harmony and melody. But, despite the seeming casual vagueness and transitory quality of Debussy's music, we will find that he, perhaps more than any other composer, strove for refinement and perfection down to the smallest detail.

CLAUDE DEBUSSY

Overview of Life and Work

The leading exponent of musical impressionism was born in 1862, in the town of St. Germain-en-Laye, a short distance from Paris. At eleven he entered the Paris Conservatoire, where he studied piano with Marmontel and theory and composition under Lavignac, Durand, and Massenet. His college experiences remind one of the rebellious Berlioz. Like his earlier compatriot, Debussy thrived on experimentation and innovation—forces that led to Berlioz's unusual orchestration and Debussy's unique harmonic language. To the consternation of his teachers, he would frequently improvise dissonant chord progressions at the keyboard, substituting personal taste for rules of harmony. An intensive interest in the harmonic aspect of musical invention eventually led to the formation of daring new tone combinations and unusual chord movement reminiscent of medieval organum.

Despite his general disinclination for the academic principles that lay behind musical art, Debussy won awards and prizes for piano, counterpoint, and fugue, and later the highest award of the Conservatoire, the Grand Prix de Rome. The award, won at twenty-two with his cantata *l'Enfant prodigue (The Prodigal Son)*, carried with it several years of study at the Villa Medici. However, like Berlioz, he left Rome before the completion of the term, returning in 1887 to his beloved Paris, where he took up residence as a professional composer.

Several events may be cited as important factors in the development of his musical style. Among these are the sojourns to Russia in 1882 and 1884 while in the employ of Mme. von Meck, Tchaikovsky's patroness. These excursions undoubtedly whetted his taste for the Russian color and exoticism so prominently displayed in his later musical compositions. He became further acquainted with the Russian style at the Paris Exposition of 1889, when he heard a series of concerts of Russian music conducted by Rimski-Korsakov, the master orchestrator whose influence extended to Debussy, Respighi, Ravel, Stravinsky, and others in the twentieth century.

While it is generally acknowledged that Debussy acquired his brilliant and exotic orchestral techniques from the Russians, especially Rimski-Korsakov, his impressionistic inclinations probably originated from his associations with the Parisian avant-garde. Mallarme's home, where Thursday afternoon symposia were frequently held, was the main center for the exchange of ideas among the impressionist painters, musicians and symbolist-poets.

Debussy's close affiliation with the symbolists is mirrored in a number of songs composed in the 1890s. Some of these use texts by the leading symbolists, Baudelaire, Mallarmé, and Verlaine. Most of these light, wispy tone-paintings focus upon typical symbolist subject matter, such as reflections on nature and romance. Representative of this close affinity is Debussy's famous orchestral composition, *Prélude à l'après-midi d'un faune (Prelude to the Afternoon of a Faun)* based on Mallarmé's poem written in 1876. Debussy's experience in hearing Javanese music at the Paris Exposition of 1889 ranks perhaps as the second strongest influence in the shaping of the Debussyan characteristics. For example, his quaint, archaic sounding melodic style, based largely on non-Western scale patterns such as pentatonic scales and whole-tone progressions, seems to have been derived from Oriental influences. His unprecedented lightness of effect, nonsymmetrical rhythms, and an all-pervasive "drifting" effect in harmony and melody may have been inspired by these Javanese musicians. Debussy, it should be pointed out, also collected Oriental art objects, which further substantiates his keen interest in Eastern cultures. There are also strong tinges of Spanish culture in his music, notably in the use of Spanish dance rhythms, the tango and the habanera (in *La Soirée dans Grenade, Iberia,* and *La Sérénade Interrompue.*) To this long list of influences we must add the name of Wagner, whose freedom in the use of chromaticism, dissonant chord movement, and sensuous tone colors was also emulated by Debussy. However, the over-all tonal effect and underlying philosophy of these two composers are as different as night and day. A partial listing of Claude Debussy's most celebrated works is as follows:

> *Cinq Poemes de Baudelaire,* songs (1889)
> String Quartet in G minor (1893
> *Prélude à l'après-midi d'un faune,*
>   symphonic poem (1894)
> *Nocturnes,* symphonic poem (1899)
> *Pour le piano* (1901)
> *Pelléas et Mélisande,* opera (1902)
> *Estampes,* piano suite (1903)
> *La Mer,* symphonic poem poem (1905)
> *Suite bergamasque,* piano suite (1905)
> *Children's Corner,* piano suite (1908)
> *Images,* symphonic poem (1909)
> *DouzePréludes (Book I),* piano preludes (1910)
> Sonata for Cello and Piano (1915)
> Sonata for Flute, Viola, and Harp (1916)
> Sonata for Violin and Piano (1917)

OTHER MUSICAL IMPRESSIONISTS:
MAURICE RAVEL

From the Sensual Toward the Rational

Maurice Ravel (1875-1937) occupies a position in music similar to Georges Seurat, the leading post-impressionist painter. Both were products of the impressionistic movement in France, and both took a similar path in seeking solutions to aesthetic problems. Although they were essentially impressionists, their formalistic treatment of typical impressionistic subject matter and themes hint at one important artistic strain of the twentieth century, that of *classicism*. More of an attitude than a codified school or style, the classicistic strain is represented in several streams of art and music in the twentieth century, notably in the early decades by the *cubists*—Cezanne, Picasso, and Braque—and in music by Satie and Stravinsky.

Both Ravel and Seurat evolved a more disciplined, formal approach to impressionism: Seurat in the 1880s (*A Sunday Afternoon on the Island of the Grande Jatte*, 1886) and Ravel beginning about 1899 with *Pavane pour une Infante défunte. (Pavane for a Dead Infanta*). Within the framework of the impressionistic view of reality (a shimmering, sensuous view of the world) they subtly brought the tonal configurations and visual forms into clearer focus, juxtaposing themes and painted figures into more defined patterns and thus diminishing the drifting amorphous quality from their work. The concept of form in music and painting was again emphasized, resulting in more precise musical themes and melodic goals in the music of Ravel and in a kind of sculpturesque solidity in the painted human figures and forms of Seurat.

This stylistic leaning toward the classical or rational originated in Seurat's work as a stated reaction against the formlessness of Monet and other impressionists and in Ravel's music as a natural predilection, which became established early in his musical creativity. In essence, the casual, informal, and sensuous expressions of Monet and Debussy were supplanted by a preplanned, formal, and essentially rational expression—as a brief prelude to the stream of classicism that appeared with the cubists in the first decade of the century.

Ravel grew up in the same impressionistic atmosphere as Debussy, received the same academic training in music and created in the same musical forms. Since Ravel was active in composition well into the twentieth century, some automatically regard him as a successor of Debussy, while actually he was contemporary with his colleague. Interestingly, only a few years separate their Paris Conservatoire experiences and their first major compositions (Debussy composed the *Afternoon of a Faun* from 1892 to 1894, and Ravel's *Pavane for a Dead Infanta* appeared in 1899).

Most scholars believe that, even though there is a marked stylistic similarity, Ravel was not directly influenced by Debussy. Much of the stylistic affinity undoubtedly stemmed from the impressionistic environment in which Ravel matured as a musician, including his French descent (he was born in Ciboure in 1875), conservatoire background, and the very influential Parisian avant-garde movement. The attraction for the Russian style, as with Debussy, accounts for his unusual exotic coloring and brilliance in orchestration. His great skill in this area, which is so wondrously manifested in his orchestration of Mussorgski's *Pictures at an Exhibition*, is unquestionably the explanation for Ravel's continued popularity in the world's music halls.

Ravel's music is basically cast in the impressionistic vein, as demonstrated in his use of many of the same techniques common to Debussy: sensuous tone colors in melody and harmony, nature themes, emphasis on atmosphere and mood, and similar choice of musical forms (see listing below). And yet, despite these broad resemblances, there is a striking classicistic quality in Ravel's work: his themes are more straightforward and clearly outlined, his rhythms are more definite and rooted in real life (he uses many authentic rhythms, such as bolero, waltz, pavane, and habanera), and a more forceful, positive expression generally prevails. Note, for example, that the volume scale is tipped away from Debussy's soft and delicate expressions; Debussy intimates or suggests, whereas Ravel proclaims.

And finally we observe that rhythm seems to be the essence, the core of his art rather than tone color which is so much a part of Debussy's musical personality.

Below, in chronological order, is a listing of some of Ravel's most important contributions.

> Pavane pour une Infante défunte, piano solo (1899*)
> *Jeaux d'eau* piano solo (1901*)
> Quartet in F, string quartet (1903)
> *Schéhérazade,,* song cycle (1903)
> *Sonatina,* piano solo (1905)
> *Miroirs,* piano solo (1905*)
> *Rapsodie expagnole,* orchestral work (1907)
> *Gaspard de la nuit,* piano solo (1908*)
> *Daphnis et Chloé,* ballet (1912*)
> *Trois Poems de Stephane Mallarmé,* songs (1913*) *Le*
> *Tombeau de Couperin,* piano solo (1917)
> *La Valse,* orchestral work (1920*)
> Orchestration of Mussorgski's *Pictures at an Exhibition* (1922)
> *Boléro,* orchestral work (1928)
> Concerto in D for Piano and Orchestra (1931)

(* indicates markedly impressionistic in style)

Summary

As with so many movements in the arts, impressionism developed as a reaction to the previous period, specifically to the powerful rhetoric of

the late romantics. However, in many ways it seems to have been a
continuation of romanticism. Another movement, concomitant with
impressionism—*expressionism*—also seems to have been a continuation
of the romantic stream. The dilemma of reconciling the two movements
as offshoots of romanticism is resolved by suggesting or postulating that
impressionism was a manifestation of the romantics' outer sensual life,
while expressionism was indicative of the inner, psychological life.

QUEST FOR THE PSYCHOLOGICAL:
ARNOLD SCHOENBERG

Vienna, the center and crossroads of many musical styles
throughout history, was the birthplace of the champion of
expressionism in music. Schoenberg's training in music was quite the
opposite of most modern-day composers. Due to the insufficient
economic resources of his family, a formal music education was not
open to him. Thus, like a number of musicians before him, he acquired
an unusual mastery of harmony and counterpoint through intensive self-
study.

Schoenberg's first phase of musical creativity, his "romantic period"
is closely aligned to the styles of Wagner, Strauss, and Brahms.
Included in this period (1896-1908) are such examples as *Verklarte Nacht
(Transfigured Night)* (1899), the huge *Gurrelieder* (1901), and the String
Quartet No. 2 (1908), which in its final movement announces the *atonal*
style, that is, music composed without key centers or key relationships.
These "romantic" works are characterized by their post-Wagnerian
profile: long, sentimental themes with the characteristically Wagnerian
inflections provided by chromatics. A heavy, ponderous orchestration
(Gurrelieder), thick harmony, and great time span reveal quite clearly the
inspirational roots of this music. Uppermost is the penchant for
romantic climaxes, use of literary sources for inspiration, and the
presence of a chromatically saturated tonality as the main organizing
force in composition. And yet throughout this music one senses a strong
compulsion to compress, to concentrate, and to cut away all but the bare
essentials (the *Chamber Symphony,* for example), as a prelude to the
"atonal" Schoenberg.

The second period of creativity, the "free-atonal period," which
extends from about 1908 to 1912, was the time of Schoenberg's strong
attraction to the expressionists. In fact, it was during this time that we
learn of a little-known facet of Schoenberg's artistic nature: his keen interest in painting as evidenced by exhibitions of his works in Vienna (in
1910), Munich, and Berlin. Indeed, during this period the struggling
musician thought of turning to painting on a professional scale to
augment his meager income. A comparison of his work with that of
other leading expressionist artists, such as Kandinsky and Munch,
shows a similar focus on pathos and deep despair. As a style-movement

expressionism shows a decided turning away from optimism toward pessimism and its disintegrating, eruptive spirit.

Schoenberg's music of this period, includes *Das Buch der hängenden Gärten (The Book of the Hanging Gardens)* (1908), *Three Piano Pieces* (1908), *Erwartung (Expectation) (1909, Five Pieces for Orchestra* (1909), *Pierrot Lunaire (Moonstruck Pierrot) (*1912*),* and *Die gückliche Hand (The Lucky Hand)* (1913). Frequently convulsive, disjunct, hypertensive, and permeated by maximum and constant searing dissonance (especially in *Pierrot Lunaire* and *Erwartung),* these works constitute the apex of musical expressionism.

Schoenberg's texts in these works provide further indication as to their psychoneurotic intent. For example, in the monodrama *Erwartung,* the plot centers around a woman who, in the dark of night, sets out to find her husband in a forest. States of anxiety and terror are portrayed as she looks in vain. Finally, she slumps down with exhaustion, only to sense the presence of a human form by her feet. The discovering of her husband's corpse touches off feelings of psychoneurosis and eventual overt pathological reactions.

Schoenberg's Third Period: The Twelve-tone System

During an interim of comparative silence, roughly from about 1912 to 1923, Schoenberg gradually worked out his complex theory of musical composition known as the *twelve-tone method.* This system or procedure forms the foundation for approximately thirty compositions composed in the final period (1923-1951). These works, representing *atonality,* are much more cerebral and detached than the earlier pieces, and therefore remain unplayed in the concert hall. Before touching on these, let us briefly outline some of the principles of the twelve-tone method:

1. The first step is to construct a "row" of twelve different tones.
2. The twelve tones of the chosen row are to be treated equally, being related to each other rather than to a central tone or key center as in tonality. Therefore, the magnetic attraction of the tonic both as to melody and chords is eliminated.
3. Traditional principles of consonance and dissonance are discarded.
4. Unity is not to be found in traditional methods such as key relationships, scales, and chord progressions, but in a structural set or series of twelve tones woven throughout on two planes: the horizontal (melody) and vertical (simultaneous sounding of the row or its parts).

The highly cerebral works from this final period include: *Serenade* (1923), Wind Quintet (1924), String Quartet No.3 1926), *Variations for Orchestra* (1928), String Quartet No.4 (1936), Piano Concerto (1942), and *A Survivor from Warsaw* (1947). Among the salient features of these works taken as a whole is their dry, abstruse style actually a highly calculated mathematical style that makes these works quite inaccessible for most listeners. As William Thomson (*Schoenberg's Error*) comments:

Schoenberg planted a revolutionary movement that turned out to be resting in shallow soil. His music, particularly the works of his last period, was rejected by not only symphony orchestras, but by 1950 had already "slipped into the grave of public neglect." We will have more to say about the demise of twelve-tone music under the "Critique of Contemporary Music" appearing in the final portions of the book.

ALBAN BERG

Following Schoenberg's invention of the twelve-tone method, two of his most celebrated pupils, Alban Berg and Anton von Webern, further developed and refined the new mode of composition. The directions the two devoted disciples took were, however, quite different from the path blazed by the founder of musical expressionism. Schoenberg's twelve-tone music is essentially arid and relentlessly abstruse. Berg's we will find is somewhat more "humanized," and therefore more readily understood by the average listener. Employing narrative-based ideas as in his most important work, the opera *Wozzeck,* and a flexible use of the twelve-tone system, Berg commanded the largest listening audience.

In contrast to Berg, Webern's approach to the twelve-tone system is more cerebral and mathematical. However, Webern's music has had a strong influence on some present-day musicians (a spell of reverence that also touched Stravinsky in later works). The reader, understandably, might tend to regard Berg and Webern as successors to Arnold Schoenberg. Quite the contrary, their atonal works began to appear soon after their esteemed teacher broke the boundaries leading into the twelve-tone method (1908-1912). As Schoenberg rejected the post-Wagnerian style for atonality, so did his pupil Alban Berg, who reflected a slightly different musical philosophy from that of the master expressionist.

Life Sketch

In contrast to Schoenberg, Alban Berg was born into a family of considerable means and strong cultural interests. And again, in marked contrast to the dynamic, forceful Schoenberg, Berg was highly emotional, nervous, and introverted. Frequently given to states of depression, the sensitive musician attempted suicide in 1903 over a failing grade in a humanities exam.

In 1904—about the time that expressionism in art was coming to the fore in Germany and Austria—Berg began studying composition with Schoenberg. The student-teacher relationship continued for about six years, until 1910. Webern, the third member of this Viennese triumvirate, was also a student of Schoenberg during this period.

Originating in the twilight era of romanticism, it is understandable that Berg's first musical explorations would mirror the lush melodic and harmonic trends of the day. However, with the approaching prewar years, his music reflected his teacher's gradual negation of tonality, a tendency we find in Berg's String Quartet, Op. 3 (1910), Five Songs for Voice and Orchestra, Op. 4 (1912), and *Three Orchestral Pieces,* Op. 6

(1914). The unusually small output noted in Berg's catalog is typical of the three leading figures in twelve-tone music, Schoenberg, Berg, and Webern. Of the three, Schoenberg wrote the most (however, a tiny fraction of the output of the earlier classicists and romanticists), while Webern wrote the least. The leaning toward brevity and small output was evidently predicated by the twelve-tone style, which, because of its constant high dissonance rate, demanded a short time span—at least until composers created new techniques or, like Berg, devised interesting ways of combining old and new.

Wozzeck

During the war years 1914-1918, Alban Berg laid the foundations for his most important work, the opera *Wozzeck*, which was finally completed in 1921. This composition brought international acclaim to Berg almost overnight. In the year 1925 the opera was performed eleven times in Berlin, indeed, an unprecedented record for a modern opera. It is a supercharged expressionistic opera of three acts, divided into five scenes each. Cast into the tragic framework and reinforced by a twentieth-century setting and atonal dissonance, the ageless theme of *Wozzeck* stands as a mirror of modern, war-torn society, and especially of the aberrations engendered by the spirit of chaos.

The entire fabric of this work—its general type of text and musical style—stem directly from Schoenberg's most bizarre expressions, *Pierrot Lunaire* and *Ewartung*. Much more listenable and successful in the music hall than the Schoenberg works, *Wozzeck* has been acclaimed as one of the leading examples of twentieth-century opera.

The opera was adapted from material by George Buchner, a nineteenth-century German author. The action centers around a poor, ridiculed soldier, Wozzeck, and his unfaithful wife, Marie. In the first act, the full gamut of the expressionistic spirit is displayed: the violent captain's deriding of Wozzeck for his stupidity and the illegitimate child born unto Wozzeck's wife, Marie; haunting, frightening visions of Wozzeck's neurotic nature; Marie's flaunting of sexuality before the handsome drum major; and the military doctor's obsessive interest in Wozzeck's mental disorders.

In the third act, the tension between the principal characters finally snaps. Accompanied by a piercing, ear-splitting crescendo and incessant beating of a bass drum, Wozzeck, in a state of mad frenzy, stabs Marie and later commits suicide by drowning. At the opera's close, Wozzeck's child is seen alone on stage playing with a hobby horse, adding another element characteristic of the twentieth century: irony in deepest tragedy.

The success of *Wozzeck* can be attributed, not only to the skillful musical setting of the story (one that was assured to interest the audience), but especially to Berg's full grasp of the potentialities of atonality and the twelve-tone system in enhancing the dramatic action. No other modern opera has achieved this effect with such directness and compression of elements.

Actually, *Wozzeck* is a mixture of tonality and atonality, that is, occasional use of major and minor chords and keys. In this regard, Berg, the humanist of the Schoenberg group, proved that a composition embodying the twelve-tone system could be successfully created. His combining of tonality and atonality also indicated the compatibility of the two systems, a pattern later composers would frequently follow.

Berg's style is much more closely related to traditional techniques than is that of either Schoenberg or Webern. Lush, romantic-sounding sections are frequently heard intermingled with the strident dissonances so characteristic of the expressionist mentality. This is true of not only *Wozzeck* but of the four major works that followed: the *Kammer Konzert* (1925), the *Lyric Suite for Strings* (1926), the opera *Lulu* (1935), and the Violin Concerto (1935).

The violin concerto was commissioned by the noted violinist Louis Krasner and dedicated to Manon Gropius (the daughter of Alma Mahler, to whom Berg was closely attached), who died suddenly at age eighteen. In essence, the concerto is a kind of requiem for the deceased girl, a fact that may help us to understand the fundamentally pathos-toned piece of music.

The concerto consists of two separate movements, each divided into two sections as follows: I Andante, Allegretto; II Allegro, Adagio. Some writers have interpreted the lyrical and delicate first movement as a musical portrait of the lovely Manon, and the searing, dissonant edifice of the second as a depiction of her death. The closing Adagio seems to represent "the search for consolation in religious belief," manifested in a strange, celestial calm.

The listener is generally impressed by the clarity and beauty of Berg's orchestral writing, and especially the successful reconciliation of tonal and twelve-tone techniques. The instrumentation of the concerto is similar to the conventional nineteenth-century orchestra (with the exception of the alto saxophone).

Berg's twelve-tone row, which serves as the foundation for the concerto, is a mixture of several ingredients that are strongly related to tonality, namely, a series of minor and major thirds, concluding with a whole-tone scale.

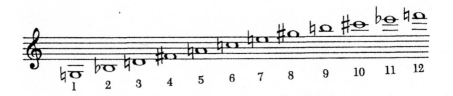

Tone Row, Violin Concerto by Alban Berg

ANTON WEBERN

Toward Fragmentation

If music strove for the condition of poetry in the nineteenth century, it became increasingly evident in the late twentieth century that it sought the condition of mathematics. In the former, communication through the emotions was paramount. In the cerebral world of pure mathematics there is no emotion or feeling, since there is no connection with life. To be sure, Webern was a champion of the twelve-tone technique; however, his mature musical style is diametrically opposed to that of his teacher, Arnold Schoenberg. Webern, though employing the expressionists' twelve-tone language, set into motion what became a major trend in late twentieth-century musical thought. Specifically, this is a tendency to extend the musical thought into rarified and abstruse regions in which tones are "engineered" with mathematical precision, first, with Webern and then with the serialists and electronic experimenters.

Poles apart from the romantics and most classicists of the era, Webern, like his contemporary, the painter Mondrian, is not concerned with the passions of man but, rather, is withdrawn into the ethereal realms of pure tonal design—designs that have no relation to the earlier patterns of symphony, sonata, or concerto.

In Webern's use of the twelve-tone technique, each tone is weighted aesthetically, as opposed to the more jabbing, piercing, gestalt-like twelve-tone patterns of Schoenberg. No actual melodies per se are to be heard; thus his music is called *Athematic*. Instead, flashes and bursts of tonal nebulae are projected in a kaleidoscopic fashion.

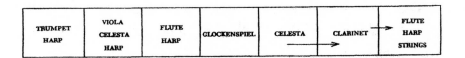

"Progressive Disclosure" of Theme assigned to various instruments in rapid succession, from Five Pieces for Orchestra Op. 10, by Anton Webern.

Webern's high degree of sensitivity to sound produced unprecedented subtleties and orchestral effects, which stretch the performers' range and technique to the absolute limit. Rehearsals of such music become less unified ensemble endeavors and more intensive individual tutorials because of the extreme complexity of splitting up tiny sounds among the various instrumentalists. Cerebral sounds flood the air, mixed with periods of dramatic silence and barely audible dynamic levels. And the crystal-clear delineation of every tone, executed with almost surgical precision, leaves the listener with the feeling that everything has been wrung out, condensed, and compressed, resulting in tiny jewell-like musical forms. (Some of Webern's pieces are less than half a minute in length.) Representative examples by Webern include:

> Passacaglia for Orchestra, Op. 1 (1908)
> *Five Movements for String Quartet,* Op. 5 (1909)
> *Five Pieces for Orchestra,* Op. 10 (1913)
> Six Bagatelles for String Quartet, Op. 9 (1913)
> String Trio, Op. 20 (1927)
> Symphony, Op. 21 (1928)
> Concerto for Nine Instruments Op. 24 (1934)
> Variations for Orchestra, Op. 30 (1940)

Summary

Berg had more romantic inclinations than the others in the twelve-tone group. In his scores the traditional beauty of melodic line, sonority, and orchestration were continued, whereas Schoenberg attempted to negate these principles. Like Schoenberg (and unlike the mature Webern), Berg gave the twelve-tone row and its arrangement an extremely high quotient of intense emotionalism. This style, musical expressionism, did not die out with Berg and Schoenberg. In the United States, through the teachings of Schoenberg (at the University of California from about the mid-1930s to 1944) and Ernst Krenek and others, the spirit and method of atonal expressionism touched various composers, among them are Roger Sessions, Carl Ruggles, Pierre Boulez, and Milton Babbitt.

THE QUEST FOR MYSTERY AND ROMANCE

> I love the mysterious sounds of the fields and
> forests, water and mountains. It pleases me
> greatly to be called a poet of nature, for nature
> has truly been the book of books for me.
> Jean Sibelius

Scope and Definition of 20th Century Romanticism

The heavy onslaught of the atonalists did not deter the continued interest in romantic ideals favored by a large number of composers in America, England, Russia and the Scandinavian region. This is a fairly lengthy list including Sibelius, Vaughn Williams, Shostakovich, Copland, Barber and others.What then, is modern romanticism (neoromanticism), and how does it differ from the German movement of the last century? In brief, we might state that the twentieth-century brand of musical romanticism is fundamentally of the same outlines and content of the preceding era: markedly *humanistic,* that is, realistic, traditional, and generally nationalistic or folkloristic in character. Other elements are common to this vein of creativity, namely the dominance of the narrative principle and the rhetorical style.

Following the path of the nineteenth century, many of these neo-romantics based their works on a story, drama, or what we may simply refer to as *narrative*. As with their predecessors, sometimes only short, fragmentary program notes or descriptive titles are provided as a guide for the listener. Also characteristic of both present and past romantics is the use of the *rhetorical style:* the tendency to couch musical ideas in lengthy, elaborate statements rather than in the highly compressed and concise assertions common to neoclassicism.The rhetorical style also implies patterns of conflict and resolution, the heroic, and strongly emotive melodic lines.

Also closely identified with all romanticism of today and yesterday is the *principle of expectation*—a particular way of listening that has prevailed throughout the history of Western music. To explain: as a piece of music is performed, certain melodic ideas (themes, motives) are heard and identified. With the unfolding of the musical work they are brought to mind or recalled and related to what has gone on before. Of course, much of the aesthetic enjoyment derived from this mode of listening comes from both expectation and surprise. We will return to this concept in the closing pages.

This principle underlies all neoromantic music, and, even though much less obvious in expressionism, it is nonetheless present (although the emancipation of dissonance in that style has removed much of the element of surprise). In avant-garde idioms of "total serialism" and electronic music, to be discussed, such a principle is nonexistent, making the music quite meaningless to the average listener. The trend away from *process* (development or working out of themes involving the principle of expectation, goals and climaxes) to the static, supra-complex manipulation of tones (in *total serialism*) is a puzzling feature needing to be discussed later in connection with the music of today.

Modern Romanticism vs Expressionism

How does modern romanticism differ from expressionism? A general comparison reveals that romanticism constitutes a much more positive view of the world. Expressionism, which focuses almost entirely upon the darker side, covers a limited range of experience. Romanticism, on the other hand, is much broader in scope, encompassing the full sweep of human experience. The expressionist tends to turn away from outer life; the romanticist revels in its many glories. For example, themes of love, passion, drama, mystery, folk, and nationalism abound in romanticism of today almost as much as they did in the nineteenth century. The subject matter and even the molds are much the same; the musical ideas are, of course, garbed in twentieth-century-styled harmony and melody.

The decisive difference between romanticism and expressionism can be found in the primal sources of creative energy. The expressionist derives his power or impact from extreme psychic disturbance (musically manifested in bizarre textual material and in jagged melodic lines and convulsive, piercing dissonances). The modern romanticist derives his strength, his inspiration, not from the subterranean regions of the soul but from a compulsion to recreate or interpret human experience (musically manifested in subject matter or themes drawn or abstracted from folk, national, historical, legendary, or popular sources).

What of the romantic's musical language? As a rule we will find that the twentieth century romantics were not the great upsetters of the period. For most, the syntax and musical vocabulary of their predecessors interspersed with or modified by characteristic modern devices met their creative requirements. Some romantics, such as Copland, Barber, Vaughan Williams, Orff, and others, greatly extended and expanded the art of music through innovation and the absorption and distillation of folk elements. Most composed in a quasi-tonal style. Even though these musicians made frequent use of the expressionistic twelve-tone system, the resulting effect is strikingly different, for the romantic cannot, like the expressionist, hide his true identity or musical personality. A good case in point is Aaron Copland and his brief excursion into the atonal stream, but we will see this especially in the great neoclassicist Stravinsky, who, in some later works adopted the twelve-tone system. His classic countenance seems to be stamped indelibly into every piece, whether tonal or atonal.

Summary

Modern romanticism is characterized by the following: (1) an obligation to reality, that is, a need to relate musical ideas to life experiences; (2) frequent use of indigenous (folk, ethnic, national) material; (3) dominance of feeling and emotion; (4) adherence to the nineteenth-century symphonic medium and rhetorical style; and (5) a programmatic basis stated or implied.

SIBELIUS, SHOSTAKOVICH, COPLAND

The listing of neoromantics is extensive, covering a wide variety of individual styles and regions. For our discussion, three names have been chosen because of their different approach to musical creativity. They are: Jean Sibelius, Dmitri Shostakovich, and Aaron Copland.

Jean Sibelius

Sibelius (1865-1957), active in the first quarter of the twentieth century, is famous for his nature tone paintings. Shostakovich (1906-1975), the leading representative of social realism in musical art, is cited for his romanticized treatment of Soviet themes. Aaron Copland (1900-1990), whose musical evolution crossed several contemporary style movements, became a leading spokesman for the American heritage. Noticeably different in style and social and geographical background, the three are closely connected with the modern romantic movement. The affinity becomes even more apparent when we place these figures against those representing the more abstruse analytical stream of neoclassicism and especially its antithesis, the dark pathos of expressionism.

Jean Sibelius may be regarded as the founder of modern romanticism. He was born in the town of Tavastehus, Finland, at the time when Europe was in the midst of Wagnerism. Thus it was perhaps inevitable that the essence of his art would be colored by the bold, sweeping romantic, gesture. Furthermore, by the time of Sibelius' tone poem *Finlandia* and his First Symphony (both 1899), the music world had witnessed still other famous giants of the epic statement, Bruckner and Mahler. From them Sibelius undoubtedly inherited his penchant for the powerful and massive, and perhaps from Beethoven and Brahms a particular predilection for musical logic; a third trait, a kind of austere, almost primitive earthiness, seems to be distinctly Sibelian, traceable to no other composer.

For a time Sibelius studied law at the University of Helsingfors in Helsinki, but at twenty-one he left to pursue a music career. In 1889, the young musician went to Berlin, and the following winter to Vienna, where he became familiar with the work of Brahms and Bruckner. At this time a strong feeling of Finnish nationalism was beginning to emerge as a result of the oppressive measures taken by the Russian czarist government. The change of postal and monetary systems from Finnish to Russian, the establishment of military conscription, and the restriction of Finnish newspapers gave impetus to Finnish political and cultural independence.

Sibelius came to prominence during this period, the 1890s, by giving a strong musical voice to the growing nationalistic spirit through such works as the symphonic poem *Kullervo* (1892), a huge composition for orchestra, chorus, and soloists based on material drawn from the national folk epic, the *Kalevala* (somewhat equivalent to the German romantics' valuable source, *Des Knaben Wunderhorn*).The strongly patriotic and heroic tone poem *Finlandia* (1899) won the popular favor of the masses. Soon after, Sibelius achieved national recognition by being awarded an annual stipend, which permitted him to put his full energy to musical creativity.

Although Sibelius composed in many forms, including the chamber, symphonic, choral, song, and piano idioms, his most important contributions lay in the symphonic realm, specifically seven symphonies and five symphonic (or tone) poems, as follows:

SYMPHONIES

Symphony No.1 in E minor (1899)
Symphony No.2 in D major (1901)
Symphony No.3 in C major (1907)
Symphony No.4 in A minor (1911)
Symphony No.5 in E flat major (1915)
Symphony No.6 in D minor (1923)
Symphony No.7 in C major (1924)

TONE POEMS

En Saga (1892, revised 1901)
The Swan of Tuonela (1893)
Finlandia (1900)
Pohjola's Daughter (1906)
Tapiola (1925)

Stylistically, the Sibelius symphonic masterpieces stand quite apart from any other twentieth-century compositions. The truth of this statement becomes immediately evident when one brings to mind the noted works of his contemporaries. For example, the post-World War I excitement over the abstractions of Schoenberg and Stravinsky did not interest the Finnish tone-poet, who preferred the austere, mysterious solitude of nature.

Sibelius' large, expansive tone canvases generally suggest a scene rather than describe or narrate an event. As one writer remarked, they are "filled with imagery of northern landscape and musings on man, nature and fate." As with Bruckner and other tone-painters of the grand manner, whose works have generally been associated with similar extramusical meanings, such subjective insights exist only in the imagination of the listener.

Following his First Symphony, which bears definite traces of Tchaikovsky, the foremost Finnish composer embarked on the gradual evolution of a highly personal style, characterized by basically powerful and elemental effects mixed with shifting moods of somberness and jubilation. The high point of this entire development is the Fourth Symphony, completed in 1911 and generally acclaimed as his chief masterpiece.

Instead of using complete melodies, Sibelius worked with motivic combinations somewhat in the manner of Beethoven. As did Bruckner, Sibelius built to a magnificent climax and used the overwhelming power of full ensemble. Unlike the late romantic, however, the nature tonepainter generally concentrated on transparency rather than opacity of orchestral texture (for example Symphony No.4). Ending passages, of course, were painted with the full, heavy romantic touch. Instrumental colors possessing the characteristic romantic pastoral effect (English horn, French horn, oboe, and deep, heavy brass) were carefully arranged to bring out the brooding, austere qualities we have come to associate with Sibelius' Northern forests, fjords, and mountains.

To be sure, the standard romantic rhetorical equipment is in full evidence: long, studied crescendos, bold, dynamic themes, and towering climaxes. Never does one feel overcome by sentimentality; Sibelius is too strong, too much like Beethoven for this effect to get in the way of his art. Indeed, the human element seems quite insignificant alongside the great peaks and valleys of the Northern romantic tradition.

Dmitri Shostakovich (1906-1975)

An obligation to social reality serves as a cornerstone for much of

Shostakovich's music. In place of Sibelius' visions of nature and northern landscapes, the leading Russian composer seems to derive his musical motivation from the Soviet world via historical, political, and folk sources. Uppermost is his regard for the simplicity and comprehensibility of musical thought, which stems from his conviction that musical art should communicate to the masses. Thus, unlike Sibelius, who often worked with austere, somber themes, Shostakovich in many scores, such as Symphonies No. 5 and No. 7, prefers more colorful, sentimental themes, themes that are easily grasped by the public.

This particular approach to much of his music stems in large measure from the official Russian artistic view called *socialist realism* that was held in official quarters during the years 1930 to about 1958. The official line of thought stressed the basic emotional appeal of the arts and the importance of communicating with the people of the nation. Nikolai Shamota ("On Tastes in Art," in *Soviet Literature* 1957) writes that:

> Art is the individual expression of social tastes and predilections....Art can exert its influence only if it is based on the broader aesthetic likes of the people, which have resulted from all their social experiences....Society's views on art indicate to art what its place in the life of the people is and determine what its subject matter should be....The viewpoint of the workers and peasants becomes the viewpoint of art.

Additional insight into the Shostakovich ideology is to be gained from the following letter which the composer sent to *The New York Times* in 1931—a time when Shostakovich was in favor among the Soviet cultural leaders:

> I am a Soviet composer, and I see our epoch as something heroic, spirited and joyous. Music cannot help having a political basis—an idea that the bourgeoisie is slow to comprehend. There can be no music without ideology. The old composers...most of them...were bolstering the rule of the upper classes. We as revolutionists have a different conception ....Lenin himself said that 'music is a means of unifying great masses of people'....Good music lifts and heartens, and lightens people for work and effort. It may be tragic, but it must be strong. It is no longer an end in itself, but a vital weapon in the struggle.

However, the political atmosphere which constantly surrounded his work changed in 1936 when he underwent a scathing attack for his opera *Lady Macbeth*, which had run for two years to packed audiences in Leningrad. *Pravda*, the official Soviet news organ, had this to say:

> The author of *Lady Macbeth* was forced to borrow from jazz its nervous, convulsive and spasmodic music in order to lend passion to his characters. While our music critics swear by the name of socialist realism, the stage serves us, in Shostakovich's work, the coarsest kind of naturalism. The music quacks, grunts and growls and suffocates itself in order to express the amorous scenes as naturalistically as possible....

In 1937, with the premiere of his Fifth Symphony Shostakovich's name was restored to good standing with the Soviet party. *Pravda* praised the "grandiose vistas of the tragically tense Fifth Symphony, with its philosophically seeking." Shostakovich gained still further honor from the official party with the Piano Quintet, which brought him the Stalin Prize of one hundred thousand rubles in 1940.

What was it that restored Shostakovich to good standing with the proletariat? What was the musical standard? Apparently the criterion remains in obscurity, to the dismay of both composer and listener, although we can gain some insight from the structure and content of the Fifth Symphony and other works.

The Fifth Symphony was written according to the traditional four-movement plan: I Moderato, II Allegretto (Scherzo), III Largo, and IV Allegro non troppo. Note, however, that the scherzo is second rather than third. No program accompanies the score, other than this brief statement made by the composer:

> The theme of my symphony is the stabilization of a personality.
> In the center of this composition, which is conceived lyrically
> from beginning to end, I saw a man with all his experiences.
> The finale resolves the tragically tense impulses of the earlier
> movements into optimism and the joy of living.

As one would expect, the rhetorical style plays a prominent role, particularly evident in the juxtaposition of large, expansive mood settings and the gradual building of tension, which finally reaches its goal in the final movement. No doubt simplicity of structure forms a part of socialist realism, evidenced by the use of the clear-cut, phrase-structured themes that pervade the composition, and also shown in the easily followed sonata form of the first movement.

In matters of orchestration, Shostakovich achieves typical Russian brilliance through octave scoring, string and brass unisons, and xylophone figures doubled with other percussion instruments and muted brass. The instrumentation he uses is basically the same as that of the late romantics: strings; large brass group; standard woodwinds, including piccolo, E-flat clarinet, and contrabassoon; and an expanded percussion section of timpani, snare drum, tamtam, cymbals, two harps, xylophone, celesta, and piano.

Shostakovich's Seventh Symphony, the "Leningrad" (1941) is a programmatic work that deals with the events of war-torn Russia. The general spirit and character of the symphony is indicated in the composer's statements as reported by *The New York Times*. The symphony commences with a theme intended to describe the existence of ordinary people—

> people not distinguished by any special features or talents—just
> good, quiet people, going about their daily life. After this
> preliminary theme I introduce the main theme, which was
> inspired by the transformation of these ordinary people into
> heroes by the outbreak of the war. This builds up into a requiem

for those of them who are perishing in the performance of their duty....The fourth movement can be described by one word, victory...as the victory of light over darkness, of humanity over barbarism, of reason over reaction.

Aaron Copland (1900-1990)

Romanticism runs deep in American music, a heritage firmly rooted in nineteenth-century practices. Also, the newness of our musical art (and especially the constant shadow of European superiority) has caused many American composers to turn to the romantic point of view for inspiration and wide-ranging subject matter.

In striving to develop a truly indigenous American style, many composers have looked for inspiration and ideas in the cultural roots of our land, including folk melody, dance, patriotic elements, early hymnody, jazz, and ethnic historical subject matter. Among the American composers who have followed this vein to some extent are Charles Ives (1874-1954), Roy Harris (1898-1979), Howard Hanson (1896-1981), and Aaron Copland (1900-1990).

Although these composers may be regarded as romantics, it should be stated that such a style label, as with other labels, is applicable in only a general way, designating certain phases or works usually regarded as romantic. While it is possible to put fairly definite labels on composers of earlier periods, it is obvious that the neoromantics cannot be treated categorically, since the musical style of these figures tends to vary from one period or decade to the next, reflecting the trends of the times. Hence modern romanticism, like neoclassicism and expressionism, differs by degree from one composer to another. Of the above listing, those who have shown the strongest leaning toward the romantic view are Harris, Hanson, and Copland, especially in his works of the 1930s and 1940s.

Copland has been rightfully called "the dean of American music." Born in Brooklyn in 1900, he, like another famed American, Howard Hanson, did much to champion the cause of modern music and the works of the younger generation of composers. Thus, through a steadfast conviction in composing music of true contemporaneity and artistic value, Copland helped to raise American music to a high level of quality and dignity. As an active proponent of the modern, he lectured at leading educational institutions, guest-conducted major orchestras, and wrote several books, including *What to Listen for in Music* (1939), *Our New Music* (1941), *Music and Imagination*(1952), and *Copland on Music* (1960).

Particular significance is to be attached to Copland's large catalog of music, which covers many idioms and styles. His use of jazz elements and folk material in a truly artistic fashion marks the most successful attempt to integrate national American idioms. While some like to regard Charles Ives as the first "modern," the real start of the modern American movement as such actually dates from Copland's first compositions of the 1920s.

Other major American figures contemporary with the young

Copland (in the 1920s) were Charles Ives, the first avant-garde composer in America and George Gershwin (1898-1937), the foremost song writer of the early twentieth century and important for his attempts at combining jazz and the symphonic medium (*Rhapsody in Blue* (1924) and Concerto in F (1926).

Following a period of European music study at Fontainebleau in the summer of 1921, and two years of study under a Guggenheim Fellowship (1925-1927), Copland returned to America, where he entered upon his first creative phase. Largely influenced by Stravinsky (through his Paris studies under the noted Nadia Boulanger), but especially by the jazz craze, which hit in the 1920s, Copland's first works exhibit a combination of Stravinskyian neoclassicism and elements of Negro blues (*Music for the Theatre*, 1925; Piano Concerto, 1926; and *Symphonic Ode*, 1929).

Copland's second period, strongly romantic and a time of his best-known works, began in the 1930s, when the nation was in the throes of the great depression. Feeling the necessity to close the gap that existed between the listener and much modern music, Copland initiated a marked change in his style by turning to folk and nationalistic material. Picturesque elements, local color, folk dance and melody, expressly Americanistic themes and subject matter, were incorporated into such works as the ballets *Billy the Kid* (1938), *Rodeo* (1942), and *Appalachian Spring* (1944); the orchestral suite *El Salon Mexico* (1936); and a work for narrator and orchestra, *A Lincoln Portrait* (1942).

In his third period, Copland returned to a more abstract and austere style, still imbued, however, with traces of the folk expression. This is particularly true of the noted Third Symphony, completed in 1946 under a commission by the Koussevitzky Foundation. The symphony represents a radical departure from the more functional ballets and typically romantic works of his previous period. Melodies of wide range, dissonant counterpoint, asymmetrical rhythms, and stress on form indicate a marked shift to the abstract point of view. Other works in this vein include the Violin Sonata (1943) and the Clarinet Concerto (1948).

From the 1950s on, the composer, like Stravinsky, incorporated twelve-tone techniques into his music; such works include the *Twelve Poems of Emily Dickinson* (1950), the Piano Quartet (1950), the Piano Fantasy (1957), and *Connotations for Orchestra* (1962).

THE QUEST FOR FORM AND STRUCTURE

> What is important for the lucid ordering of the work—for its crystallization—is that all the Dionysian elements....must be subjugated...and must finally be made to submit to the law: Apollo demands it.   Igor Stravinsky, *Poetics of Music*

A belief in the power of restraint, order, and lucid simplicity has been the conviction of a multitude of artists, musicians, and writers for more than two thousand years. We have observed that certain epochs characterized as "classical" such as those of the Italian High Renaissance, seventeenth-century France, and late eighteenth-century Europe as a whole, generally followed the precepts of ancient Greece and Rome. However, what they emulated was the ancients' classic spirit adapted to contemporary forms of literary, artistic, and musical expression.

The same holds true of the neoclassical strain in twentieth-century music. Although Stravinsky's "classicism" differs in form from Mozart's, the rational approach remains the same. There are, of course, varieties of classicism in the contemporary period, ranging from the interjection of modern content into Mozartian forms (as with Prokofiev and Piston), and the adaptation of ancient Greek and biblical themes (Stravinsky), to an almost mathematical manipulation of tones (Webern and the modern serialists). In the more abstruse music of Webern and late Stravinsky, the formal considerations seem at times to outweigh the expressive. Therefore, the term *abstract classicism* would probably be more appropriate to designate a heavy concentration on analytical, calculative procedures in composing.

Apollonian Ethos

The neoclassical movement in music is generally thought of as beginning about 1920, with Stravinsky's new works in this vein. However, the way was prepared in the preceding years by a circle of Parisians, including the musician Erik Satie (1866-1925) and the writer Jean Cocteau. (1891-1963). In seeking to restore the Apollonian ethos of order and structure, they rejected the vagueness and dreaminess of Debussy and the sentimentalizing of the postromantics.

Satie, about the time Paris was reveling in impressionism, turned to simplicity, wit, and directness of expression in such piano compositions as *Gymnopidies* (1888), *Three Pieces in the form of a Pear* (1903), and *Desiccated Embryos* (1913). The lightness, humor, and economy of means so characteristic of Satie's music were soon to be adopted by another composer, Igor Stravinsky.

Jean Cocteau added verbal fuel to the neoclassic explosion in his little book of 1918 entitled *Coq et Arlequin* (*Cock and Harlequin*), containing a series of pungent aphorisms attacking impressionists and romanticists alike; some of these are as follows:

> Wagner's works are long works which are long and long drawn out, because this old sorcerer looked upon boredom as a useful drug for the stupefaction of the faithful. Debussy missed his way because he fell from the German frying pan into the Russian fire. Once again the pedal blurs rhythm and creates a kind of fluid atmosphere congenial to *short sighted* ears. Satie remains intact. Hear his "Gymnopedies" so clear in their form and melancholy feeling. Debussy orchestrates them, confuses them, and wraps their exquisite architecture in a cloud.

The growing atmosphere of classicism was enhanced by other noted figures who gathered in Paris at the close of the war, including the author and avid proponent of modernism, Gertrude Stein; the famed teacher and advocate of neoclassicism in music, Nadia Boulanger; the musical giant of modern classicism, Igor Stravinsky, who became a French citizen; and the originators of cubism, Pablo Picasso and Georges Braque.

IGOR STRAVINSKY

Stravinsky, Picasso and Neoclassicism

Igor Stravinsky's creative life is usually divided into several periods: the first is his romantic phase (1910-1918), including the famous ballets *The Firebird* (1910), *Petrushka* (1911), and *The Rite of Spring* (1913). The second, the time of his emerging neoclassical style, covers approximately the years 1918 to 1950. The period from 1950 to his death may be called *abstract classicism.*

As we have already noted, the drawing of parallels between music and art is particularly helpful in determining the underlying philosophy in contemporary music. Earlier, for example, we mentioned that Schoenberg's excursion into atonality paralleled Kandinsky's move into the uncharted regions of nonobjective or abstract expressionist art.

A similar relationship exists between Picasso, the prime mover of the classical or structuralist point of view in painting, and Stravinsky the originator of modern neoclassicism in music. In contrast to the radical departure of Kandinsky and Schoenberg, the two classicists retained objective reality: Picasso through recognizable *visual imagery,* Stravinsky through recognizable *musical imagery* (tonality). And, quite opposed to their expressionist predecessors, they exalted design and logic rather than the ironic and psychic.

In Picasso's the *Three Musicians* (1921), for example, the emphasis is not upon romantic feeling and emotion but upon the formal arrangement of lines, cubes, colors, and planes. The subject matter, in this case three masked musicians, is discernible but there is a calculated rearrangement of the figures. Clearly, there is a subordination of natural relationships and appearance for manipulation of volume, space, planes, and colors into geometrical patterns, which cross and merge—as if one were walking around a piece of sculpture for successive views but getting all of these views at once.

Beginning about 1918, a dominance of formalism also characterizes Stravinsky's music. Well-known compositions from the second period include the ballet (*The Soldier's Tale*) (1918), the Octet for Wind Instruments (1923), Symphonies for Wind Instruments (1920), (*Oedipus Rex* 1927), and the *Symphony of Psalms* (1930).

Opening Measures, *l'Histoire du soldat* by Igor Stravinsky. Used by
permission of G. Schirmer, Inc.

Interesting similarities can be noted between such examples as
Picasso's *Three Musicians* and Stravinsky's Symphonies for Wind Instruments, both completed about the same time, 1921 and 1920 respectively.
For instance, Stravinsky's neat, clean-cut melodic lines are similar to
Picasso's clear, uncluttered outlines; and Stravinsky's pitting of one clearly
delineated sound mass against another is similar to Picasso's juxtaposition
of one plane against another; too, the almost frozen, motionless musical
architecture of the *Symphonies* relates to Picasso's frozen, stationary
cubes.

Absent in both are questing, impetuous romantic lines; instead,
angular, pointing lines meet the eye and the ear. Absent, too, is the
melodramatic emphasis, the literary subject, moral statement, and grand
climax. Moreover, the impersonal, detached, abstract sounds of Stravinsky
are matched by Picasso's expressionless figures; and the color planes of
the painting are mirrored in Stravinsky's delineated colors and restrained
orchestration. In both examples a kind of cool, precise, calculated outlook
seems dominant—a point of view quite removed from the melodramatic,
sentimental attitude of the postromantics.

Eric Salzman (*Twentieth-Century Music*) summarizes very nicely the
Picasso-Stravinsky artistic ideals.

> Just as cubism is a poetic statement about objects and forms,
> about the nature of vision and the way we perceive and know
> forms, and about the experience of art and the artistic
> transformation of objects and forms, so is Stravinsky's music a

poetic statement about musical objects and aural forms, about the way we hear and the way we perceive and understand aural forms.

Abstract Classicism

Stravinsky's preoccupation with the classical ideals continued into his third period, which dates from about 1950. Even though during this period the composer became increasingly preoccupied with the twelve-tone system—regularly from 1958 on—the Schoenberg method did not affect his fundamentally classical outlook. As a true artist he bent the twelve-tone system to his creative will, so to speak, producing some of the most interesting music in this vein since Berg's humanization of the Schoenberg theories.

Some examples from this period include (*In Memorian Dylan Thomas* 1954) for tenor, string quartet, and four trombones; *Canticum Sacrum* (1956) for tenor, baritone, and orchestra; *Agon* (1957); *Threni* (1958); *Movements* (1959); *The Flood* (1962); and *Variations for Orchestra* (1964).

Ingrained in most of these works is the fundamental spirit of modern classicism, with its emphasis on logic, compression, and purity of design, and colored, of course, by the incisive, biting dissonance of the twelve-tone system. Other ingredients have been added or reaffirmed: a religious, ceremonious quality, a veneration of medieval mysticism, and a preference for a static harmonic style reminiscent of the Gothic composers. Above all, a greater degree of austerity and concision is noticeable, which probably stems from his admiration of Anton Webern, whom he called "the discoverer of a new distance between the musical object and ourselves and therefore, of a new measure of musical time."

BÉLA BARTÓK

As we near the final phase of our discussion of twentieth-century music, it would be well to reflect upon the great pathfinders and molders of modern musical thought. Several names, already discussed, immediately come to mind: Claude Debussy, who is to be cited for the unique harmonic innovations he contributed to the impressionist movement; Arnold Schoenberg, for his theories (less for his music); Igor Stravinsky, for his distinctive renewal of the classical spirit; and the last composer to be discussed, Bela Bartók, for his successful fusion of the folk element with musical art.

Few composers of the first half of the century possess such a dynamic and clearly marked style as Béla Bartók. His sensitive, impetuous musical personality seems to permeate the entire fiber of practically every piece he composed, seemingly in the same undefinable way that Beethoven, Mozart, Leonardo da Vinci, and Delacroix personally inscribed their works.

All of the elements employed in the creative process—melody, rhythm, harmony, and form—bear the inimitable Bartók imprint. It would seem that this memorable personal stamp, combined with originality and a mastery of medium, constitute the chief marks of a superior artist. In fulfilling these requirements, Bartók ranks with the leading masters.

Every composer of stature has a particular imprint or musical signature: with Beethoven it is a robust rhythmic vitality, with Mozart an ingratiating melodic line, and with Stravinsky a precise, crystal-clear delineation of musical elements in the true classical manner. The Bartók trademark is his stylized treatment of the Central European folk spirit, which he transformed into powerful, driving rhythmic figures and exotically colored melodic lines.

The characteristic Bartókian mannerisms, which are manifested in such outstanding examples as his six string quartets (dating from 1908 to 1939), Concerto for Orchestra (1943), and *Music for Strings, Percussion and Celesta* (1936), began to evolve as early as 1904, when the young musician discovered the intrinsic character and expressive power of folk dance and melody. Possessed with a good deal of nationalistic pride, Bartók and a fellow composer named Zoltan Kodaly, set out to revive the musical heritage of their native Hungary.

Bartók's zeal for folk song study and collection led him on numerous journeys to various parts of Hungary and later to North Africa (1913) where he investigated the music of Arabic tribes. The lifelong association with this branch of music study (called *ethnomusicology*) continued even into his later years. In 1940, following the collaboration of Hungary with Nazi Germany, Bartók moved to America. For a time he held an appointment in the department of music at Columbia University, and he continued to compose until his death in 1945.

Eclectic and Abstract

Since Bartók's creative interests covered a variety of different techniques, forms, and influences, it is very difficult to classify his style. Actually, Bartók seems to have been the most eclectic of the composers active in the first half of the twentieth century. Never plagiaristic, he assimilated elements of the major trends past and present: expressionism, the classical chamber style, jazz, Hungarian and Romanian folklore, impressionism, and elements of the Stravinsky art.

If we choose to place the composer in one of the three main categories of twentieth-century music, it will become evident to the listener that expressionism is not akin to the composer's basically optimistic nature. He is much too inspired by the outer world to be set alongside Schoenberg and Berg. Some scores, however, (*Allegro barbaro* 1911, and *The Miraculous Mandarin* 1919) are clearly expressionistic.

It is very difficult to place this composer into a neat, defined style system; he seems to be nearer the classical point of view, as evidenced in his preponderant use of classical forms such as the suite, divertimento, concerto, quartet, and sonata-genres based upon pure patterns of tone rather than romantic narrative. This, then, his penchant for logically organized designs, is perhaps the first key to understanding Bartók. A second key, is his abstraction of folk elements, which in some ways stamps his work as classic in style.

Abstraction in Tonal and Visual Arts

The term *abstract* means basically the same in the visual and tonal arts: to take or extract from a subject some phase of its characteristics and to shape it into a new entity. In effect, the new adaptation stands as a symbol more or less like the original. For example, in a cubist painting by Picasso, abstraction becomes a kind of "tampering with visual truths," where parts of the human anatomy are transformed into solid geometrical masses. A good illustration is Picasso's *Nude in the Forest* (1908), in which the figure's limbs are depicted as planklike forms.

Abstraction in modern music works much the same way. For example, when Bartók the classicist employs folk material, he is likewise attracted to the possibilities of treating the element intellectually. Thus, he takes delight in reshaping or fragmenting some or all of the elements into unusual patterns—in short, in abstracting the original material. In Bartók's scores abstraction takes two major forms: melodic and rhythmic.

The most characteristic interval in Hungarian and other East European folk songs is the perfect fourth. In the two examples that follow, observe the fourths (bracketed) in the original Hungarian folk song and their abstraction in Bartók's Third Quartet. Other melodic intervals common to Slovak folk songs are used by the composer, such as the augmented fourth (tritone), to be noted in the following:

Hungarian Folk Song

In the next examples compare the use of fourths; first from his second quartet, and the second a Slovak folk song.

Slovak Folk Song

Rhythmic abstraction of folk tunes also occupies a prominent position in Bartók's art, chief of which are the asymmetrical groupings of beats (5, 7, etc.) and fluctuating meters (as opposed to the consistent use of one meter throughout, as in earlier periods). Changing metric patterns, for example 4/4 2/4 3/4 5/8 3/8 so common to Hungarian and Romanian folk song, appear regularly in his scores. Compare the following original folk example with Bartók's usage:

Hungarian Folk Song

From Concerto for Orchestra by Béla Bartók.

Below is a selected list of Bartok's major works.

Two Portraits for Orchestra (1908)
Fourteen Bagatelles, for piano (1908)
String Quartet No.1 (1908)

Allegro Barbero, for piano (1911)
String Quartet No.2 (1917)
The Miraculus Mandarin, pantomime (1919)
Concerto No.1 for Piano and Orchestra (1926)
String Quartet No.3 (1927)
String Quartet No.4 (1928)
Twenty Hungarian Folksongs (1929)
Concerto No.2 for Piano and Orchestra (1931)
Music for Strings, Percussion and Celesta (1936)
Sonata for Two Pianos and Percussion (1937)
Mikrokosmos, 153 pieces for piano (1926-1937)
Contrasts for Violin, Clarinet and Piano (1938)
Concerto for Violin and Orchestra (1938)
Divertimento for String Orchestra (1939)

Principles of Style

To cover the many facets of Bartók's musical language would go beyond the scope of this book; however, his significant innovations in each of the main aspects of musical composition may be lightly touched upon. Rhythm, characteristically incisive, bold, and dynamic, seems uppermost in his art. In addition to asymmetrical groupings of beats and changing meters, his unusual rhythmic style is characterized by an intensive motoristic drive. This powerful kinetic movement is propelled by irregular meters, ostinato figures, and offbeat accents. Also characteristic is the employment of polymetric schemes whereby different meters are heard simultaneously: for example, one instrument or section in duple and another in triple, thus setting up unusual cross-accents.

Bartók's harmony, though fundamentally organized tonally and covering a wide range of expression, is usually intense and strident. These qualities result both from his use of chords constructed of fourths and major and minor seconds and from the simultaneous juxtaposition of two or more different streams of harmony (*polyharmony*). Contrapuntal techniques involving imitation and canon play an important part in such works as the (*Mikrokosmos*, 153 graded piano pieces), the first movement of *Music for Strings, Percussion and Celesta*, and the first and last movements of the Concerto for Orchestra.

In summary, Donald Grout (*A History of Western Music*) writes, "The guiding thread in all of Bartók's work is the variety and skill with which he integrated the essence of his national folk music heritage." Undoubtedly Bartók's highly original style, with its ever-present invention, freshness, and spontaneity derived from the folk realm will assure the composer a lasting position in the history of music. Curiously, such words as "freshness" and "invention" which have often identified noteworthy musical production, are now in jeopardy among some quarters of present day music. This predicament will be our lead-off thought taking us into some of the most prickly isssues facing music audiences and critics today.

AND BEYOND---

The Viennese audience was shocked and astounded by the hammerstroke opening chords, the dynamic shifting and thrusting of accents....critics referred to the composition as being "daring," "wild," of extreme difficulty and lacking unity.

·······

The New York Times reported that listeners streamed out of New York's Avery Fisher Hall after the New York Philharmonic finished playing the raucous first movement.

The Listener Dilemma

The first report above pertains to the premier performance of Beethoven's Eroica Symphony in 1805. The second, to a performance of John Adams' *Naïve and Sentimental Music* in 2006. What are some of the similarities between the two incidents? The first, obviously, is the ever-present audience discontent when something new appears in the concert hall—an outcry heard ever since Plato complained about musical trends 2000 years ago. Some differences are noted: Beethoven's innovative, ground-breaking approach to creativity centered around his dynamic emotional expression, which, however, was couched in a musical language inherited from the eighteenth century. The Adams piece appears to focus on total shock value—the extreme juxtaposition of musical styles (supposedly Bruckner and Stravinsky in almost a surrealistic manner). As one writer commented, "the sharp string crescendos in the slow movement suggested the sound of an orchestral tape being played backward." Another difference: Beethoven cared deeply about his audience; today's composers seem to be detached, caring less if their music is performed or accepted. What has caused the present predicament that has increasingly split composers from the mainstream of musical culture?

A retrospective view of the twentieth century offers an ideal vantage point for understanding the background to our question. For example, what influence did the social upheaval of two monstrous wars have upon music? What happened to the many experiments which supposedly were going to change the world of music? Several decades ago, for example, who would have thought that Schoenberg's music (the hot item in the 1950s) and that of the entire serialistic group would become a lifeless art form. The historical context is the first place to look for answers as to what prompted the current listener's quandary (and perhaps provide some insight as to the causes for the many style changes that have swept though music over the past decades).

Beethoven enjoyed relative security as a composer in a society whose musical tastes had been shaped by a long heritage. Beethoven filled the role magnificently, paying homage to the well-established classical style, but at the same time announcing in most powerful terms the new romanticism. Even though he was far advanced of any other musician of his day, we would not consider him to be *avant-garde*—someone working beyond the conventional forms and limits of music. Music history reveals a few names that fit the definition, but generally speaking the term avant-garde applies primarily to a group of composers in the twentieth century who deliberately destroyed all vestiges of traditional musical form. The word "avant-garde" seems to have come into popular currency about 1910-1914—the approximate time of this unprecedented surge of experimental creativity.

Origins of an Ideology

Even though Beethoven went to the "edge" at times, he followed what had generally existed for hundreds of years, namely, fundamental principles of musical perception—that music has form, ideas, and is capable of human expression. The problem that has caused such a disruption today, is that these principles have been completely negated. To put it mildly, the problems faced by audiences are unlike anything found in earlier music history, comparable, perhaps, to someone who is taking on a study of a new language. The difference, however, is that much of the new music has no "grammar" or "syntax," no guidelines—in short, the systems that have been in place for centuries have been completely torn up and discarded. Where, why, and under what conditions did all of this occur? Let's begin with the early years of the twentieth century.

The urge to be new, ahead, advanced, unconventional, radically experimental—to be avant-garde—was born of an age when the world was greatly disturbed by a series of social and intellectual events: when optimism was shattered by a series of wars, when artists began to replace representation with abstraction; and when scientific thought began to be mirrored in all of the arts including music—a trend that led to Schoenberg's theory of evolution in music, namely, that music "progresses," "advances" in a scientific path through history (one of the most damaging thoughts to come out of the artistic upheaval).

The pieces composed by our present day musicians such as Adams, Boulez and Babbitt are the products of this upheaval in musical thinking and construction. It was driven by the extreme pursuit of an idea that caught the imagination of many would-be composers: to be *different* at any cost, including the loss of an audience. To summarize, the spirit of experimentalism—spanning roughly 1915 to the present—is represented by various "isms" which we will examine. They include: *serialism, minimalism, Cageism,* and *electronicism.* We will find that not all is negative. Like all periods in history, several conditions work together to somehow keep music alive as a major cultural force.

The Beginning: Expressionism

Following the appalling carnage of the war of 1914-1918, men of good will thought the militarism, tyranny, and aggression had been crushed for all time and lasting peace would be assured. Unfortunately, the dream was exploded in an even greater holocaust, the Second World War and other massive disorders of our time. In essence, our existence was weakened by the gradual decline of optimism in the wake of a series of social and political paradoxes that deeply disturbed the modern conscience. The first to disclose this conscience were the early twentieth-century writers, painters and musicians, especially, as we noted earlier, the expressionists whose works clearly indicated the powerful new trend: the depiction of harsh and painful reality. The "language" of atonality and its many complexities invented by Schoenberg fit the aesthetic goals of expressionism perfectly.

Spinoffs of Atonality

Even though the Schoenberg phenomenon all but expired about 1960, there has been a continued, but subdued movement called *total serialism* led by Milton Babbitt, Pierre Boulez, Elliot Carter and others. Composers following the Schoenberg method were interested in carrying the tone-row principle to its ultimate conclusion. That is, in addition to regulating pitch (as we observed in the manipulation of the twelve-tone row throughout an entire composition), all other elements such as tempo, meter, dynamics and tone color were treated in similar fashion. Babbitt worked out these techniques in *Three Compositions for Piano* (1947), the first piece to make use of the new procedures. Babbitt feels that he must explain everything he composes in the most complete, complex detail, this is also true of his fellow compatriots. As Thomson writes, "they created a bountiful crop of verbiage never before witnessed in music circles." One final thought: these composers, and those who dabbled in electronic music (to be discussed), are perhaps the chief representatives of the psuedo-scientific attitude applied to music, as Rochberg remarks: "music like everything else today is reducible to formulas, equations, to statistical probabilities." This becomes evident in the description furnished by Babbitt for his *Relata: I*:

> the inversionally related...lines of this underlying "polyphony" however, though still maintaining hexachordal combinatoriality, do not preserve this dyadic relationship, clearly they could have been so chosen...but the final pair was chosen to function as a linear summation of the "simultaneous" dyads.

Minimalism

A trend in our time that is in the opposite direction from total serialism, is *minimalism*. It seems only natural that a new style would come along that would be a reaction to the complexities of total serialism; interestingly, it came onto the scene about the same time as Babbitt was declaring a new path. The logical step in the evolution of what Wylie Sypher and other cultural historians refer to as "the loss of self"—so characteristic of the modern avant-garde—has been toward complete depersonalization of music. This has been achieved by the simple elimination of the human performer and secondly, by taking away the persona of the composer. These trends are represented in *minimalism, electronicism, and Cageism* (named by some critics after John Cage).

Because it is built around highly repetitive tones or simple figures, minimalism has caused some to refer to it as "trance" or "hypnotic" music.

Whereas serialism tried to incorporate intellection in requiring the listener to follow complex permutations of the tone-row, minimalism, as Salzman states, is not an intellectual exercise since there is no theme as such to follow other than the mantra-like tonal figure. There is so much eclectism among composers (combining bits of serialism, electronic synthesizers, tape players, and human performers) that it is very difficult to pin down one style such as minimalism. Among the practioners are Steve Reich (*Variations for Winds, Strings and Keyboard*, 1979), and Philip Glass. In the 1970s Glass began to expand minimalist theory into an actual sense of harmonic movement and organized phrase structure resembling musical form. Typical is his *Glassworks* (1983). Concentration and meditation over a long period of listening are required; however, as Salzman remarks, this music is not demanding, it is not necessary to "figure things out." One critic pointed out that the only element of intellection seems to be if the listener notices subtle shifts in dynamics.

Electronic Experimentation

Electronic music derives its sound material from a range of electronic devices such as a frequency oscillator. A piece of music is constructed by re-recording these sound fragments at higher or lower pitches, faster or slower speeds, louder or softer volumes, or backwards or forwards, and playing them through speakers.

Those who advocate the medium point out that it eliminates the middleman, the performer, and enables direct communication between the composer and the audience. The tonal range can be extended to an unlimited degree, and an infinite number of sounds, rhythms and total regulated control of these new elements achieved. As to its disadvantages, we note the following criticism by leading performers and musicologists: the medium creates the problem of a gigantic amoeba because of its lack of order, and its constant additive methods; it reaches beyond the threshold of human perception (in contrast to the composer-created forms, which remain within human limits), the stress is on the manipulation of artificially produced tones rather than on the art of creation. The latter underscores the essential problem heard over and over: "mechanized music lacks the spontaneity of individual human performance in which each performance illuminates a work from a slightly different angle...Lost are the elements of anticipation and surprise that the human performer instills in each successsive phrase of a piece." (Arthur Edwards and W. Thomas Marrocco).

Cageism

Amazingly, the experimental shifts have gone from total control (serialism and electronicism), to non-developmental (minimalism), to complete loss of the rational (Cageism). All of these trends occured within a few years of each other, roughly from 1950 to 1970. John Cage (died in 1992) is not to be considered a composer in the usual sense, but rather a "manipulator" who desired notoriety (like so many spurious "artists" who have come upon the scene in recent years).

Indicative of his contributions to depersonalizing music are "chance procedures" in his *Piano Concert 1957-58*, consisting of a piano part where elements could be played in any order desired. The directions for performance include: the parts maybe played separately, together, or not at all. Eventually, as Salzman remarks, there need be no activity at all—only an open piano and the contemplation of four minutes—the ultimate in non-music. What he has succeeded in doing is not of musical importance but of personal, therapeutic importance to the hearer—to appreciate the value of silence and pure contemplation in the maddingly, dizzy world in which we live. Perhaps an offshoot might be the application of the experience to the perception of musical sounds—as the first and primal step to appreciate tones, their subtleties and their capability of meaning.

Some Lights at the End of the Tunnel

Douglas Lee (*Masterworks of 20th Century Music*, 2002), has made a compilation of modern music performed by present-day symphony orchestras. Specifically, he surveyed various orchestras to find out what works were in the repertory during the last decade of twentieth century. The criteria he used was: which musical scores were most performed during that period. His survey disclosed 119 works by 29 composers. Not surprising, he found compositions by the following artists who represented more than half of the repertory: Samuel Barber, Béla Bartók, Sergei Prokofiev, Maurice Ravel, Dmitri Shostakovich and Igor Stravinsky. (To this list we might add: George Rochberg, Joan Tower, Ned Rorem, John Corigliano and many others which space does not permit.)

The survey has much value: firstly, it indicates which musical scores have endured through the century, and, in most likelihood, will continue to be performed. Secondly, it indicates the kind of link that exists between music performed and audience tastes. And thirdly, it has considerable musicological and philosophical value for anyone interested in musical culture and its movement through history.

If we examine the top six composers we may gain insight into how the struggle between the avant-garde and audience taste may be resolved, or at least modified from the sharp angles that now exist. In brief, what are the kinds of musical ideas, forms and perceptive experiences that seem to be important if we are to continue a cultural holding pattern that we have observed for several centuries? If we consider "culture" not in its current catch-all vogue, but in its original meaning—as Rochberg states, as a self sustaining organism, which thrives because of memory and the preservation of things human—then these works speak volumes.

The list of "positives" that follow, extracted from the works of the six composers, is by no means a look into future or to be thought of as essentials for writing great music, but rather a composite picture that corroborates in many ways our musical heritage:

-- pronounced themes or motives
-- expressive use of instruments and voices
-- interesting, varied treatment of musical form
-- a presence of the composer's persona
-- the ageless principle of conflict and resolution
-- memorable, repeatable creativity
-- presence of dramatic gestures
-- balance of technique and expression
-- strong sense of humanism

To summarize, we have witnessed several things: a weakening of humanism as a motivating force; the constant search for newness has led to a kind of superficial application of the scientific attitude in experimental music; and concomitantly, the search for new sources of "meaning" in music has resulted in the elimination of meaning altogether. The problem is to enable art (as a subjective life-experience) and science (objective) to coexist, and finally, to value the heritage that has brought us to where we are. Jacques Barzun, who has made an extensive study of cultural changes over the past several hundred years, characterizes our present era not as a culmination but rather a decline. He adds further, that decadence is a necessary condition of any great period, for with it comes the creative innovation or novelty that will burst forth tomorrow or the next day. Somewhat contrary to Barzun, we have found that despite the confused state of contemporary music, the period did manage to produce some of the greatest works in the repertory—possibly adhering to an idea so eloquently stated by George Rochberg, composer and writer, and a towering figure in American music:

> The gesture of music can only proceed authentically
> from one direction: from *inside*. This is where
> they [composers] get their energy, power,
> their immediacy.

GLOSSARY

A Cappella - Sung without accompaniment.

Accent - Stress or emphasis on one tone or chord.

Accidental - A sharp, flat, double sharp or double flat, or natural sign prefixed to a note in a passage of music.

Adagio - A slow tempo. In ballet, the "grand" adagio is the climax of the dance.

Alberti bass - Broken chord texture in piano music of the late eighteenth century.

Allegro - A lively, brisk tempo.

Alto - Second highest part in choral music.

Allemande - A dance in moderate tempo, in duple meter; of late Renaissance and Baroque periods.

Antiphony - The exchange of musical phrases or passages between two or more soloists or groups.

Appoggiatura - A dissonant tone that occurs on the strong beat and resolves up or down by half or whole step. Also a Baroque ornament consisting of a small added note played on the beat.

Aria - An elaborate song with instrumental accompaniment. First introduced in seventeenth-century opera.

Arpeggio - The tones of a chord played consecutively; also called a broken chord.

Assai – expressive marking meaning "very."

Atonality (Atonal) - The absence of key feeling; used generally in conjunction with the 12-tone technique of Schoenberg and modern "serialists" in which all 12 tones of the chromatic scale are treated equally; traditional scales, chords, key centers are avoided.

Ballade - A type of medieval poetry and music; also designation for dramatic piano pieces of the nineteenth century.

Bar line - A vertical line through the staff which separates one measure from another.

Beat - The unit of measurement in music; a felt pulsation.

Binary form -A type of musical structure in which there are two distinct sections or themes, usually designated by A B.

Cadence - The ending portion of a melody or section of music. Different types of cadences, derived from a particular arrangement of melody tones and/or chords, provide a kind of musical punctuation in which the musical flow is completely stopped (full cadence) or momentarily suspended (incomplete cadence).

Cadenza - An elaborate improvisatory passage played by a solo instrument in the concerto; usually occurs near the end of the first movement.

Canon - The exact imitation of one musical part by another.

Cantabile - Expressive term indicating a "singing" style of performance, smooth and flowing.

Cantata - An extended vocal form (with instruments in supporting role); those of Johann Sebastian Bach usually employed a sacred text, small orchestra, chorus, vocal soloists, and were arranged into a series of short movements or verses.

Canzona - Lively sixteenth and seventeenth-century instrumental pieces for keyboard or ensemble.

Chamber music - Instrumental ensemble music (more than one instrument) with one player to a part; includes string quartets, quintets, violin sonatas, flute sonatas.

Chorale - A short hymnlike form for voices; usually written for four voice parts and in metrical rhythm; common to German Protestant music.

Chord - Three or more tones sounded simultaneously.

Chorus - A group that sings choral music; also the choral sections of a cantata, oratorio, or opera.

Chromatic - Tone foreign to the key of the music.

Classical ballet - A dance form that began in the royal courts of sixteenth-century France, eventually established by Louis XIV in 1661. The classical ballet was based on five strict positions.

Clef - Sign written at the beginning of each staff that designates the pitches of the lines and spaces; the treble clef circles the pitch "g" (second line of the staff).

Coda - An added section or concluding statement at the end of a movement in the symphony or sonata and other forms.

Concertino - Name given to the solo group in the concerto grosso.

Concerto - An orchestral composition either for one soloist (solo concerto) and accompanying body of instruments, or for several soloists, usually two or three (concerto grosso), and supporting orchestra.

Concerto grosso - A multimovement form (normally three movements) featuring a solo group of instruments (two or three) against the full orchestra.

Conjunct - Refers to step-wise melodic movement.

Consonance - A musical effect resulting from a particular arrangement of tones (usually in terms of harmony or chords) that provides a feeling of repose, balance, stability.

Continuo (also known as basso continuo) - A keyboard instrument which with one other instrument (normally a cello) provided the nucleus of Baroque music. The term continuo may also refer to the bass melody and numbers (indicatingtypes of chords to be filled in) played by the keyboard instrument in the Baroque period.

Counterpoint - The technique of combining two or more lines of melody; also referred to as polyphony.

Courante - A lively dance in triple meter; of French origins, used in Baroque suites.

Credo - Third part of the Ordinary of the Mass.

Crescendo - Expressive term indicating a gradual increase in volume or loudness abbreviated cresc., or indicated by two diverging lines $<$.

Development - The working out or elaboration of thematic material by rhythmic, harmonic, or contrapuntal techniques. It generally appears in the second phase of the sonata form where an important feature of the melody is elaborated upon.

Diatonic - Describes any melodic or harmonic movement that uses only the tones of the given key of the composition.

Disjunct - Refers to a melody that progresses mainly by skips, that is large intervals between melody notes.

Dissonance - Combinations of tones in harmony or melody that produce a state of tension and unrest.

Dominant - The fifth tone of the scale, or the chord built on the fifth tone of the scale.

Dorian - An ancient mode highly esteemed by the Greeks.

Dynamics - Terms and abbreviations that indicate degrees and changes in volume or loudness: crescendo: gradual increase in volume; decrescendo or diminuendo: gradual decrease in volume; sfz: strongly accented.

Empfindsamer stil - "Sensitive style" common to the music of the preclassicist Carl Phillip Emanuel Bach; characterized by sudden changes in volume and rhythmic movement, and highly personal quality.

Enharmonic - A note that has the same pitch (but different spelling) as another note, for example F# and Gb.

Equal temperament - A system of tuning that came into musical practice during the early Baroque; all tones of the scale are tuned equally.

Exposition - The first phase or part of the sonata form, in which the main themes are announced or presented.

Fantasia - An instrumental form for keyboard or ensemble.

Form - The structure or pattern in which musical ideas or themes are presented and arranged.Vocal forms include the oratorio, cantata, mass, motet, and so on; common instrumental forms include sonata, fugue, symphony, concerto, and symphonic poem.

Fugue - A musical form in which a single theme called the subject is stated in one key by a particular part and then imitated or answered by a second part in a different key; a series of successive statements and answers involving all of the parts (usually four) constitutes the overall design of the fugue.

Galliard - A dance, moderately fast, triple meter.

Gavotte - A fairly lively dance, quadruple meter, introduced in 17th century operas and ballets.

Gigue - A Baroque dance of English origin (Jig), six-eight meter, very lively.

Gloria - "Glory," the second part of the Ordinary of the Mass.

Grace note - An ornamental note (appoggiatura) that is played very quickly; written as a very small note. In the Baroque and Classical periods it is played on the beat; from Beethoven on:into Romantic period: just ahead of the beat.

Harmonics - A musical tone, has, in addition to its fundamental tone, a series of overtones or harmonics which contribute to the richness and resonance. Harmonics also refers to high-pitched artificial tones produced by over-blowing on the flute, for example, or using certain finger positions on the violin.

Harmony - The technique of combining tones into chords and chord progressions.

Homophony - A type of texture consisting of melody and chords.

Interval - The distance between one pitch and another, measured in scale steps.

Key - A grouping or family of notes in which a piece of music is composed. Traditional keys have seven different tones, for example the key of C: C D E F GAB C.

Key signature - The sharps or flats (or complete absence of these as in C major) that designate a particular key. They are grouped together on the staff at the beginning of each line of music.

Kyrie - The first part of the Ordinary of the Mass.

Largo - Italian term designating the slowest tempo.

Ländler - Austrian folk dance, triple meter, strong emphasis on first beat of measure.

Legato - Smooth, connected fashion.

Libretto - The text of any dramatic vocal work such as opera.

Major, minor - Refer to two basic types of scales differentiated by their third interval (in the Cmajor scale there is a major third between C and E, in the C-minor scale, there is a minor third, C to E-flat).

Mass - A musical setting of the Ordinary of the Mass, consisting of the Kyrie, Gloria, Credo, Sanctus, and Agnus Dei, in which the texts are invariable.

Measure - The space between two bar lines.

Melody - The succession of meaningful tones; also called melodic line.

Meter - The regular grouping of pulses or beats into either *duple* (1-2, 1-2), *triple* (1-2-3, 1-2-3), *quadruple* (1-2-3-4, 1-2-3-4), or compound combinations (more than four beats).

Minuet - A French dance of moderate tempo and triple meter, reputedly introduced as a formal dance by Lully about 1650. Used in some Baroque suites and widely employed in the Classical symphony (late eighteenth century) as the third movement.

Mode - A type of ancient Greek and medieval scale; a characteristic mode is the Dorian: D E F G A B C D.

Modulation - The technique of passing from one key to another in the course of a musical composition.

Monophony - A type of texture having just one part or line of music.

Mordent - A three-note ornament consisting of a principal note, the note next below, and then the principal.

Motive - The smallest musical idea consisting of several notes.

Musical form - The mold or pattern into which musical ideas or themes are organized.

Musicology - A discipline devoted to research in all phases of musical endeavor; in general historically oriented.

Note - The written symbol for a specific pitch and its time duration.

Opera - A drama set to music, staged with scenery and costumes, and usually based on a secular theme; includes orchestra, chorus, and soloists.

Opera buffa - A bright, lively comic type of Italian opera of 18th century.

Opus - The chronological number given to a composition; abbreviated Op.

Oratorio - A drama, usually of a sacred nature, set to music with a narrator, soloists, chorus, and orchestra. Those of late Baroque (Handel, for example) are without scenery and costumes.

Ornament - Refers to decorative figures applied to melodic lines of 17th and 18th century music, eg. trills, turns, etc.

Ostinato - A repeated melodic, rhythm or harmonic idea, usually in the bass register.

Part - A single line of notes to be played or sung; the printed music designated for an instrument or voice.

Pavane - A sixteenth-century court dance in a slow, duple meter (stately).

Phrase - A melodic division in traditional music. Much of the music of the classical and Romantic periods is based on melodies having two phrases, each of four measures, the first ending with an incomplete cadence and the second, a complete cadence.

Polyphony - The technique of combining two or more melodic lines; also known as counterpoint.

Pulsatile - Possessing a definite beat feeling.

Recapitulation - The third and last phase or part of the sonata form; the restatement in whole or part, of the exposition section.

Recitative - A type of singing in a speechlike manner; common to opera of the Baroque and Classical periods.

Register - The level or range of the musical sound, identified by such classifications as treble or bass clef.

Resolution - Pertains to the progression of tones from a point of dissonance to consonance.

Rhythm - The regular, constant feeling of forward motion or propulsion in music, achieved by the repetition of a beat or pulse and a particular pattern of note values.

Ripieno - The full orchestra portion in the baroque concerto, also referred to as tutti.

Ritornello - A recurring theme common to the baroque concerto

Rondo - A musical form in which a central theme keeps recurring.

Round - A short vocal canon in which one part imitates another at the same pitch level or at the octave (eight steps higher or lower).

Scale - A series of successive tones placed in order from low to high; also, a particular key written out in ascending order of tones: C D E F G A B C.

Scherzo - A musical joke or jest.

Sinfonia - Italian for symphony; predecessor of the classical symphony.

Sonata - This word has at least two meanings: it may refer either to a musical genre or form (for example, piano sonata) having three or four movements, or, to a type of musical structure having three sections or divisions.

Staff - The five parallel lines upon which music is written .

Sanctus - The fourth part of the Ordinary of the Mass.

Sarabande - A dignified, slow dance in triple meter; found in the baroque suite.

Score - A musical work in its complete printed form with all parts indicated in full, precise form.

Semitone - A half-tone, for example C to C#.

Symphonic poem (also known as tone poem) - A programmatic work (based on an extramusical idea such as a poem, story, painting, historical event) for orchestra, in one extended moyement.

Symphony - A large-scale composition for orchestra having several movements.

Syncopation - A deliberate upsetting of normal rhythmic and metric flow through the use of accents occurring on the uneven beats, for example: 1 2 3 4 of the measure.

Ternary - Three-part form: A B A.

Texture, musical - The manner in which tones are woven or arranged in musical space. See *monophony, polyphony* and *homophony*.

Timbre - The characteristic tone quality or tone color of an instrument or voice.

Toccata - A brilliant, virtuosic piece in free form; common during the Baroque period and usually composed for the organ.

Tonality - A system of tonal organization consisting of major and minor keys, in which tones gravitate to a central key.

Tone - A musical sound of definite pitch.

Tonic - The name of the central chord (or scale tone) to which all tones or chords gravitate; common to the period of tonality, 1600-1900.

Triad - A fundamental type of chord having three different tones: C E G.

Trill - The rapid alternation of two tones that are a scale degree apart, indicated by the abbreviation *tr*.

Trio - The second division of the minuet, originally played by three instruments.

Trio sonata - A Baroque form of the sonata, for two violins, cello (or bass) and keyboard instrument such as the harpsichord.

Turn - A rapid embellishment, usually a group of four notes, indicated by an inverted, reversed "S" sign.

Unison - The sounding of the same note either in exact pitch or at the octave lower, by two or more players or singers.

Vibrato - A wavering of the tone.

About the Author

Donald H. Van Ess is Professor of Music Emeritus, State University of NewYork, Brockport. In addition to teaching at SUNY Brockport he has held positions at Boston University (Doctoral Fellowship), Mansfield State University, and Carthage College. He earned his Ph. D. at Boston University and is the author of several books including *The Commonwealth of Arts & Man: Readings in the Humanities; A Listener's Guide to the Heritage of Musical Style; English Wind Music Through the Ages; The Romantic Revolution in Music* (in preparation); and contributor to *The Athlone History of Music in Britain, The Romantic Age.*